Accessibility, Diversity, Equity and Inclusion in the Cultural Sector

Accessibility, Diversity, Equity and Inclusion in the Cultural Sector: Initiatives and Lessons Learned from Real-life Cases

EDITED BY

JULIE BÉRUBÉ
Université du Québec en Outaouais, Canada

MARIE-LAURE DIOH
Université du Québec en Outaouais, Canada

AND

ANTONIO C. CUYLER
University of Michigan, USA

emerald
PUBLISHING

United Kingdom – North America – Japan – India – Malaysia – China

Emerald Publishing Limited
Emerald Publishing, Floor 5, Northspring, 21-23 Wellington Street, Leeds LS1 4DL

First edition 2024

Reprints and permissions service
Contact: www.copyright.com

British Library Cataloguing in Publication Data
A catalogue record for this book is available from the British Library

ISBN: 978-1-83753-035-9 (Print)
ISBN: 978-1-83753-034-2 (Online)
ISBN: 978-1-83753-036-6 (Epub)

Printed and bound by CPI Group (UK) Ltd, Croydon, CR0 4YY

INVESTOR IN PEOPLE

Contents

About the Editors   *ix*

About the Contributors   *xi*

Foreword   *xvii*

Chapter 1   ADEI in the Cultural Sector: Theories, Concepts, and Real Case Studies   *1*
Julie Bérubé and Marie-Laure Dioh

Section 1: Performing Arts

Chapter 2   Cultural Organizations on the Leading Edge of Accessibility Management: The Case of the Teatro Villa Mayor of Bogotá   *13*
Julien Doris, Julie Bérubé and Álvaro Andrés Martínez Coronel

Chapter 3   Black Opera Leaders in the United States: What Is Their Role in Black Opera?   *31*
Antonio C. Cuyler

Chapter 4   Performing Arts in a Francophone Minority Context: A Case Study of *L'Association la Girandole d'Edmonton*   *47*
Srilata Ravi and Olivia Leclair

Section 2: Music

Chapter 5   A Transformation of an Orchestra Through Gender Equity and Diversity   *69*
Sophie Galaise

Chapter 6   Navigating Gendered Spaces: Activists' Synergies in Montreal's Electronic Music Scene   *83*
Nancy Aumais and Coline Sénac

Chapter 7   The Expanding Economic Borders of South African Musicians: A Policy Effect   *97*
Akhona Ndzuta

Chapter 8   To Understand Solidarity Through Hip-Hop Culture in Haiti   *117*
Sandy Larose

Section 3: Visual Arts

Chapter 9   Collections and Inclusion: A Portrait of Museum Initiatives in Quebec and Ontario   *135*
Mélanie Boucher

Chapter 10   Beyond Fakequity: Redefining "Excellence" to Create Space for Equity   *151*
Brea M. Heidelberg

Chapter 11   Toward an Inclusive Cultural Participation: The Case of Chilean Museums   *167*
Jesús Heredia-Carroza, Javier Reyes-Martínez and Fátima Gigirey

Section 4: Events

Chapter 12   The Super Bowl: An Opportunity for Equity, Diversity, and Inclusion Initiatives for Arts Organizations   *185*
Tiffany Bourgeois

Chapter 13   Local and Popular Cultural Festivals as Venues for the Promotion of Equity, Diversity, and Inclusion: The Case of the Petronio Álvarez Pacific Music Festival in Colombia   *199*
Luis F. Aguado, Alexei Arbona and Jesús Heredia-Carroza

Chapter 14   Digital Transformation of Events and Live Performances   *215*
Stephen Boyle, Carmen Reaiche and Mohammadreza Akbari

Section 5: Synthesis, Tools, and Policy

Chapter 15   Teaching ADEI in Taiwan   *229*
Tobie S. Stein

Chapter 16   Managing Diversity in Federal Cultural Administrations: The Example of Heritage Canada and Library and Archives Canada   *243*
Julien Doris

What Can We Learn From the Case Studies About ADEI Issues?: Conclusion   *255*
Marie-Laure Dioh

About the Editors

Julie Bérubé is a Full Professor in the Department of Administrative Sciences at the Université du Québec en Outaouais (UQO). She holds a master's degree in Project Management from UQO and a PhD in Management from HEC Montréal. Her research interests focus mainly on arts and culture management. She has conducted research projects on artists' identity tensions and the effects of the pandemic on the cultural sector. She also studies issues of accessibility, diversity, equity, and inclusion, in particular the role of cultural organizations and the attractiveness of audiences. Finally, she pays particular attention in her research to culture in a regional context. Her teaching focuses mainly on management and entrepreneurship.

Marie-Laure Dioh is an Occupational Psychologist and an Associate Professor in the Department of Administrative Sciences at the Université du Québec en Outaouais. She is also a regular member of the Équipe de recherche en partenariat sur la diversité culturelle et l'immigration dans la région de Québec (ÉDIQ) and the Centre de recherche en innovations sociales (CRISES). Her main research interests are the socio-professional integration of immigrants, skilled workers and refugees in Quebec, and the life story method. In connection with this theme, she has presented numerous papers at national and international conferences and publishes her work in refereed journals.

Antonio C. Cuyler, PhD, is a Professor of Music in Entrepreneurship and Leadership in the School of Music, Theater & Dance at the University of Michigan. He is the Author of *Access, Diversity, Equity, and Inclusion in Cultural Organizations: Insights from the Careers of Executive Opera Managers of Color in the US*, the Editor of *Arts Management, Cultural Policy, & the African Diaspora*, the Author or Co-Author of 25 peer-reviewed articles that appear in the *American Journal of Arts Management, Cultural Management: Science and Education, Cultural Trends, ENCACT Journal of Cultural Management & Policy, GIA Reader, Grant Professionals Association (GPA) Journal, International Journal of Arts Management, International Journal of the Inclusive Museum, International Journal of Social, Political and Community Agendas in the Arts, Journal of Arts Management, Journal for Cultural Research, Journal of Arts Management, Law,* *and Society*, and the *Polish Journal of Management Studies*, chapters in *Music as Labour: Inequalities and Activism in the Past and Present*, *Business Issues in the Arts*, *Voices for Change in the Classical Music Profession: New Ideas for Tackling Inequalities and Exclusions*, *Oxford Handbook of Arts and Cultural Management*, and the Co-Author of *Racial/Ethnic and Gender Diversity in the Orchestra Field in 2023*. He also consults cultural organizations on access, diversity, equity, and inclusion (ADEI).

About the Contributors

Luis F. Aguado holds a doctorate in Applied Economics and Economic History from Universidad de Sevilla (Spain). He is a Professor in the Department of Economics and director of Programs and Projects, *Riqueza Completa*. Center for Applied Research at the Pontificia Universidad Javeriana (Cali, Colombia), and undertakes research and provides consultancy services in the cultural economics and creative industries. In Colombia, he has measured the economic impact of mega-cultural and sporting events such as the Cali Fair, the *Petronio Álvarez Pacific Music Festival*, and the World Games 2013 Cali. He is the Co-Founder of the Workshop on Popular Culture Economics and Business (WPCEM). He has published in prestigious journals on cultural participation and appreciation of intangible cultural heritage: *Journal of Cultural Economics, Empirical Studies of the Arts*, and *Journal of Arts Management, Law and Society*.

Mohammadreza Akbari is an MBA Academic Director (Singapore Campus) and Senior Lecturer (Supply Chain Management) at James Cook University, College of Business, Law, Governance. His research interests include logistics and supply chain management, sustainable development, emerging technologies, digital transformation, smart cities, pollution control, and the hybrid work environment.

Alexei Arbona holds a PhD in Entrepreneurship and Management from the Universitat Autònoma de Barcelona, UAB (Spain). He is an Associate Professor in the Department of Economics and the Director of *Riqueza Completa*. Center for Applied Research at the Pontificia Universidad Javeriana (Cali, Colombia). He leads the line of research on Enterprise and Sustainable Competitiveness of the Territory. He has published in prestigious journals such as *Socio-economic Planning Sciences* and *Journal of the Operational Research Society*.

Nancy Aumais is a Professor in the Department of Management of "École des sciences de la gestion de l'Université du Québec à Montréal (ESG UQAM)." She is also a member of the Chair of Entrepreneurship, Otherness, and Society. Her research primarily explores identity transformation and gender as social practice. This includes examining the construction of managerial and entrepreneurial identities, understanding how gender practices contribute to the (de)construction of difference, otherness, and inequality in organizations, and advocating for engaged pedagogy.

Mélanie Boucher is a Full Professor in museology and art history at the Université du Québec en Outaouais. She is the Founder of the CIÉCO Research and Inquiry Group, which brings together the main centers of study in francophone museology in Quebec and Canada for research on art collections and museums. She is the Director of the research creation project "Creating with collections" (FRQSC 2022–2026) and of axis 3 (the expanded collection) of the research Partnership "New uses of collections in art museums" (SSHRC 2021–2028). Mélanie Boucher is also a Principal Investigator of the Art and Museum Team, which brings together curators, visual artists, and graphic designers from three Quebec universities, and a Principal Investigator of the group "The origin and currentness of the subject's becoming object: recreating oneself at the museum and in exhibitions" (SSHRC 2021–2024). She is also a Researcher within the Research Chair in Creative Economy and Well-being (FRQSC 2022–2026). Her most recent book, *Réinventer la collection: l'art et le musée au temps de l'évènementiel* [Reinventing the collection: art and the museum in the time of events], coedited with Marie Fraser and Johanne Lamoureux, was published at the PUQ in 2023.

Tiffany Bourgeois works at the Ohio State University's Department of Arts Administration, Education and Policy as an Assistant Professor of Arts Management. Her scholarly work uses mega-event legacy theory as a lens to examine the relationship between sports mega-events and arts organizations. It also highlights exercises in soft power and cultural diplomacy. Bourgeois' recent publications can be found in *Place Branding and Public Diplomacy, American Journal of Arts Management*, and *Visual Inquiry: Learning & Teaching Art.*

Stephen Boyle is the Dean of the College of Business, Law and Governance at James Cook University. He undertook his MBA at University of South Australia and then completed his PhD in Cultural Economics at Macquarie University. He studied with cultural economist, Professor David Throsby, examining the economics of symphony orchestras in Australia. Professor Stephen Boyle won best paper in the *Economic Papers* journal in 2012 for his work on productivity analysis of symphony orchestras. His teaching and research interests are in cultural policy, arts management, and the creative economy. He chaired the 41st International Conference on Social Theory, Politics and the Arts and is an Executive Editor of the *Journal of Arts Management, Law and Society.* He is an Adjunct Researcher at the Culture and Leisure Industry Research Center at the University of International Business and Economics in Beijing, China.

Julien Doris is a Postdoctoral Researcher. He works as a Research Administrator at the Université du Québec en Outaouais. He holds a doctorate degree in Public Administration (University of Ottawa). His thesis analyzes the institutionalization of public policies aimed at increasing the representativeness of the public service and their application to organizational management systems. It also examines the emergence and professionalization of ADEI as a new venue in managing cultural organizations.

Sophie Galaise is the Managing Director of the Melbourne Symphony Orchestra (2016–). She has been a Director of not-for-profit boards for more than 20 years.

She is a member of the Australian Institute of Company Directors and, since 2021, the Chair of Symphony Services International. She has extensive global experience working with orchestras at the executive level and as a professional musician and musicologist. She is a member of the International Advisory Committee of the Master in International Arts Management (Southern Methodist University, SDA Bocconi and HEC Montreal). Prior to the MSO, Galaise was the CEO of the Queensland Symphony. Previous roles include Executive Director of the Orchestre symphonique de Québec, Executive and Artistic Director of the Orford Arts Center, and Music Coordinator of the Quebec Arts Council. Starting her career as a Flautist in Germany, she has worked in Switzerland and France. Sophie has a PhD in Musicology (University of Montreal) and an Executive MBA (McGill University/HEC Montreal). She is the Co-Author of two books and has published several articles. In 2022, she was appointed Honorary Consul of Canada to Melbourne and recognized as an Asia Society Game Changer. Asia Society Australia. https://www.Asiasociety.org.

Fátima Gigirey, PhD, graduated in Law and Economics from the University of Sevilla (Spain). At this same university, she has completed a master's degree in Economic Consulting and is currently a PhD in Economics. Among the main research topics, she addresses those related to the economics of culture and competition policy.

Brea M. Heidelberg, PhD, is an Arts Management Educator, Researcher, and Consultant. She is an Associate Professor of Entertainment & Arts Management at Drexel University. Dr Heidelberg earned her PhD in Arts Administration, Education, and Policy from the Ohio State University. Her research focuses on diversity, equity, and inclusion throughout the arts management ecosystem, human resources in cultural organizations, the professionalization of the field of arts management, and the training and development of arts administrators. In addition to earning an MA in Arts Policy & Administration, Dr Heidelberg has also earned an MS in Human Resource Management from Villanova University. She is the Founder and Principal of ISO Arts Consulting. Her consulting practice focuses on human resources issues, particularly those related to diversity, equity, and inclusion. Dr Heidelberg enjoys the emotional roller coaster that is raising her two sons, office supplies, supporting craft artists, and occasionally baking.

Jesús Heredia-Carroza, PhD, researches and oversees the cultural economics and leisure and tourism sectors. At present, Jesús is a Professor of Economics and Economic History at Universidad de Sevilla. Also, he was a Postdoctoral Researcher at the University of Sevilla for the competition-based project fund: "Ayudas para la Recualificación del Sistema Universitario Español en su Modalidad Margarita Salas" granted by the Spanish Ministry of Universities by means of Resolution of November 29, 2021, of the Universidad de Sevilla, financed by the European Union – Next Generation EU. He is the Co-Founder of the Workshop on Popular Culture Economics and Management, the Director of the Social Theory, Politics and the Arts Conference, and the Vice President of the Fundación Pública de Estudios Universitarios Francisco Maldonado de Osuna.

He has published in prestigious journals on cultural participation, copyright, and the appreciation of intangible cultural heritage: *Journal of Arts Management, Law and Society, Empirical Studies of the Arts, International Journal of Heritage Studies*, among others.

Sandy Larose holds the position of Professor of Social Psychology at the State University of Haiti and is a member of the management team of the Observatoire de recherche sur les rapports élites-populations et les migrations (ORREM). His research focuses on social inequalities, hip-hop, identity, gender, and working-class neighborhoods. He is currently on the executive committee of the International Association for the Study of Popular Music (Canada) and a member of the CELAT research center at Université Laval.

Olivia Leclair is the Programming and Communication Coordinator at l'Association la Girandole d'Edmonton since April 2022. Dance is at the heart of what Olivia does, being a member of Zéphyr since 2013, a dance teacher and workshop animator, as well as an artist in residence since 2018, reaching audiences on a national and international scale. She has recently collaborated with the Fédération Culturelle Canadienne-Française and the Société Historique de la Saskatchewan on interdisciplinary and dance pedagogy tools and workshops.

Álvaro Andrés Martínez Coronel is the General Manager at the Teatro Villa Mayor in Colombia. He has a Master of Management in International Arts Management from SMU and HEC Montreal, in alliance with SDA Bocconi. A Business Administrator with an option in Anthropology and a Bachelor in Literature with an option in Classical Studies from the Universidad de los Andes. He has worked in the Ministry of Culture of Colombia in different positions such as managing the Colombia Creativa program, an alliance between the Ministry and nine universities to offer higher education programs to artists without a university degree. Advisor to the Direction of Arts supervising projects related to public investment for the arts, international relationship agreements, investment resources from the general royalty system and arts education programs for the development of different communities. He is a Fellow 2018, 2019, 2021 of International Society for the Performing Arts (ISPA). Currently, he is leading the revitalization project of the Villa Mayor Theater.

Akhona Ndzuta is a Lecturer in Cultural Policy and Management at the Wits School of Arts (University of the Witwatersrand). At the time of writing this chapter, she was a Postdoctoral Research Fellow at the Chief Albert Luthuli Research Chair (University of South Africa). Her research interests lie in the intersections of the management of South African music and public policy. She holds a PhD from the Ohio State University and has taught a broad range of courses in cultural studies and arts management across five universities. As a music practitioner, she has performed as a vocalist in popular music ensembles in Cape Town and Johannesburg. She was a contributing Editor to volume 1 of the book "Culture and Liberation Struggle in South Africa: from colonialism to post-apartheid." In 2022, she managed "MusoCulture: A Music and Public Policy

Series," a project funded by a grant from the National Institute for the Humanities and Social Sciences (NIHSS).

Srilata Ravi is an Emeritus Professor of Francophone Literature at the University of Alberta (Campus Saint-Jean). Prior to joining the University of Alberta in 2010, she worked at the National University of Singapore (1994–2003) and then at the University of Western Australia (2004–2010). She has published extensively on global Francophone literature as well as on Canadian francophonies from comparative, postcolonial, and transnational perspectives.

Carmen Reaiche holds an MBA from the University of Adelaide and a PhD from the University of South Australia in the area of Project Management/Soft Systems Self-Organization. Beyond her research successes (including more than 70 papers to date and others in preparation), A/Prof Reaiche has obtained several research grants and a wide range of cross-cultural teaching and supervisory experience (teaching and supervising research students in Australia, Venezuela, Singapore, Hong Kong, China, Singapore, and Malaysia). Her present research interests include project management, digital transformation, cross-cultural leadership, and the social network aspects of business management models. Prior to joining the College of Business, Law and Governance at James Cook University in the role of MBA Academic Director, she was the Associate Head (Teaching and Learning) in the Entrepreneurship, Commercialisation and Innovation Center at the University of Adelaide.

Javier Reyes-Martínez holds a PhD in Social Work from Boston College and a PhD in International Social Welfare from Universidad Iberoamericana. He is a Research Professor in the Public Administration Division of the Centro de Investigación y Docencia Económicas (CIDE) in Mexico, specializing in socioeconomic and cultural inequalities, well-being, and vulnerable groups. Additionally, he is a member of the Mexican National System of Researchers at level I.

Coline Sénac is completing an interdisciplinary doctorate in semiotics and communication at the Université du Québec à Montréal (UQÀM). Her interdisciplinary research focuses on knowledge and gender inequalities in organizations. Her work has been published in international journals such as *Language and Dialog* and *Labyrinth*, as well as in research reports by the Institut national de la recherche scientifique (INRS) and the Volunteering on the move (VOTM) research group. She recently coedited a pedagogical work on communication published by Presses de l'Université du Québec.

Tobie S. Stein, PhD, is a Visiting Distinguished Professor at National Sun Yat-sen University in Kaohsiung, Taiwan. She is a three-time Fulbright Specialist (South Korea, Israel, and Taiwan) and is a member of the Fulbright Specialist Roster. She is the Author of five books, including *Racial and Ethnic Diversity in the Performing Arts Workforce* (Routledge) and *Leadership in the Performing Arts* (Allworth). Two of her books, *Performing Arts Management: A Handbook of Professional Practices*, second edition, and *Leadership in the Performing Arts* have been published in Mandarin. She is also a Professor Emerita at Brooklyn College, where for over 20 years she was the Director of the MFA Program in Performing Arts Management. She is a member of the Diversity Scholars Network at the National Center for Institutional Diversity, University of Michigan.

Foreword

Julie Bérubé

No need to argue the importance that issues of accessibility, diversity, equity, and inclusion (ADEI) play in our societies. More than ever, we need social justice in all spheres. We need a balm to heal wounds inflicted by transgressions like hate crimes, oppression, exclusion, and more. This perspective shaped the idea for our book.

In studying the cultural sector for almost a decade, I have taken an interest in the identity tension experienced by artists who are torn between giving their creativity free rein and needing to earn a living. Cultural activity in rural areas is also of significant interest to me because the concentration of resources in major urban centers leaves artists in rural areas with limited resources and, unfortunately, leads to a less robust cultural offering. Nonetheless, culture should remain accessible to all citizens regardless of factors such as their origins, social status, gender, and location. Art and culture bring well-being and have positive economic and social impacts (Boix et al., 2022; Tubadji et al., 2015). This book affirms the importance of promoting culture and its accessibility for all; it is essential, even vital, that culture becomes a common good.

I have always dreamed of a just society where differences are accepted and appreciated for their uniqueness. However, as I grew up, I quickly realized that differences could frighten, making it easy for people to discriminate against others who did not belong to dominant groups. This led me to take an interest in understanding issues of ADEI. Similar to many people, I have both privileged and unprivileged social identities. I didn't want to assume that I understood other peoples' experiences with discrimination and marginalization, but I could dream of an inclusive and just society. So, with humility, I began to study ADEI issues.

My first research project on ADEI focused on the role that cultural organizations played in relation to ADEI issues in the cultural sector. This project led me to meet artists and cultural workers who are interested in ADEI issues and who are striving for a fair and inclusive sector. I quickly became interested in the initiatives they were implementing to promote inclusion. Cultural workers and artists around the world are advocating for ADEI and seeking greater social justice. We must recognize their work and efforts and share these initiatives to inspire others to join in making cultural sectors more fair and more inclusive. This desire to acknowledge and highlight the work of others gives the book purpose.

By sharing these initiatives that promote ADEI in the cultural sector, we aim to reach two target audiences: practitioners and academics in the cultural sector. Practitioners may find interest in concrete initiatives that can be used to replicate or to inspire other actions. Several best practices emerge from the cases presented, and initiatives from one artistic discipline can also inspire other cultural disciplines. Our goal is to break down barriers and foster exchanges across all disciplines for all cultural disciplines. Similarly, initiatives in one country can inspire cultural workers in others to adopt certain practices or initiatives.

For academics, real cases fuel reflection on the challenges related to ADEI in the cultural sector. Several cases present ideas that academics can further explore, especially in collaborative research projects. In these cases, we can identify not only best practices but also the ADEI challenges that the cultural sector faces. Thus, academics could undertake research projects to find ways to overcome these challenges. The cases can also serve as teaching material, providing concrete examples that illustrate the theories taught in arts and cultural management classrooms. University programs that focus on arts and culture management are increasing in number. These programs must teach the concepts of ADEI, and this book is a perfect tool to promote the practical application of theories. Real cases from various disciplines and regions help students to understand the breadth of possibilities for promoting and integrating ADEI in the cultural sector.

As the idea for the book took shape, it became clear that I couldn't work alone on a project of such significance and scope. I instinctively turned to my close network and invited my colleague Marie-Laure Dioh to join me. Marie-Laure has a strong research background on themes of equity, diversity, and inclusion (EDI), Quebec immigration, and socio-professional integration. Her knowledge of these subjects made a valuable contribution to steering this book. Her openness, empathy, ability to engage in dialog, and her desire to continually learn about others make her a perfect editor.

Next, I approached someone I didn't know personally but who is a leader in the field of ADEI in the cultural sector, Antonio C. Cuyler. I have immense respect for all of Antonio's work on ADEI, particularly his relevant and timely contributions to the opera field. His knowledge of the sector, experience, and network were major assets for our work. The contributions of Marie-Laure and Antonio were essential for success; without their efforts and input, the book could not have been realized. I am immensely grateful to them for accepting my invitation and for their dedication for more than a year to deliver a high-quality manuscript.

Of course, the book could not have come to fruition without the participation of all the authors and practitioners who contributed to writing the separate chapters. We reached out to you, and you all responded with enthusiasm for the project. Your experiences make this book even more relevant. On behalf of the editing team, I warmly thank you for your participation and the quality of your chapters.

To maintain an open-minded approach, we intentionally placed few constraints on the contributing authors. Indeed, we only asked them to present an initiative that promotes ADEI in the cultural sector. Recognizing that the concepts of accessibility, diversity, equity and inclusion are social constructs and inherently polysemic, we acknowledge the existence of multiple and coexisting definitions to understand these concepts. We chose to let the authors refer to their own definitions rather than impose our vision of ADEI on them.

In the same vein, we did not determine the specific type of initiative that authors could present. As readers will observe, some chapters focus primarily on accessibility, others on social justice, and others on inclusion or equity. Thus, we embrace the plurality of perspectives related to ADEI and the various ways of conceptualizing them in the cultural sector.

It is, however, relevant and important for us to share with the reader at the outset how we frame these concepts. We opt for broad and inclusive definitions. For accessibility, we concur with Cuyler (2023) who conceives it as: "Access is the removal of all barriers to participation" (p. 86).

There is a range of definitions for diversity; some identify specific components such as race, gender, ethnicity, age, national origins, religion, and disability (van Ewijk, 2011). We prefer a broader definition suggesting that diversity includes all the ways in which individuals differ from one another and encompasses the characteristics that make an individual or group of individuals different from one another (Cuyler, 2013; van Ewijk, 2011).

For equity, we adopt the definition used by a Canadian funding agency, the Natural Sciences and Engineering Research Council of Canada (2017):

> Equity means fairness; people of all identities being treated fairly. It means ensuring that the processes for allocating resources and decision-making are fair to all and do not discriminate on the basis of identity. There is a need to put measures in place to eliminate discrimination and inequalities which have been well described and reported and ensure, to the best degree possible, equal opportunities. (p. 3)

Finally, for inclusion, we propose one of the definitions suggested by Dobusch (2014): "a process and condition where people gain access to areas from which they were formerly un/intentionally excluded" (p. 220). As mentioned, we did not impose these definitions, but in the foreword, we wanted to offer an initial way of conceptualizing accessibility, diversity, equity, and inclusion. While readers can understand these as individual concepts, in most cases, they are interconnected, where, for example, accessibility promotes inclusion, and so on. Thus, we advocate for a unified and comprehensive conception of ADEI.

Given the richness of chapters we received, we have chosen to organize them according to artistic discipline: performing arts, music, visual arts, and events. Initially, we aimed to highlight similarities or differences in ADEI initiatives across various artistic disciplines, but it is clear that such classification is not feasible at this stage. Indeed, faced with the diversity of cases presented, we have not been able to identify specific practices unique to each artistic discipline. The initiatives are therefore presented as independent of each other. Chapter 1 introduces the structure of the book and provides a brief overview of some literature on ADEI in the cultural sector.

References

Boix, D., De Miguel Molina, B., & Pau Rausell, K. (2022). The impact of cultural and creative industries on the wealth of countries, regions and municipalities. *European Planning Studies, 30*(9), 1777–1797.

Cuyler, A. (2013). Affirmative action and diversity: Implications for arts management. *The Journal of Arts Management, Law, and Society, 43*(2), 98–105. https://doi.org/10.1080/10632921.2013.786009

Cuyler, A. (2023). Access, diversity, equity, and inclusion (ADEI) in cultural organizations. In A. Rhine & J. Pension (Eds.), *Business issues in the arts*. Routledge.

Dobusch, L. (2014). How exclusive are inclusive organisations? *Equality, Diversity and Inclusion: An International Journal, 33*(3), 220–234. https://doi.org/10.1108/EDI-08-2012-0066

Natural Sciences and Engineering Research Council of Canada. (2017). *Guide for applicants: Considering equity, diversity and inclusion in your application*. https://www.nserc-crsng.gc.ca/_doc/EDI/Guide_for_Applicants_EN.pdf

Tubadji, A., Osoba, B. J., & Nijkamp, P. (2015). Culture-based development in the USA: Culture as a factor for economic welfare and social well-being at a county level. *Journal of Cultural Economics, 39*(3), 277–303. https://doi.org/10.1007/s10824-014-9232-3

van Ewijk, A. R. (2011). Diversity and diversity policy: Diving into fundamental differences. *Journal of Organizational Change Management, 24*(5), 680–694. https://doi.org/10.1108/09534811111158921

Chapter 1

ADEI in the Cultural Sector: Theories, Concepts, and Real Case Studies

Julie Bérubé and Marie-Laure Dioh

Université du Québec en Outaouais, Canada

Abstract

In this first chapter of the book, we present our perspective of the cultural sector along with the terminological choices we have made. Subsequently, we provide a brief literature review on issues of accessibility, diversity, equity, and inclusion (ADEI) in the cultural sector. Finally, we outline the structure of the book, which is divided into five sections. The first four sections group chapters that discuss ADEI initiatives in specific sectors. The first section focuses on the performing arts sector and includes three chapters presenting cases from a theater, the opera sector, and a dance organization. The second section delves into the music sector, with four chapters covering cases from an orchestra, the electronic music sector, musicians from South Africa, and hip hop in Haiti. The third section comprises three chapters presenting cases from the visual arts sector, including Canadian and Chilean museums and a cultural organization. The fourth section explores the events sector, presenting three chapters, two of which discuss festivals and one focuses on the Super Bowl. The final section presents two chapters not tied to a specific discipline. The first chapter shares an experience of teaching ADEI in art in Taiwan, while the second chapter deals with policies related to ADEI from a federal cultural administration in Canada.

Keywords: ADEI; cultural sector; literature review; structure of the book; concepts

Introduction

In the foreword for this book, we proposed definitions for the central concepts of accessibility, diversity, equity, and inclusion (ADEI). These concepts traverse all

Accessibility, Diversity, Equity and Inclusion in the Cultural Sector, 1–9
Copyright © 2024 Julie Bérubé and Marie-Laure Dioh
Published under exclusive licence by Emerald Publishing Limited
doi:10.1108/978-1-83753-034-220241001

areas of society and all sectors. However, as these are social constructs (van Ewijk, 2011), it is important to specify the context in which the authors study them. The book is based entirely on real cases from the cultural sector. In this first chapter, we present a brief review of the literature on the concept of cultural sector and introduce a few ADEI studies for this sector. Next, we present the different sections of the book and the theme of each chapter.

One can study this sector according to a variety of approaches, and ADEI is generally considered within the broad spectrum of arts management or arts administration. In the early 1990s, some questioned the very legitimacy of the field by showing the lack of seriousness that some universities reserved for it (Dorn, 1992), but since then, several authors have argued in favor of its legitimacy (Jung, 2017; Kirchner & Rentschler, 2015; Paquette & Redaelli, 2015). Jung (2017) identified the interdisciplinary and multidisciplinary theories of the field: "I postulate that this is due to the nature of arts administration. Its topics and issues are too broad and interconnected with other areas to be addressed or solved in one artificially confined discipline" (p. 11). In articles published in the *Journal of Arts Management, Law, and Society* between 1990 and 2014, she classified theories associated with nine disciplinary categories: art, law, sociology, psychology, policy, political science, management and organization, marketing, and economics. In this book, we embrace the diversity of theoretical approaches. We did not attempt to divide the chapters according to theoretical approaches. Given that the cases presented in this book originate directly in the field, we opted for an empirical division, based on distinctions between the artistic or cultural disciplines themselves. First, it is important to define the broader concept of the cultural sector.

Cultural Sector

UNESCO (2012) defined creative and cultural industries as: "sectors of activity whose main purpose is the creation, development, production, reproduction, promotion, dissemination or marketing of goods, services and activities that have cultural, artistic and/or heritage content" (free translation, p. 17). We prefer the term sector to industry in order to avoid any confusion regarding the purpose of this sector. Indeed, one can categorize cultural activities as either private or public ownership, and many of the organizations that make up the cultural sector are not-for-profit (Thibodeau & Rüling, 2015). Some authors use the terms creative and cultural sectors interchangeably indiscriminately, while others see the cultural sector as a subcategory of the creative sector (Lazzeretti et al., 2008). The United Kingdom's Department for Culture, Media and Sport (2001) first proposed a sectoral definition of creative industries: "industries which have their origin in individual creativity, skill and talent and which have a potential for wealth and job creation through the generation and exploitation of intellectual property" (p. 5). For Lazzeretti et al. (2008), the creative sector remains an extension of the cultural sector which is traditionally associated with artistic disciplines such as music, the performing arts, and the visual arts. After systematically reviewing the literature on cultural and creative ecosystems, de Bernard et al. (2022) reported that in general, authors tend to refer to the cultural sector when discussing the "not-for-profit and/or 'arts' portion of the cultural and creative sectors" (p. 339), whereas the creative sectors are considered to be aimed at market-oriented activity. However, they add that many authors do not necessarily distinguish between the creative and cultural sectors. In the context of this book, we focus on the cultural sector by embracing its diversity, which includes a large number of subsectors or disciplines such as visual arts, performing arts, music, etc. In turn, one can divide these disciplines into several other subdisciplines or genres.

ADEI in the Cultural Sector

Before presenting the rationale for the structure of the book, we offer a brief overview of some research projects on ADEI in the cultural sector. In recent decades, several industries and sectors have expressed ideals and commitments about ADEI and implementing these concepts at a systemic level. These concerns have developed in private sector organizations (Thompson, 2022), as well as public sector higher education (Bombaro, 2020), training (Morukian, 2022), and the surgical and medical sector (Mulholland, 2020). However, there are challenges that impede ADEI-related progress in both the private and public sectors. First and foremost, the changing vocabulary surrounding these concepts does not provide for a stable base for communication and understanding (Bombaro, 2020; Morukian, 2022). We do not pretend to address all the concerns related to ADEI issues in all these sectors of activity, but we join the debate by assembling authors whose questions delve into ADEI issues in the cultural sector around the world and who present relevant initiatives. We hope to contribute to reflection on the subject.

In the cultural sector, several authors have studied ADEI, particularly in Europe and North America. A growing number of studies have explored the lack of ethnic diversity in many subsectors ranging from film to television (Cobb, 2020; Henry & Ryder, 2021), publishing (Saha & van Lente, 2020; Shaw, 2020), music (Cuyler, 2020; Hesmondhalgh & Saha, 2013), museums (Heidelberg, 2019), or media (O'Brien & Arnold, 2022). As an example, the literature highlights a lack of racial diversity in the performing arts in the United States. Stein (2020) goes so far as to speak of "white privilege" in the arts sector by exposing barriers and biases that have created inequalities for minority groups. Other authors (Cuyler, 2007, 2013, 2020) have pointed out the nonrepresentation of racially diverse communities in the management of arts and entertainment organizations in the United States, including opera, and how such factors as ethnicity, different abilities, race, gender, sexual orientation remain barriers in pursuit of career. As a result, people of color remain underrepresented in leadership positions.

In museums, researchers have reached similar conclusions (Davies & Shaw, 2013; Heidelberg, 2019; Kinsley, 2016). Indeed, Heidelberg (2019) stressed that individuals from diverse backgrounds are underrepresented. The author asserts that despite several initiatives to diversify the workforce to accommodate individuals limited by disability, economic means, or other diversity, museums must develop decision-making processes that dismantle discriminatory practices. The author's findings echo what other authors (Davies & Shaw, 2013; Kinsley, 2016) have said about museums and the lack of diversity or inclusion, especially in management positions.

Other researchers, meanwhile, have focused on the media sector (Banks, 2017; O'Brien & Arnold, 2022). For example, in Europe, some professionals in the sector experience inequality, exclusion, and discrimination on the basis of their social identity; ADEI initiatives to facilitate their integration are lacking. And these workers do not see themselves as key players in bringing about the social change needed. On a different note, authors in the creative and cultural industries literature have looked at youth inclusion, particularly in community arts in Canada (Campbell, 2021), and also point to a lack of diversity and equity.

Researchers in the cultural sector have also studied the impact of underfunding in the sector. Indeed, according to some authors (Helicon Collaborative, 2017; Sidford, 2011), the majority of arts funding supports large organizations with budgets over $5 million, that primarily present Western European art forms and serve white audiences. In other cases, larger scale permanent institutions and certain types of management structures and business models receive funding at the expense of the independent precariat (Greer, 2021, pp. 235–236). Using the publishing industry as an example, Shaw (2020) explained how the lack of financial opportunities contributes to underrepresentation of working-class writers in the United Kingdom. The author argued that this lack impacts their networking abilities and opportunities to showcase their skills. Consequently, the literary industry is the least diverse of all creative and cultural industries in the United Kingdom. In this case, increasing the investment in mentoring programs, unconscious bias training, and policy development to counter the "class ceiling" (p. 224) would address this situation.

Several other studies have examined the integration of ADEI into municipalities' overall goals and master plans for their arts and culture programs (Ashley et al., 2022; Loh & Kim, 2021). They found that, occasionally, these values are only considered guiding principles and that the level of commitment varies across municipalities. Quite often, municipalities continue to ignore marginalized and low-resource groups in providing services and encouraging participation (Ashley et al., 2022). Similarly, when looking at organizational structures in the cultural sector, such as museums (Haupt et al., 2022; Scott & Luby, 2007), authors found that internal culture, management, and leadership practices or change strategies can inhibit the evolution of ADEI. Some research in the arts and creative industries has highlighted various initiatives to address imbalanced representation of minority groups in production, distribution, and consumption of public cultural goods (Gregory, 2019; Saha, 2017 cited in Hadley et al., 2022).

Scholars have also studied the effect of the pandemic on artists' livelihoods (Connor, 2021; Jones, 2024; Walmsley et al., 2022). The literature shows the vulnerability and discrimination experienced by artists in the field, underlining that during the pandemic, this structural precarity was exacerbated, due to lack of funding and relief assistance (Jones, 2024). Indeed, in many countries around the world, support from governments and funding agencies in the arts and culture sector has been lacking, which has increased individual and organizational vulnerability (Bailey, 2020). Other research has argued that the pandemic has had an impact on inclusion and diversity of the workforce in the cultural sector. In this regard, Eikhof (2020) found that women, older people, people with disabilities, and workers with family responsibilities, who were already underrepresented in cultural careers, experienced further job losses and precariousness. We see that ADEI research in the cultural sector is flourishing, whether done in Europe or North America, but to solve these issues, we have much more work to do. This book and its illustrative cases from different artistic disciplines and countries contribute to the research efforts for effective solutions.

Structure of the Book

We organized the material according to four categories of artistic discipline: performing arts, music, visual arts, and events. Each discipline forms a section of the book, while the concluding synthesis section presents two chapters that are not specific to any artistic discipline. It's difficult to draw a line that clearly separates certain disciplines. Given the breadth of the music discipline, we chose to treat it in a separate section, but for some, the discipline of music is an inherent part of the performing arts. For example, opera straddles the line between the performing arts and music. We made editorial choices when allocating the chapters to sections, but we are aware that some could have separated the sections differently.

The first section of three chapters focuses on the performing arts, such as theater, dance, circus, opera, etc. Doris, Bérubé, and Martinez's chapter presents the case of Teatro Villa Mayor in Bogota. In recent years, this theater has undertaken an initiative to promote its accessibility, following a three-step approach (mindset, possibility and capacity, and productive learning). The implementation of their accessibility management plan is outlined. The second chapter by Cuyler concerns Black opera leaders in the United States. In addition to defining the concept of Black opera, this chapter describes the unique and powerful role that Black opera leaders play in shaping audiences' appreciation, engagement with, and understanding of Black opera. The third chapter by Ravi and Leclair presents the history of a dance troupe and school in a francophone minority context. In the other nine English-speaking provinces and three territories, there are minority francophone communities. The case of L'association la Girandole, in Edmonton, Alberta (Canada), demonstrates the challenges faced by this cultural organization dedicated to teaching and promoting French–Canadian dance there.

The second section focuses on the music sector and consists of four chapters. The first chapter is by Sophie Galaise, who has been the Managing Director of the Melbourne Symphony Orchestra (MSO) in Australia since 2016. Galaise explains the MSO's desire to transform itself to embrace greater diversity and strive for greater equity. She particularly emphasizes the gender equity targeted by the

MSO, as orchestras are traditionally recognized as predominantly male environments. She explains how the pandemic provided an opportunity to launch the transformation of the MSO. In the second chapter of this section, Aumais and Senac also explore the role of women in the Canadian music industry in Montreal. They focus, among other things, on the place of women and their identity in electronic music and the strategies women employ to build a career in a male-dominated environment. The third chapter, by Ndzuta, focuses on South African musicians who struggle to find employment opportunities after they graduate from university. Public and institutional policies during and after apartheid encourage musicians to exile themselves to other countries where they can fulfill their career and economic ambitions. In the last chapter of this section, Larose examines the case of hip-hop in Haiti, where practices of solidarity and mutual aid in Port-au-Prince help rappers to cope with social and financial challenges.

The third section is comprised of three chapters on ADEI in the visual arts discipline. In the first chapter, Boucher presents initiatives by three Canadian museums to develop and use their collections. Boucher relies on the three strategies established by Maura Reilly – areas of study, revisionism, and polylogue – to promote inclusion in exhibitions. In the second chapter, Heidelberg explains the concept of fakequity, where organizations talk about equity but do not take the necessary steps to bring about real changes. She relates the case of a midwestern museum, which illustrates the elements that contribute to false starts in equity work within predominantly white arts institutions. The third chapter by Heredia-Carroza, Reyes-Martinez, and Gigirey focuses on attendance in Chilean museums by disabled people, using data from the National Survey of Cultural Participation in Chile. They are researching the impact of certain disabilities on museum attendance. To make Chilean museums more accessible and inclusive, their findings have implications for museum infrastructure, funding, and management policies.

The fourth section offers three chapters on the events industry. In the first chapter, Bourgeois analyzes a partnership between a mega-event, Super Bowl LIII, and a local arts organization, WonderRoot. WonderRoot created a mural to promote ADEI that accented elements of Atlanta's civil rights and social justice journey. In the second chapter, Aguado, Arbona, and Heredia-Carroza discuss how the Petronio Álvarez Pacific Music Festival in Colombia promotes ADEI in the city of Cali. This festival serves as a source of income for traditionally marginalized Afro-Colombian communities and fosters intercultural dialog between the local community and tourists. The last chapter by Boyle, Reaiche, and Akbari details the digital transformation of the North Australia Festival of Arts. This transformation requires adjustments in roles, personal skills, management techniques, technologies, and digital inclusion initiatives.

The final section comprises two chapters that address different aspects of ADEI without a specific discipline focus, as well as our conclusion for the book. In Stein's chapter, she shares her experience as a visiting professor in Taiwan, teaching 16–18 week courses on creativity, marketing, theater management, the cultural and artistic environment, and research methods to undergraduate and graduate college students. Her inclusive pedagogical methods incorporated ADEI concepts, and she reports on two relevant cases from her experience teaching the arts in Taiwan. In the final chapter, Doris discusses how two federal government departments, Heritage Canada and Library and Archives Canada, implemented an ADEI management strategy. His chapter illustrates how the mandate of a public cultural administration evolved to promote ADEI. In the conclusion, Dioh proposes a synthesis of the different concepts presented in the book.

Conclusion

We hope that you will learn from each of authors' insights about the cases presented in this book, and that the initiatives presented will inspire and shape future ADEI goals of the cultural sector worldwide. The book is also an invitation to international collaboration and the sharing of best practices. Several ADEI initiatives for the cultural sector are already underway, and we wanted to present a few of them to inspire future generations.

References

Ashley, A. J., Loh, C. G., Bubb, K., & Durham, L. (2022). Diversity, equity, and inclusion practices in arts and cultural planning. *Journal of Urban Affairs, 44*(4–5), 727–747. https://doi.org/10.1080/07352166.2020.1834405

Bailey, J. (2020). *Government responses to the impact of COVID-19 on the arts and creative industries*. BYP Group. https://www.bypgroup.com/blog/2020/3/21/government-arts-responses-to-covid-19?fbclid=IwAR1mc44Yc4ulSHhUDmhJws7mqgiOMFCi6LMnkRRz0OL2n5NTW7RcgdeHIw. Accessed on February 17, 2023.

Banks, M. (2017). *Creative justice: Cultural industries: Work and inequality*. Rowman & Littlefield.

Bombaro, C. (Ed.). (2020). *Diversity, equity, and inclusion in action: Planning, leadership, and programming*. ALA Editions.

Campbell, M. (2021). Reimagining the creative industries in the community arts sector. *Cultural Trends, 30*(3), 263–282. https://doi.org/10.1080/09548963.2021.1887702

Cobb, S. (2020). What about the men? Gender inequality data and the rhetoric of inclusion in the US and UK film industries. *Journal of British Cinema and Television, 17*(1), 112–135. https://doi.org/10.3366/jbctv.2020.0510

Connor, B. (2021). *Gender & creativity: Progress on the precipice* (Special ed.). UNESCO.

Cuyler, A. C. (2007). *The careers of non-European executive opera administrators in the U.S.* Unpublished doctoral dissertation, Florida State University.

Cuyler, A. (2013). Affirmative action and diversity: Implications for arts management. *The Journal of Arts Management, Law, and Society, 43*(2), 98–105.

Cuyler, A. C. (2020). *Access, diversity, equity and inclusion in cultural organizations: Insights from the careers of executive opera managers of color in the us*. Routledge.

Davies, S., & Shaw, L. (2013). Diversifying the museum workforce: The diversify scheme and its impact on participants' careers. *Museum Management and Curatorship, 28*(2), 172–192.

de Bernard, M., Comunian, R., & Gross, J. (2022). Cultural and creative ecosystems: A review of theories and methods, towards a new research agenda. *Cultural Trends, 31*(4), 332–353. https://doi.org/10.1080/09548963.2021.2004073

Department for Digital, Culture, Media & Sport; Unites Kingdom Government. (2001). *Creative industries mapping.* https://www.gov.uk/government/publications/creative-industries-mapping-documents-2001

Dorn, C. M. (1992). Arts administration: A field of dreams? *The Journal of Arts Management, Law, and Society, 22*(3), 241–251. https://doi.org/10.1080/10632921.1992.9944406

Eikhof, D. R. (2020). COVID-19, inclusion and workforce diversity in the cultural economy: What now, what next? *Cultural Trends, 29*(3), 234–250. https://doi.org/10.1080/09548963.2020.1802202

Greer, S. (2021). Funding resilience: Market rationalism and the UK's "mixed economy" for the arts. *Cultural Trends, 30*(3), 222–240.

Gregory, D. L. (2019). *Learning from The Drum: Towards a decolonization of the arts in the UK.* PhD thesis, University of Warwick.

Hadley, S., Heidelberg, B., & Belfiore, E. (2022). Reflexivity and the perpetuation of inequality in the cultural sector: Half awake in a fake empire? *Journal for Cultural Research, 26*(3–4), 244–265. https://doi.org/10.1080/14797585.2022.2111220

Haupt, G., Bequette, M., Goeke, M., & Her, C. (2022). '… Yet, it is still very White': Structural and cultural impediments to DEAI change in science museums. *Museum Management and Curatorship, 37*(2), 196–213. https://doi.org/10.1080/09647775.2022.2052161

Heidelberg, B. M. (2019). Evaluating equity: Assessing diversity efforts through a social justice lens. *Cultural Trends, 28*(5), 391–403. https://doi.org/10.1080/09548963.2019.1680002

Helicon Collaborative. (2017). *Not just money: Equity issues in cultural philanthropy.* https://heliconcollab.net/our_work/not-just-money/

Henry, L., & Ryder, M. (2021). *Access all areas: The diversity manifesto for TV and beyond.* Faber and Faber.

Hesmondhalgh, D., & Saha, A. (2013). Race, ethnicity, and cultural production. *Popular Communication, 11*(3), 179–195. https://doi.org/10.1080/15405702.2013.810068

Jones, S. (2024). Cracking up: The pandemic effect on visual artists' livelihoods. *Cultural Trends, 33*(1), 1–18.

Jung, Y. (2017). Threading and mapping theories in the field of arts administration: Thematic discussion of theories and their interdisciplinarity. *The Journal of Arts Management, Law, and Society, 47*(1), 3–16. https://doi.org/10.1080/10632921.2016.1241970

Kinsley, R. P. (2016). Inclusion in museums: A matter of social justice. *Museum Management and Curatorship, 31*(5), 474–490.

Kirchner, T. A., & Rentschler, R. (2015). External impact of arts management research: An extended analysis. *International Journal of Arts Management, 17*(3), 46–67, 93.

Lazzeretti, L., Boix, R., & Capone, F. (2008). Do creative industries cluster? Mapping creative local production systems in Italy and Spain. *Industry & Innovation, 15*(5), 549.

Loh, C. G., & Kim, R. (2021). Are we planning for equity? *Journal of the American Planning Association, 87*(2), 181–196. https://doi.org/10.1080/01944363.2020.1829498

Morukian, M. (2022). *Diversity, equity & inclusion for trainers.* ATD Press.

Mulholland, M. W. (2020). *The diversity promise: Success in academic surgery and medicine through diversity, equity, and inclusion.* Wolters Kluwer Health.

O'Brien, A., & Arnold, S. (2022). Creative industries' new entrants as equality, diversity and inclusion change agents? *Cultural Trends.* https://doi.org/10.1080/09548963.2022.2141100

Paquette, J., & Redaelli, E. (2015). *Arts management and cultural policy research.* Palgrave Macmillan. https://doi.org/10.1057/9781137460929

Saha, A. (2017). The politics of race in cultural distribution: Addressing inequalities in British Asian theatre. *Cultural Sociology, 11*(3), 302–317. https://doi.org/10.1177/1749975517708899

Saha, A., & van Lente, S. (2020). *Rethinking "diversity" in publishing.* Goldsmiths Press.

Scott, E., & Luby, E. M. (2007). Maintaining relationships with native communities: The role of museum management and governance. *Museum Management and Curatorship, 22*(3), 265–285. https://doi.org/10.1080/09647770701628602

Shaw, K. (2020). Common people: Breaking the class ceiling in UK publishing. *Creative Industries Journal, 13*(3), 214–227. https://doi.org/10.1080/17510694.2019.1707521

Sidford, H. (2011). *Fusing arts, culture and social change: High impact strategies for philanthropy.* http://heliconcollab.net/wp-content/uploads/2013/04/Fusing-Arts_Culture_and_Social_Change1.pdf

Stein, T. S. (2020). *Racial and ethnic diversity in the performing arts workforce.* Routledge.

Thibodeau, B. D., & Rüling, C.-C. (2015). Nonprofit organizations, community, and shared urgency: Lessons from the arts and culture sector. *The Journal of Arts Management, Law, and Society, 45*(3), 156–177. https://doi.org/10.1080/10632921.2015.1080640

Thompson, J. (2022). *Diversity and inclusion matters: Tactics and tools to inspire equity and game-changing performance.* Wiley.

UNESCO. (2012). *Politique pour la créativité. Guide pour le développement des industries culturelles et créatives.* http://www.unesco.org/new/fr/culture/themes/cultural-diversity/diversity-of-cultural%20expressions/tools/policy-guide/como-usar-esta-guia/sobre-definiciones-que-se-entiende-por-industrias-culturales-y-creativas/. Accessed on 21 février 2023.

van Ewijk, A. R. (2011). Diversity and diversity policy: Diving into fundamental differences. *Journal of Organizational Change Management, 24*(5), 680–694.

Walmsley, B., Gilmore, A., O'Brien, D., & Torregiani, A. (2022). *Culture in crisis: Impacts of Covid-19 on the UK cultural sector and where we go from here.* Centre for Cultural Value.

Section 1

Performing Arts

Chapter 2

Cultural Organizations on the Leading Edge of Accessibility Management: The Case of the Teatro Villa Mayor of Bogotá

Julien Doris[a], *Julie Bérubé*[b]
and *Álvaro Andrés Martínez Coronel*[c]

[a]University of Ottawa, Canada
[b]Université du Québec en Outaouais, Canada
[c]Teatro Villa Mayor of Bogotá, Colombia

Abstract

As part of the accessibility, diversity, equity and inclusion (ADEI) conceptual umbrella, how accessibility is envisioned and requires increasingly greater attention and involvement from both cultural managers and audiences of inclusive arts organizations? But what is the scope of an accessibility management plan? What exactly does an accessibility plan include, and how do cultural institutions engage with accessibility requirements today? Such questions drive this chapter, illustrated by the case of Teatro Villa Mayor, located in Bogota. Since this cultural institution opened in 2000, its goal has been to "bring people together around shows of quality and diversity that make the theater a symbol of the city." In 2016, the city approved a new managerial plan for this facility. In response, Teatro Villa Mayor implemented a three-part management strategy for its teams, outlined in this chapter. First, the "Mindset" phase redefined this place as a cultural institution accessible by not one but multiple communities. Second, the "Possibility and capacity" phase activated awareness and training to prepare the theater to be able to receive any kind of event. Third, the "Productive learning" phase encouraged concrete actions to design, implement, and promote new experiences for the audiences. By detailing the strategic changes and evaluation measures adopted by the Teatro Villa Mayor to sustain accessibility, the positive results from accessibility management in

Accessibility, Diversity, Equity and Inclusion in the Cultural Sector, 13–29
Copyright © 2024 Julien Doris, Julie Bérubé and Álvaro Andrés Martínez Coronel
Published under exclusive licence by Emerald Publishing Limited
doi:10.1108/978-1-83753-034-220241003

cultural industries, such as an increased capacity to organize more events and to welcome new participants, can be discussed.

Keywords: Accessibility; cultural organizations; management; communities; infrastructures; evaluation

Introduction

For more than two decades, accessibility has been recognized as a managerial standard. The International Standards Organization (ISO) provides best practices to promote accessibility in the workplace. Initial accessibility policies and action plans were implemented to give disabled persons an opportunity that was equal to abled people to access infrastructure and services that operated according to the rules and needs of nondisabled people. Many countries including Colombia adopted and adapted some of these standards. More recently, the concept of accessibility has been extended to all "situations in which the characteristics of any field can be accessed by all people without discrimination on grounds of sex, age, scientific status, etc. In other words, a situation where everyone can use infrastructure, services, equipment, goods and engage in activities independently, safely, and conveniently" (UNESCO, 2022). Accessibility, as defined in section 1 of this chapter and as shown through the experience of the Teatro Villa Mayor, is a key question for each cultural organization's management. It deserves priority attention to ensure equal and universal access to arts for everyone (Plaisance, 2015).

The Teatro Villa Mayor is in the southeast side of the Antonio Nariño locality, one of 20 electoral districts in Bogotá, Colombia's largest city. As a public cultural facility, it is administered under the locality Mayor's Office. Between 2000 and 2020, Teatro Villa Mayor was the only public venue with the capability to present artistic shows in southern Bogotá. Other theaters were concentrated in the center and northern areas of the city. Villa Mayor was a very important reference point for testing and presenting (mainly performing arts) shows for audiences in the area who craved artistic programming. The building is designed as a 291-seat black box, with a medium-size stage (12 × 8 × 5 mts), with minimal offstage space (both in the back and in the wings), and a small lobby (seasonally used as an art gallery). The theater is located in the park of the Villa Mayor neighborhood, between the headquarters of the Local Board for Community Action and the Church.

In 2016, Bogotá's District Planning Secretary provided the following data: The Antonio Nariño locality (made up of 15 neighborhoods) has a population of 109,254 people (51.4% women and 48.6% men), with a high social mobility factor (0.84). Education achievement was mainly at the secondary level (45.2% of the local men and 46% of the women), while 15.9% of the men and 13.9% of women reached university level.

In this sociodemographic context, the theater had evolved. Three moments in its history are relevant:

(1) Construction (2000), instigated by the Antonio Nariño local Mayor's Office, to host different artistic presentations from the area. Artists who had performed informally in neighborhood facilities that served other purposes finally had a stage on which to perform. Even though the equipment was basic and conditions were simple, the place was purpose-built to accommodate artists and audiences. The notable features of this moment were the important contributions and participation of local artists, producers, community leaders, and city hall.

(2) Remodeling (2013), thanks to the Antonio Nariño local Mayor's Office, expanded the administrative area and the lobby, improved auditorium seats and the lobby, built an exterior balcony, and improved some aesthetic aspects of the venue. These changes were designed to make the theater more welcoming to audiences. The remodeling and contributions of technical equipment from strategic allies were the salient attributes of this moment.

(3) The succeeding years (2016 – current) involved a change of vision that impacted the operating model. Programming was diversified and reactivated, creating long-term alliances with public and private entities who promote the arts in Bogotá and internationally; the theater was included in national and district cultural plans and projects; legal and institutional problems with the building and the land were solved; the theater was integrated in regulations for presenting Public Artistic Shows, and upgraded to comply with regulations for public buildings; an architectural remodeling plan was implemented to solve structural problems; a new sustainable managerial model was introduced to encompass this evolution. Updating the model, improving the venue, and professionalizing procedures and regulatory compliance were the significant elements of this moment.

Due to the consistency in programming by the venue between 2016 and 2019, the Secretary of Culture, Recreation, and Sports for the City of Bogota awarded a grant to the locality's Mayor Office Development Fund for the Teatro Villa Mayor in 2019. This grant showed City Hall's commitment to support a five-step plan that involved: (I) Preparing the venue for transformation (2016–2019); (II) Designing and licensing the architectural changes (2020–2021); (III) Funding and executing remodeling of the building (2022–2024); (IV) Obtaining and installing upgrades equipment (2024–2025); and (V) Implementing a new management model of remodeled theater (2025).

The aim of this chapter is to illustrate ways to manage accessibility in cultural organizations by discussing multiple strategic steps that the Teatro Villa Mayor followed. After a brief introduction to accessibility management in cultural organizations in section 1, in section 2, we discuss institutions' audiences and communities to explore accessibility as an initial "mindset stage" (Klironomos et al., 2006). The third section draws attention to workplace responsibilities. In this stage, the *potential* of engaging cultural workers and artists in accessibility management is linked to the organization's *capacity* to design awareness and training initiatives. The fourth section on the "productive learning stage" refers to programming and infrastructural renewal to welcome and serve all kinds of publics. Finally, the question of *the strategic plan evaluation* can be interpreted as an additional stage to measure and report implementation and results of accessibility management.

Section 1: Accessibility Management in Cultural Organizations

Accessibility: One Word, Several Meanings

The concept of accessibility is usually studied in conjunction with the concepts of diversity, equity, and inclusion (ADEI) (Cuyler, 2023). These concepts are polysemous, and there are several definitions for each. For the Teatro Villa Mayor of Bogotá, all four concepts are interrelated, but for the purposes of this chapter, we focus specifically on accessibility. More than two decades ago when scholars and public decision-makers discussed accessibility, its meaning was limited to the physical environment (Zallio & Clarkson, 2021). Now, accessibility is much more broadly conceived to include physical, sensory, and cognitive needs. Most cultural organizations have their own definitions of accessibility. For example, the American Alliance of Museums (2018) defines accessibility as: "Giving equitable access to everyone along the continuum of human ability and experience. Accessibility encompasses the broader meanings of compliance and refers to how organizations make space for the characteristics that each person brings." For this chapter, we refer to the definition proposed by Cuyler (2023): "Access is the removal of all barriers to participation" (p. 86). As he explained, accessibility is a universal design for all.

Accessibility Management Is Mainly About Opening Cultural Organizations

Accessibility is a responsibility of cultural organizations to ensure that they promote accessibility to all. According to a 2015 report by the National Endowment for the Arts, 38% of Americans surveyed did not attend an arts event because the costs were too high, and 37% did not attend because access was too difficult, including access difficulties resulting from a disability or illness. Cumulatively, 75% of respondents were unable to attend an arts event because of accessibility issues. Cuyler (2023) explained that cultural organizations need to be aware of the composition of their audience if they are to foster accessibility. He indicated that people are more likely to consume cultural goods if they identify with them, and consequently, it is important for cultural organizations to consider this factor when planning their programming. Accessibility therefore requires an awareness of the various barriers that may prevent a person from attending an artistic event.

Multiple Ways of Guiding Organizational Practices Through Accessibility

Cultural organizations may be encouraged to include accessibility in their strategic plans for a range of different reasons. International organizations are adopting accessibility standards as guidelines for their members. The United Nations signed a declaration on the rights of people with disabilities in 2006 (Folcher & Lompré, 2012). Governments are increasing implementation of public regulations concerning accessibility. In 2019, the federal government of Canada legislated *The Accessible Canada Act*, to "guarantee the right to equal benefit of the law without discrimination, in particular discrimination on the basis of disability." Columbia adopted the *ley 1618* in 2013. *The Americans with disabilities Act* became law in the United States in 1990. Besides these external influences, cultural institutions have inherent concerns about accessibility: as a workplace, as a place of public assembly, as a place to welcome artists and audiences, where art is exhibited and performed. Moreover, cultural institutions reflect their social environment so their own organizational practices must encompass social changes (Curie, 2000; Ferté, 2008). To do so, there certainly is no one best way but multiple avenues that admit all their communities. These organizational choices may be articulated in a strategic plan. This plan may identify the organizational context, objectives, estimated results, and finally, the indicators to measure the results (Larouche et al., 2016).

Cultural organizations can address accessibility in their strategic plan by thinking about their level of knowledge about the concept and their commitment to change. The capacity of cultural workers to act as institutional entrepreneurs was previously shown in the study of the cultural sector by US sociologist Paul DiMaggio (1982). He explained how cultural institutions historically differentiated between high and popular culture and how this thinking contributed to obstructing access to their organization for many groups of people. Training about how to consider accessibility in terms of expanding cultural programming or adapting physical and technological infrastructure to include more communities and publics are examples of options that can be part of the strategic plan. Whatever the lines of action, indicators of results must be chosen to express alignment with and measure achievement of strategic goals.

Section 2: The "Mindset" Stage: Thinking in Terms of Communities

As explained above, the Teatro Villa Mayor has passed through three stages to build accessibility. The initial stage is to address "mindset" which implies that to be as inclusive and accessible as possible, organizations must think about communities and audiences. As a first step, cultural organizations need to be aware of how the public and communities perceive them. Indeed, beyond concrete obstacles or barriers, such as cost or physical accessibility, organizations must consider the psychological dimension of accessibility. In advanced capitalist societies, cultural organizations are frequently perceived as elitist, and therefore not very accessible to individuals who feel that they do not belong to this social network (Foreman-Wernet, 2017). Foreman-Wernet (2017) explained that many cultural organizations are aware of the importance of being more responsive to the needs of the public in order to attract a diverse audience without diminishing artistic quality. Thus, the first step in organizational thinking is to understand community perception of art and to recognize how the organization is identified. This step can lead to reflections on whether actions to broaden accessibility can be implemented.

Bouder-Pailler and Urbain (2015) interviewed professionals in charge of providing cultural products. According to these authors, audiences in arts and cultural activities are not diversified enough, and this is often the same people who attend culture activities. To become more accessible, cultural organizations need to understand their communities and barriers to their participation. If organizations do not know why people do not participate in cultural activities, they will be unable to change their environment to make it more accessible. Or they will make changes that do not address the real problems of the people they are trying to reach. For example, Bouder-Pailler and Urbain (2015) studied barriers to participation by the underprivileged. Among the most cited barriers were the following perceptions: the activities were too expensive, the feeling that the activities were not intended for them, and that there were psychological barriers. On the other hand, respondents felt stigmatized if cultural activities were exclusively targeted to those considered underprivileged; they preferred activities intended for the general public. Bouder-Pailler and Urbain (2015) explained that the nonparticipating public "is a difficult segment to convince (cognitive register) and attract (emotional register) because of very strong financial, psychological, symbolic and identity obstacles" (p. 66).

Cuyler (2023) explained some myths about ADEI that relate to the "mindset" stage for cultural organizations. The first myth is "we welcome everyone, and do not need ADEI" (Cuyler, 2023, p. 88), a thought that presumes a knowledge of what actions are universally perceived as welcoming. This "mindset" ignores an organization's need to get to know which publics attend and which publics do not attend their cultural activities. It is not enough to say that everyone is welcome; processes must be put in place to make them feel welcome and interested in consuming the cultural goods offered. Obviously, organizations must be willing to invest money and time to be truly accessible; this echoes the fourth myth presented by Cuyler (2023) that pertains to budgeting for ADEI. Committing the time and energy necessary to making cultural organizations more accessible therefore starts with knowing the communities. This initial step must be done diligently for the next stages to be successful.

A Theater Engaging Communities

Understanding that saying "everybody is welcome" is insufficient to promote inclusion; in 2016, Teatro Villa Mayor started to identify its potential capacity to host artistic shows and linked that capacity to the artistic offer (artists and shows available) in the area and in the city. To do this, two models were considered: the Concentric Circles Model of the Cultural Industries (Throsby, 2008) and the Plan for the Arts 2016 of the Ministry of Culture of Colombia (Mincultura, 2016). The first model provides a concrete definition of artistic disciplines and activities in the milieu, in this case, relating to the organizational structure of cultural organizations in Colombia and focusing on the artistic languages present in the Antonio Nariño area. The second provides a clear definition of management dimensions in the artistic field. While the artistic practices are a "final result," it was necessary to understand that there are several other jobs central to presenting artistic performance in order to prepare the venue to receive a wide variety of artistic proposals and effectively serve their artistic needs.

In addition to this framework, the theater worked with a mindset of inclusion that considered communities in plural. Acknowledging differences, both among groups and individuals and their communication methods, was essential to understanding the dynamics of the venue and its role in the area. Having an open mind about hosting a wide variety of artists and artistic performances and not overspecializing but rather adapting to the needs of different artistic groups was key to providing a diverse artistic offering and including as many artistic proposals in the portfolio as possible. This approach also made it possible to create projects that linked artists in different disciplines, communities in different economic situations, and mediate encounters, through artistic practices, combinations that would have at first sight seemed impossible. Soon, the theater made this motto official with the local Mayor's Office:

> Teatro Villa Mayor hosts all artistic languages (music, dance, theatre, visual arts, literature and cinema), all audiences and communities (artistic interests, groups of participation, education levels, local initiatives) and all dimensions of artistic management (arts education, performance, creation, production, endowment and infrastructure, information management, sectoral organization and management).

This accumulation of interests attracted more artists and made the theater more accessible. To succeed at making the theater accessible, the team needs to continually monitor how consistent their actions are with the motto. The curatorial work of the artistic programmer goes beyond including performances of diverse communities and linking a diversity of artists to create new innovative works. The programmer understands how social and cultural dynamics change and affect performers and producers. Venezuelan migration, for instance, positively affected cultural dynamics during recent years, resulting in joint efforts of Colombian and Venezuelan artists. The pandemic disrupted regular dynamics and seasonal programming for the venue. Programming inclusiveness includes being aware of how some seasons are more active for certain communities, how educational and working calendars affect attendance, and what solutions are possible to present shows.

In 2022, for instance, Teatro Villa Mayor facilitated an interesting collaboration between Chilean performance artist, Valentina Utz, and women from the

Antonio Nariño community. Performing this international collaboration, the *Casa de igualdad de oportunidades*, raised awareness about violence against women in the city and connected with international experiences.[1] It created an impact in the area, even if it didn't ultimately solve the problem. Inclusive artistic performance may draw critical attention to a problem or issue to be addressed by a community or society. This performance transcended the space of the theater and was performed in other neighborhoods of the district. Most importantly, the collaboration expanded the network of the local organization and the artist, with the potential to make more performances and integrate them with experiences abroad.

Section 3: The "Possibility and Capacity" Stage: Awareness and Training Programs in Cultural Organizations

Why and How to Promote Accessibility in the Workplace?

Cultural organizations as professional milieus must increasingly respond to institutional norms and pressures. These responses are as much the result of influences from other professional organizations as to regulations and mechanisms related to labor and the notion of a socially responsible organizational culture (Gănescu & Gangone, 2017). Schein (2017) explains how essential the notion of organizational culture is in any organization. Organizational culture is based on the promotion of certain basic principles, certain values, and certain organizational artifacts shared between all its professional actors. Organizational culture is defined by some authors as a force for integrating and valuing diversity (Zanoni & Janssens, 2015). Organizational culture thus refers to a process of translating and communicating the objectives and values of any organization – not only to the external public and clients but, primarily internally, to show the organization's commitment or missionary spirit (Mintzberg, 2021) toward certain priorities or social issues that can be adapted and translated into the management model.

To implement an objective such as accessibility within the organization, its professionals must be able to share and promote it before it can be conveyed through their own practices and those of the organization. In this sense, training, awareness-raising, or involving organizational actors in the development of the strategic plans appear to be necessary. Training enables professional workers to reflect on "certain axes of their work and to take certain criteria into consideration" in the programming and in the standards of organizational activities (Lemaître, 1985, p. 3).

---

[1]House for the equality of opportunities for women.

Awareness and Training Programs, Between Strengths and Constraints

Training and awareness-raising therefore appear to be a prerequisite for broader organizational action to promote accessibility policies. The organization's capacity to implement training activities and share strategic orientations can greatly depend on the extent to which human, temporal, material, and financial resources are deployed by the organization. While training often appears to be undertaken voluntarily by organizations, it can also result from obligations and constraints imposed on them. This imposition may add to pre-existing management constraints. Some studies, for example, have explained that the sustainability of training could be impacted where staff turnover is high or where teams are small (Tremblay & De Sève, 2006).

When we turn to the opportunities presented by training and awareness-raising activities, it should be noted that any organization may respond to a certain social demand and can innovate its own activities, whether imitating good practices seen in other organizations or whether adapting management objectives to organizational practices (Powell & DiMaggio, 2012). Moreover, training is a necessary condition to prepare professional actors to act as institutional entrepreneurs and therefore participate in organizational renewal. With a view to implementing a strategic accessibility management plan, training can be considered as a preliminary brainstorming stage in order to guide the process of strategic orientations for the whole organization.

Awareness and Mentorship Activities Implemented by the Teatro Villa Mayor

In the case of Teatro Villa Mayor, once the strategic orientation and inclusive mindset were in place, management (the Mayor's Office and the theater director) established five principles to guide the daily operations of the theater. The actions of the team, the district council, producers, and artists were informed by these principles: Teatro Villa Mayor is a theater for the communities (in plural), for the arts (also in plural), diverse, inclusive, and with impeccable technical standards.

The first principle (communities) was a declaration of the plurality mindset and openness to receive new proposals. The second one (for the arts) was to focus the theater's main activity and the plurality of artistic languages to be received by the cultural center. The temptation to use the venue as an event hall for social, political, or other kinds of reunions was a problem for the theater in its early years. The third and fourth principles (diversity and inclusion) reinforced the message of openness and acceptance to aesthetic proposals and a broad variety of communities in the city, to eliminate censorship or discrimination practices. The final declaration (quality) emphasizes the importance of keeping good standards and adapting to the demands of the productions. The priority to include a wide range of proposals has to be balanced with technical excellence in performances. Too often, pursuit of accessibility, diversity, equity and inclusion (ADEI) involves an inherent assumption that quality will decrease without careful consideration of how it can increase excellence and quality.

In addition to these principles, other statutory requirements were widely communicated to artists and producers. Since Teatro Villa Mayor is part of the public infrastructure, it was not permitted to use it for proselytizing events of political or religious nature. Due to local regulations, it was also impossible to use it for commercial purposes, a topic that is being debated in the current plan for remodeling. These principles were disseminated broadly in presentations to the "Juntas Administradoras Locales" (local administrative council), the Cultural Council of the locality, the district and national institutions in charge of culture, producers, artists, and in other meetings with colleagues to share the strategy.

Section 4: The "Productive Learning" Stage: Adapting the Infrastructure and Events Programming

Why and How to Make Infrastructure, Programs, and Activities Accessible?

Adapting spaces and activities to welcome the diversity of the groups and their needs appears to be the most crucial challenge to the implementation of a management plan prioritizing accessibility. While reflection about accessibility initially involved questioning the conditions of access and use of spaces for users with different forms of disability, organizations can extend their reflection on accessibility to more groups or audiences to shape truly universal spaces. Universality in access can be seen as having and promoting spaces defined by and for the user groups. This ameliorative aim of cultural organizations (Haslanger, 2000) to redefine both physical and digital infrastructure of performance spaces, as well as the content and programming offered, must be subject to internal and external consultations that consider the needs expressed by the different groups (Folcher & Lompré, 2012).

Performance spaces and scheduled activities must therefore be able to be adapted to accommodate new audiences, as explained at the end of section 2. An inventory of accessibility barriers or gaps can constitute a first step prior to the implementation of a strategic plan for accessibility. The organizational statement of commitment to accessibility can then facilitate consultation about needs among users and stakeholders of cultural organizations. Following the consultation on different needs, the strategic plan on accessibility can integrate SMART objectives: specific, measurable, acceptable, realistic and defined in the time (Aghera et al., 2018). Implementation of the strategic plan is thus a process which involves significant resources and which should not be neglected by cultural organizations when reporting results.

Opportunities and Constraints for Cultural Organizations

Beyond their aim to transform managements of cultural organizations and open them up to new audiences, strategic plans can help to promote and convey new artistic practices and make new repertoire and works known to the public. They can also contribute to thinking about new nontraditional uses for cultural spaces.

Moreover, and as underlined above, accessibility can be incorporated in the basic principles and culture of the organization as managers demonstrate professional values to workers (Schein, 2017). However, and as noted above, certain issues concerning the definition and implementation of accessibility strategic plans need to be addressed by organizations to properly adapt their spaces and their cultural programming:

- Who are the groups seeking access? As highlighted in section 2, identifying groups requires thinking about audiences in terms of communities by asking what could be done to promote their access and improve their experience.
- How to inventory accessibility needs? This question arises because it is necessary to locate and interview the public who are prevented from coming to cultural organizations due to potential barriers. The work may be tedious and require the expertise of external consultants.
- How to adapt accessibility standards in consideration of the available technical and architectural resources and constraints faced by organizations? Improving accessibility of cultural institutions is often mandatory but may point out constraints with which organizations may have to deal with. These constraints in adapting the organizational environment can be cumulative: technical, financial, legal, temporal, or even logistical.
- Finally, how to adapt the programming to the needs and preferences of the users?

Infrastructure, Activity, and Event Changes in Teatro Villa Mayor

As mentioned in section 2, the cultural dynamics of the venue and the social dynamics of the area required continual monitoring to adapt to contextual changes. During the years 2017–2019, it was clear how growth affected the capacity of the venue. Admissions increased 65% from 13,860 in 2017 to 23,034 in 2019 demonstrating critical architectural needs which were not being met by the venue in its current state. Even though the base of groups performing was maintained over time, new players and bigger productions challenged the capacity of the technical and administrative team and the building.

During the prepandemic period, the experience of hosting a wide diversity of artistic offerings (594 shows) allowed the team of Teatro Villa Mayor to understand exactly what the venue needed to host better performances from diverse artistic dimensions. The technical team received a tremendous amount of feedback regarding the architectural characteristics and the stage equipment from producers, performers, and audiences. Their recommendations were the main drivers to start a remodeling plan and the main inputs to design a new cultural center.

Feedback from audiences urged for more seats and better and larger social areas, dancers and dance companies required a bigger and safer stage, theatrical performers wanted to stage events that require height, opera producers required an orchestra pit, artists with disabilities wanted self-propelled or wheelchair access to the stage, visual artists found that the space was insufficient for certain exhibitions, reading clubs wished for better spaces to read and store books, and all the companies expressed the need for a place to rehearse as well as to perform. These were among many more conscious and practical insights that provided precise knowledge of how the cultural center could work and what was lacking to provide an optimal service, in accordance with the principles established to guide strategy and operation.

Consequently, Teatro Villa Mayor came to realize that not only did it have to adapt its operations to the changing social and cultural dynamics. At a certain point, it was also clear that the vibrant cultural life of the area required a safer and bigger venue that could respond to the needs of the artists it was hosting and to the complex regulation associated with performing in a public theater.

Section 5: The Stage of Evaluation: Reporting Accessibility Achievements

Why and How to Report Accessibility Results?

The last step is evaluation. Organizations may be able to report achievements on accessibility. Professionals and artists can perceive this stage of implementing accessibility as futile or as a waste of time, energy, and money. Why do we need to put effort into evaluating accessibility achievements? To answer this question, we turn to one of the key concepts in management, developed by Fayol in the early 20th century, which is the administrative process of planning, organization, direction, and control (PODC). Planning anticipates the future and sets objectives. Organization designs the work and structure. Direction is mainly about communicating, guiding, and motivating. Finally, control evaluates performance, to learn and make corrections (Déry et al., 2020). If we omit the last step of control, it is impossible to know if the efforts invested in being more accessible have paid off or not. This stage therefore allows us to assess whether an organization is or is not more accessible. If the measures show that accessibility has not been improved, then the methods and initiatives must be reviewed by the organization so that it can really promote accessibility and being accountable to their stakeholders and honoring their mission.

Opportunities and Constraints for Cultural Organizations

While it is easy to agree that it is important to measure accessibility to know whether the organization's actions have been successful, it is more difficult to actually measure the level of accessibility. The first thing to consider is what do we want to measure? For example, do we want to measure the success of a specific program or initiative to attract a specific group of people? Do we want to measure demographic changes in the characteristics of people who attend the cultural organization in general (e.g., ethnicity, sexual orientation, gender, disability, social class, etc.)? Do we want to measure the visitors' perception of the accessibility of a cultural organization? Depending on what we want to measure, we will have to choose suitable indicators or tools.

Some organizations will want to develop very specific tools. For example, Brook (2016) presented an accessibility index that has been developed for museums and galleries in London. This index is based on the geographic proximity of museums and galleries to citizens. This measure assumes that all organizations are accessible, and that the central element is geographic proximity. This model has been refined to also consider the size of the organization and its attractiveness. This type of index provides some limited information about accessibility.

There are other tools to measure accessibility; for example, Ludwig (2012) presented a tool developed by the Cultural Access Network created by the National Endowment for the Arts. This tool asks cultural organizations to assess their accessibility in several areas like management practices, employment, grievance procedures, and communications including publications, marketing, and outreach (Ludwig, 2012). Ludwig (2012) explained that this tool is to be used by managers in conjunction with the *Design for Accessibility* handbook and addresses architectural accessibility, program accessibility, etc. An organization can use this tool to initially evaluate its accessibility and make changes accordingly. Later, a second assessment can be done by managers to note improvements. This tool is one example of many. Cultural organizations must be aware of the importance of their accessibility, and managers can initiate improvements, but to validate their relevance, it is essential to carry out an evaluation to measure their effectiveness. Ludwig (2012) specified that to help cultural organizations in this process, it is important that employees be adequately trained. Generic training on misconceptions and prejudices about disabilities, for example, could be required for all employees of cultural organizations.

Reporting Progress in Teatro Villa Mayor

In the case of Teatro Villa Mayor, documenting performance and measuring the basic activities started recently. What happened 10, 15, or 20 years ago lies in the living memory of actors and cultural agents, in archives (contracts, communications, and other official City Hall documents), and a few independent texts. There are approximate figures for attendance and many stories. Hence, it is important to systematize data.

The organization has filed two reports with the City Hall, each for 3-year periods (2016–2019 and 2020–2022), that summarize activities and include: context, policy and theoretical explanations, and basic statistics (number of events, monthly or seasonal attendance, averages, maximum and minimum levels, and comparisons). The reports also describe the programs held by the theater and a list of events, with date and attendance details. Even if issues like equity, diversity, and inclusion are not explicitly measured, these reports help to form a general idea about how accessibility has increased.

Coincidentally, the two reports frame two distinct periods, the pre-pandemic and the pandemic, making evident how difficult it was for cultural organizations to operate during the forced confinement. During the last 6 years, the theater hosted a total of 737 events with 70,599 admissions; however, 80% occurred pre-pandemic.

In terms of ADEI, measurement implies serious interrogations on many levels (ethical and technical, for instance), and difficulties are encountered when attempting to align criteria from different stakeholders. The theater's operating principles, especially about communities, diversity, and inclusivity, were reflected in qualitative and quantitative results.

Quantitatively, the percentage of local artists increased from 17% in 2017 to 19% in 2019 to 49% in 2022, showing a serious commitment by the administration to intensify participation by local and emergent artists in the theater's programming and an attentive response to strong demand from local communities.

Qualitatively, there are many programming examples that trace the evolution of accessibility and inclusion. For artists who have always felt excluded from the scene (such as blues performers, traditional dancers, Afro dancers, artistic proposals from alternative circuits, and Venezuelan migrant artists), ADEI programs have made explicit their aim of inclusion through art and creative languages. Examples illustrate this evolution: the choir *Voces Unidas*, an initiative to gather children from different socioeconomic contexts, creating and singing together, using the space of Teatro Villa Mayor to rehearse periodically; presentations by artists, and companies of artists, with cognitive or mobility challenges; and commitment to programs with institutions that promote empowerment of women and LGTQBI+ visibility.

Table 2.1 summarizes several indicators linked to ADEI collected by Teatro Villa Mayor for the period between 2017 and 2019:

Table 2.1. Accessibility, Diversity, Equity and Inclusion Programming and Participation Indicators Collected by Teatro Villa Mayor (2017–2019).

Indicator/Year	2017	2018	2019
Number of events	154	238	202
Number of participants	13,860	20,276	23,034
Percentage of local artists	17%	15%	19%
	2017–2019 inclusive		
Family programming	148 events – 19,152 participants		
Blues programming	6 concerts, 4 workshops, 667 participants		
Artistic projects with local artists	11 special projects, 4 musical projects, 4 transversal projects		
Festivals	• Human rights international cinema festival: 16 events, 1,168 participants • Festival of poetry: 16 events, 1,963 participants		

Conclusion: Highlighting the Role Played by Cultural Organizations to Sustain Accessibility

The main goal of this chapter was to provide a discussion rather than a framework for thinking about accessibility in cultural organizations. From the experience of Teatro Villa Mayor, we have seen how accessibility management is both multidimensional and transformative. Indeed, accessibility is much more than adapting the initial physical infrastructures that only accommodated abled people. Accessibility also involves transforming the workplace, the organizational culture, and the social value of the cultural organization for various audiences.

As a recent field of conceptual and practical research, accessibility has experienced expanded meaning and uses. First, the notion of disability has undergone progressive enlargements and now addresses "a wide range of diverse situations which originate in traumas and alterations, which may be physical and psychological, native or acquired, transient or sustainable" (Folcher & Lompré, 2012). In addition to the distinction between people with disabilities and people in situation(s) of disability, many other groups and audiences have accessibility requirements that cultural organizations need to consider. Instead of viewing accessibility as a restrictive dynamic, it becomes possible to have a universal perspective where no barrier can hinder anyone's access to and participation in the arts and culture.

We have highlighted in the second section the efforts that have been made by Teatro Villa Mayor to think about its community of spectators and to expand it over the years. This "mindset stage" appeared as a decisive step to attract and offer cultural content adapted to more audiences and to open wide the doors of the cultural institution. In the third section, we presented the issues related to the workplace, emphasizing the role played by cultural organizations to train and engage professionals in accessibility. We emphasized that awareness-raising and training activities were a prerequisite for involving professionals in strategic planning. Even more than thinking about and promoting the ability of cultural institutions to integrate accessibility into their management priorities, we emphasized that accessibility could be integrated into the organizational culture and thus bridge the gap between the basic principles, organizational values, and artifacts. This transformative capacity of accessibility management does however raise certain questions and challenges: how to think about user groups? How to consult audiences who do not normally frequent cultural organizations (for all sorts of reasons)? How to adapt spaces and programs to eliminate a set of barriers that prevent adopting a universal vision for access and use of arts and culture? These questions have been illustrated through the experience of Teatro Villa Mayor in the fourth section. Certain good practices or possible solutions have been identified and implemented in recent years. Finally, in the fifth section, we underlined the importance of establishing indicators and evaluation strategies to report accessibility achievements.

In short, accessibility is an important part of diversity policies in cultural organizations. As the experience of Teatro Villa Mayor shows, there is no one-way street to promote accessibility but multiple interwoven paths. Each organization may have different priorities, methods, and needs in terms of accessibility. It is also important to remember that despite the unique and singular experience of each organization, standards and good practices have been promoted internationally for the past 20 years. In addition to these standards and best practices, there are also legal and regulatory frameworks that vary from one jurisdiction to another. It is interesting to understand the extent that these regulations and laws on accessibility impact the evolution of management practices in cultural organizations.

Finally, this chapter aimed to highlight the broader contribution that cultural organizations make to the management of ADEI. Indeed, since the dividing line between these different concepts is sometimes indistinct and their implementation intersects all organizational practices (as shown by the experience of Teatro Villa Mayor), we believe it was necessary to focus attention specifically on accessibility.

References

Aghera, A., Emery, M., Bounds, R., Bush, C., Stansfield, R. B., Gillett, B., & Santen, S. A. (2018). A randomized trial of SMART goal enhanced debriefing after simulation to promote educational actions. *Western Journal of Emergency Medicine, 19*(1), 112–120.

American Alliance of Museums. (2018). *Diversity, equity, accessibility, and inclusion definitions.* https://www.aam-us.org/wp-content/uploads/2018/04/AAM-DEAI-Definitions-Infographic.pd

Bouder-Pailler, D., & Urbain, C. (2015). How do the underprivileged access culture? *International Journal of Arts Management, 18*(1), 65–77. https://search.ebscohost. com/login.aspx?direct=true&db=bth&AN=110117752&lang=fr&site=ehost-live

Brook, O. (2016). Spatial equity and cultural participation: How access influences attendance at museums and galleries in London. *Cultural Trends, 25*(1), 21–34. https://doi.org/10.1080/09548963.2015.1134098

Curie, J. (2000). *Travail, personnalisation, changements sociaux. Archives pour les histoires de la psychologie du travail* (Octarès Éditions, p. 554). Toulouse.

Cuyler, A. (2023). Access, diversity, equity, and inclusion (ADEI) in cultural organizations. In A. Rhine & J. Pension (Eds.), *Business issues in the arts.* Routledge.

Déry, R., Pezet, A., & Sardais, C. (2020). *Le management* (2e édition). Éditions JFD.

DiMaggio, P. (1982). Cultural entrepreneurship in nineteenth-century Boston: The creation of an organizational base for high culture in America. *Media, Culture & Society, 4*, 33–50.

Ferté, D. (2008). *L'accessibilité en pratique, de la règle à l'usage* (p. 200). Éditions le moniteur.

Folcher, V., & Lompré, N. (2012). « Accessibilité pour et dans l'usage: concevoir des situations d'activité adaptées à tous et à chacun ». *Le travail humain, 75*, 89–120.

Foreman-Wernet, L. (2017). Reflections on elitism: What arts organizations communicate about themselves. *The Journal of Arts Management, Law, and Society, 47*(4), 274–289. https://doi.org/10.1080/10632921.2017.1366380

Gănescu, C., & Gangone, A. (2017). A model of socially responsible organizational culture. *"Studia Universitatis, Vasile Goldis" Arad – Economics Series, 27*, 45–59.

Haslanger, S. (2000). Gender and race: (What) are they? (What) do we want them to be? *Noûs, 34*(1), 31–55.

Klironomos, I., Antona, M., Basdekis, I., & Stephanidis, C. (2006). White paper: Promoting design for all and e-accessibility in Europe. *Universal Access in the Information Society, 5*, 105–119.

Larouche, C., Savard, D., Héon, L., & Moisset, J.-J. (2016). Analyse typologique des plans stratégiques des universités québécoises. *Revue Canadienne d'enseignement supérieur, 46*(3), 18–40.

Lemaître, N. (1985). La culture d'entreprise: facteur de performance. *Revue internationale de gestion, 10*(1), 1–12.

Ludwig, E. (2012). Stigma in the arts: How Perceptual barriers influence individuals' with disabilities participation in arts organizations. *The Journal of Arts Management, Law, and Society, 42*(3), 141–151. https://doi.org/10.1080/10632921.2012.729498

Mincultura. (2016). p. 8. http://www.mincultura.gov.co/areas/artes/Documents/Plan%20Nacional%20para%20las%20Artes%202025%20-%202019%20-%20jul13%20de%202015.pdf

Mintzberg, H. (2021). *Le pouvoir dans les organisations* (2ème édition, p. 688). https://www.eyrolles.com/Entreprise/Livre/le-pouvoir-dans-les-organisations-9782708130135/

National Endowment for the Arts. (2015). *When going gets tough: Barriers and motivations affecting arts attendance.* https://www.arts.gov/sites/default/files/when-going-gets-tough-revised2.pdf

Plaisance, É. (2015). Culture et Handicap. Les enjeux de l'accessibilité à la culture. In J. Zaffran (Ed.), *Accessibilité et handicap* (pp. 71–89). Presses universitaires de Grenoble.

Powell, W. W., & DiMaggio, P. (Eds.). (2012). *The new institutionalism in organizational analysis* (p. 486). University of Chicago Press.

Schein, E. H. (2017). *Organizational culture and leadership* (5th ed.). John Wiley & Sons.

Throsby, D. (2008). The concentric circles model of the cultural industries. *Cultural Trends*, 147–164. https://doi.org/10.1080/09548960802361951

Tremblay, D.-G., & De Sève, M.-K. (2006). *Rapport de recherche final sur les obstacles à la formation dans les petites et moyennes entreprises* (p. 228). NR_CB_2007_01.pdf (teluq.ca).

UNESCO. (2022). *Cultural accessibility guide.* Cultural Accessibility Guide "Kaunas for All" | Diversidad de las expresiones culturales (unesco.org).

Zallio, M., & Clarkson, P. J. (2021). Inclusion, diversity, equity, and accessibility in the built environment: A study of architectural design practice. *Building and Environment, 206*, 108352. https://doi.org/10.1016/j.buildenv.2021.108352

Zanoni, P., & Janssens, M. (2015). The power of diversity discourses at work: On the interlocking nature of diversities and occupations. *Organization Studies, 36*(11), 1463–1483.

Chapter 3

Black Opera Leaders in the United States: What Is Their Role in Black Opera?

Antonio C. Cuyler

University of Michigan, USA

Abstract

Though scholarship has documented Black opera leaders' contributions to the art form in the United States (André, 2018; Caplan, 2017; Cuyler, 2021; Southern, 1997; Turner, 2015), they have received scant attention in rubrics that theorize a definition of Black opera (André, 2018; Cheatham, 1997; Schmidt & Schroeder, 1999). However, as their recent advocacy for racial justice (Cuyler, 2022) through their *Letter to the Opera Field* in 2020 revealed (Cuyler, 2023), Black opera leaders play a powerful and unique role in shaping audiences' appreciation, engagement with, and understanding of Black opera (André, 2018; Cuyler, 2023; Floyd & Cuyler, 2023). In addition to their positionality as observers of and participants in opera companies' decision-making processes, their advocacy for racial justice can compel an opera company to program Black opera, or not (Cuyler, 2021, 2022, 2023). Therefore, in this chapter, I explore the research question, what is the role of Black opera leaders in Black opera? Lastly, I propose a theory of the dynamic process that includes artistic programming and casting, hiring, community engagement, and audience development which enables the development of an audience for Black opera when Black opera leaders view their leadership of these areas of work through the lens of racial justice.

Keywords: Black Americans; community engagement; leaders; opera; racial justice

Introduction

As far back as the impresarios Theodore Drury (1867–1943), H. Lawrence Freeman (1869–1954), and Mary Cardwell Dawson (1894–1962), scholarship has

Accessibility, Diversity, Equity and Inclusion in the Cultural Sector, 31–45
Copyright © 2024 Antonio C. Cuyler
Published under exclusive licence by Emerald Publishing Limited
doi:10.1108/978-1-83753-034-220241005

documented Black opera leaders' contributions to the art form in the United States (André, 2018; Caplan, 2017; Cuyler, 2021, 2022, 2023; Miller, 2019, 2023; Smith, 1994; Southern, 1997; Turner, 2015). Yet, Black opera leaders have received scant attention in rubrics that theorize definitions of Black opera. In defining Black opera, scholars acknowledge the contributions of artistic personnel (André, 2018; Cheatham, 1997; Schmidt & Schroeder, 1999; Smith, 1994; Southern, 1997; Story, 1990) while offering a footnote, if at all, on Black opera leaders. As their recent advocacy for racial justice showed (Cuyler, 2022, 2023; Floyd & Cuyler, 2023), Black opera leaders play a unique role in shaping audiences' appreciation, engagement with, and understanding of Black opera (André, 2018; Cuyler, 2021, 2022, 2023).

By "Black opera leaders," I mean US born and non-US born descendants of enslaved Africans, as well as African immigrants who live in the United states and opera companies' contract as administrators, executives, or managers. Given their participation in opera companies' decision-making processes, Black opera leaders can use their racial justice advocacy to compel an opera company to program an opera by a Black composer, or not. Therefore, in this chapter, I explore the research question, what is the role of Black opera leaders in Black opera? This chapter draws upon qualitative semi-structured interviews with current and former Black opera executives such as Torrie Allen, Wayne Brown, Linda Jackson, and Willie Anthony Waters (Cuyler, 2021). In addition, an interview with Quodesia (Quo) Johnson, Founder of the Black Opera Administrators informs my answer to the research question (Cuyler, 2023). Lastly, I propose a theory of the dynamic process that includes artistic programming and casting, hiring, community engagement, and audience development which enables the development of an audience for Black opera when Black opera leaders view their work through the lens of racial justice. But first, I will define Black opera.

Defining Black Opera

When asked in an interview by Wallace Cheatham, "how would you define Black opera," Ben Matthews, a cofounder of Opera Ebony responded:

> I have never seen a definition of Black opera that you really could not punch holes through, depending on which direction you were coming from. An opera written by a Black composer, on Black subject matter, and performed, by a Black company with Black artists, and everything Black from back wall to the entrance door, this would come closest to defining a Black opera for me. I haven't run across that even with Opera Ebony in my lifetime. (Cheatham, 1997)

Wayne Sanders, Opera Ebony's cofounder, suggested their production of *Sojourner Truth* fits the definition. Then they identified a list of qualities that consummate Black opera, "Black subject matter, Black orchestra, Black singers,

Black conductor, and Black composer" (Cheatham, 1997, pp. 86–87). Curiously, they did not include themselves as cofounders of Opera Ebony. Still, here, one finds factors that help to articulate a definition of Black opera. The composer of *X, the Life and Times of Malcolm X*, Anthony Davis, maintained that a Black opera is about the "African American experience and dealing with the African American tradition." In *Aida's Brothers and Sisters*, he made it clear that Thomson's *Four Saints in Three Acts* could not count as Black opera, nor could Gershwin's *Porgy and Bess*. He also argued that the Black community responded positively to *X* in a way that they could never identify with *Porgy and Bess* (Schmidt & Schroeder, 1999). Implicit in Davis' premise is that a Black composer must compose the opera in and of itself for it to count as Black opera. If this is true, then the controversial *Universal Child: The Emmett Till Story*, which premiered in 2022, complicates Davis' definition of Black opera. Though the composer, Mary Watkins, identifies as Black, the librettist, Clare Coss, identifies as white (Watkins, 2019).

In *Black Opera: History, Power, Engagement*, André (2018) went beyond only mentioning Black composers and singers as major factors in the equation of defining Black opera. She discussed the historical context and political directive for having Black voices telling their own stories and becoming full participants in a musical genre that remained mostly closed to them through segregation. On Seattle Opera's blog, she elaborated that, "Black Opera," is "the construction of Black experiences in opera, encompassing a variety of activities, such as operas by Black composers and librettists with stories about Black people sung by Black singers. Yet, having Black people involved in all these facets is not the only configuration for defining Black opera. Black opera can also include interracial partnerships that involve non-Black collaborators; for example, works incorporating Black narratives by non-Black writers or productions where, even if a character's race is not specified as Black, opera companies give Black singers the opportunity to perform (André, 2022)." This definition permits the inclusion of *Universal Child: The Emmett Till Story* into a theory of the definition of Black opera.

Furthermore, Saha (2018) suggested that one should consider the ways in which cultural policy has constrained or enabled the construction of race in defining Black opera. By cultural policy, I mean policies that constrain and/or embolden cultural engagement, practices, and values. Given the ways in which racism remains embedded in US cultural policies, thinking of Black opera pre and post segregation allows for a capacious and elastic definition that fully accounts for the ways in which Black folx can participate in opera, including as leaders, but also as artists, audiences, board members, partners, vendors, and volunteers. Yet, the creative impetus of a Black composer's operatic work remains central to defining Black opera. In sum, Black opera is the process that begins with an operatic composition written by a Black composer. Programming this opera invites the maximum quotient of Black creative genius to authentically and powerfully tell the story of the embodied and lived experiences of people of African descent maximizing its potential of engaging multiple audiences, but centrally a Black audience. But, one should ask would Black operas exist without the advocacy of Black opera leaders?

Black Opera Leaders

When defining the African diaspora, Palmer (1998) proposed that, "the modern African diaspora, at its core, consists of the millions of peoples of African descent living in various societies who are united by a past based significantly but not exclusively upon 'racial' oppression and the struggles against it; and who, despite the cultural variations and political and other divisions among them, share an emotional bond with one another and with their ancestral continent; and who also, regardless of their location, face broadly similar problems in constructing and realizing themselves." Furthermore, in 1970, Rustin argued that "the Black artist, whether or not he considers himself as such, is an essential member and a most important member of the freedom struggle." He further contended that, "one of the fundamental reasons that the artist is always a forerunner in the movement for freedom among oppressed people is that all men, including Black men, judge a society or an ethnic group or a nation on the basis of their artistic creativity."

This social responsibility applies to Black opera leaders, too, yet no role in opera has achieved parity with Black people's representation at 13.6% of US population (Cuyler, 2021; U. S. Census Bureau, 2023). As further evidence of the systemic nature of Black people's low representation in opera, only 3.7% identify as leaders, 4% as board members, 4.5% as staff, (OPERAAmerica, 2022), and 9.5% as singers (Riley, 2023). Unfortunately, the American Society of Composers, Authors, and Publishers (ASCAP) as well as Broadcast Music Inc. (BMI) does not collect or share demographic data on its members. Thus, opera does not know the percentage of music creators or composers who identify as Black.

Still, shared racial oppression does not compel the same approach to achieving racial progress among people of African descent, especially in opera (Cuyler, 2022, 2023). Nor do all Black folx, based on their racial identity development, and specifically some Black opera leaders, feel compelled to advocate for racial justice in opera. Still, even in a segregated society, Black opera leaders' courage, creativity, ingenuity, innovation, and resilience uncovered and maximized entrepreneurial opportunities to envision and imagine possibilities that would not have otherwise existed in opera. This is why ancestrally and professionally, I consider Theodore Drury, H. Lawrence Freeman, and Mary Caldwell Dawson the elders of Black opera leaders.

On May 14, 1900, the Theodore Drury Grand Opera Company gave its first performance of *Carmen*. After then, the company performed productions of *Il Guarany, Faust, Aida, Pagliacci, Cavalleria Rusticana*, and *Carmen* (André, 2018; Caplan, 2017; Smith, 1994; Southern, 1997; Turner, 2015). The company's performances became more sporadic after these productions. Still, of note is that a Black opera leader founded an opera company in the United States during the racist cultural policy of segregation. Though the Theodore Drury Grand Opera

Company gave performances of canonical operas, I have not found evidence that the company produced operas by Black composers, nor that he considered it. This suggests an explanation for why H. Lawrence Freeman may have established the Negro Grand Opera Company.

According to Gilmore (2019), H. Lawrence Freeman is the first Black opera composer to produce an opera in the United States. In 1928, a New York Times review of his opera, *Voodoo*, condescendingly described it as, "presented for the first time last night at the Palm Garden with an all-negro cast of thirty singers. The composer utilizes themes from spirituals, Southern melodies and jazz rhythms which, combined with traditional Italian operatic forms, produce a *curiously naïve mélange* of varied styles." Though the reviewer shaded *Voodoo*, the fact that the New York Times reviewed the performance speaks to his renown during the Harlem Renaissance. Furthermore, a 1935 letter alluded that the Metropolitan Opera considered performing Freeman's, *The Octoroon*, but ultimately concluded, "to our regret, we do not see our way clear to accept this work (Gilmore, 2019)." The racist social milieu he lived in would not permit him to produce his prolific body of operas at the highest level. Yet, Freeman innovated by incorporating the Negro Grand Opera Company in 1920 which afforded him a reliable vehicle to consistently present and produce his operas during his life time.

Likely inspired by Thedore Drury and H. Lawrence Freeman, Mary Caldwell Dawson launched her National Negro Opera company with a production of *Aida* at the National Association of Negro Musicians conference in 1941 (André, 2018; Miller, 2019, 2023; Smith, 1994; Southern, 1997; Turner, 2015). Among several leadership and managerial skills such as casting, fundraising, and negotiating union fees for lead singers, she challenged racism by engaging a white orchestra to accompany the operas that she produced (Miller, 2019). Similar to the Theodore Drury Grand Opera Company, Madame Dawson's company's repertoire not only included canonical operas such as *Aida*, *La Traviata*, and *Faust*, but also Dett's oratorio, *The Ordering of Moses*.

Unlike the Theodore Drury Grand Opera Company, however, Madame Dawson produced white's *Ouanga*, an opera by a Black composer (André, 2018; Caplan, 2017; Miller, 2019, 2023; Smith, 1994; Southern, 1997; Turner, 2015). Learning of this fact raised for me the question, why did Theodore Drury only program canonical operas and not include operas written by Black composers in his company's repertoire? Turner (2015) argued that Drury and the Black press positioned his productions as racially and musically uplifting experiences that confirmed their elite audience's worthiness to participate fully in white society.

This observation brings focus to one aspect of what Black audience members might expect to gain from attending an opera. But, if Turner (2015) is correct, then Drury's case supports my assertion that shared racial oppression does not compel the same vision of racial progress among people of African descent. Consideration of a Black opera leader's racial identity development must also factor into the equation. Given this, it is fair to ask if Drury internalized anti-Black racism to the point that he did not see the value in an opportunity to not only advance Black singers in opera, but also advance Black composers and other creatives in opera. Conversely, as a Black woman, did intersectionality

(Crenshaw, 1989) heighten Mary Caldwell Dawson's awareness of opportunities to uplift as many Black creatives and leaders in opera as are possible no matter their demographic or professional positionality?

In addition to her many accomplishments, Madame Dawson extended and professionalized the legacy of Black opera companies through her leadership by incorporating her company in 1942, and produced performances over a 20 year period until her death in 1962 (Miller, 2023; Southern, 1997). Inquiry into Madame Dawson's leadership philosophy warrants further scholarly exploration. However, her willingness to advocate for union pay for the lead singers of the operas that she produced suggests a proclivity toward equity. Furthermore, her opera company's mission to "afford for the Negro the opportunity for the fullest expression in cultural development" (Miller, 2023) speaks volumes about her belief about the role of Black people in opera. It also resonates with *creative justice* which I defined as the manifestation of all historically and continuously discriminated against, marginalized, oppressed, and subjugated peoples living creative and expressive lives on their own terms (Cuyler, 2022).

Black opera leaders have come a long way since the times of Theodre Drury, H. Lawrence Freeman, and Mary Caldwell Dawson. Torrie Allen, Linda Jackson, and Willie Anthony Waters held executive positions with non-Black opera companies in the United States, the first three to do so since the first opera performance in the United States in 1735 (Cuyler, 2021). Wayne Brown has served as President and CEO of Detroit Opera since 2014. Most recently, Afton Battle served as General/Artistic Director of Ft. Worth Opera from 2020 to 2022, and she now serves as Vice-President of Lyric Unlimited and Artistic Operations at the Lyric Opera of Chicago. In addition, the unincorporated collective, Black Administrators of Opera (Cuyler, 2023), formed after the 2020 summer of racial discontent inspired by the murders of Ahmaud Arbery, Breonna Taylor, George Floyd, Tony McDade, Rayshard Brooks, and far too many others. But, what exactly makes Black opera leaders' contributions to Black opera unique within Black opera, and among non-Black opera leaders?

When I asked, "why was the *Letter to the Field* necessary?", Quo Johnson, Founder for the Black Administrators of Opera, responded in part:

> Because we knew that there would be pushback for the Black Opera Alliance *Pledge*, but we also knew that the industry needed to hear from its administrators. Because there is a habit of dismissing the artists who do not often see all of the moving pieces. The administrative voice was necessary because we're in the space, doing the work. We wanted to present what accountability and change looks like from an administrative focused space because we know the reasons behind the budget, hiring, and casting decisions. We're the ones doing the work to administer this art form to others.

Quo described the unique positionality that Black opera leaders hold in opera companies' decision-making processes. But she also identified a few of the competencies expected of Black opera leaders such as budgeting, casting, and hiring.

Identifying community engagement as another unique skill for Black opera leaders to possess and optimize, Quo stated the following regarding the practice:

> Where so many people were literally asking, how do we talk to communities? That's a very simple thing to do depending on your space and experiences. You've been sending your Black staff to go talk to the community and using that to present the art that ultimately is still hurting the community because it's showing false depictions of community, or these harmful depictions of identities. And not just the Black communities, but all communities.

Borwick (2012) defined community engagement as, "a process whereby institutions enter into mutually beneficial relationships with other organizations, informal community groups, or individuals (p. 14)." In this chapter's case, this means opera companies partnering with communities to develop mutually beneficial initiatives. As Hamerlinck (2022) showed in Table 3.1, community engagement differs from community outreach, which many cultural organizations condescend to practice to their detriment with white Saviorism. Cultural organizations' shift toward community engagement warrants distinguishing the practice from audience development, which Walker-Kuhne (2005) described as, "a specialized form of marketing that requires more than mastery of traditional marketing techniques, such as direct mail, subscription drives, membership drives, or advertising, and press. Audience development merges marketing and relationship-building skills to enable a lasting impact on a prospective audience (p. 25–26)". In Table 3.1, Hamerlinck (2022) described the differences between community engagement and community outreach, a more paternalistic approach informed by white savior complex.

Clearly, Black opera leaders need to understand how to effectively lead and manage the strategic integration of artistic programming, casting, hiring, community engagement, and audience development to create, intrigue, and sustain audiences for Black opera. The decision to choose unique programming to attract audiences is how opera leaders begin the process; Torrie Allen shared this story about a Zarzuela that he wanted to program in Alaska:

Table 3.1. Community Engagement Versus Community Outreach.

Community Engagement	Community Outreach
Long-term	Short-term
Relationship building	Marketing
What can A and B do together?	What can A do for B?
Community benefits	One group benefits the most
Connecting	Transactional
Cyclical	Directional

I said to my colleagues, "I'm gonna do a Zarzuela. I found this really cool Zarzuela, *La Tabernera del Puerto* (the tavern girl on the port). It's really cool. The music is fabulous. It's relevant. The folks in Alaska are going to like it." Some of them started laughing. A few started gossiping with each other, like, "Oh, this guy's crazy. He's gonna do a Zarzuela?" "Now, they weren't racist, but clearly what they were doing is manifesting a systemic racism. I was disappointed and wanted to say (but didn't), "You guys are killing the industry." What's wrong with the opera world trying to make itself relevant, I mean, the automotive industry is constantly remaking itself. We're not driving 1920 Fords, right? In the opera world, we're still driving 1920 Fords. Occasionally some new car will surface and you think that's gonna change things, but it doesn't.

Wayne Brown expressed this sentiment about artistic programming and communities:

For me it's an honor to do what I do and to see how Michigan Opera Theater, and other opera companies, can play a vital role within their communities to honor the master works, but to provide a platform so that today's stories will resonate with current audiences. Creating an environment that focuses not only on artistic works of what we refer to as the core repertoire, but the inclusion of works that speak to current day audiences and current day concerns and interests. The opera we're closing with this week is an initiative based in parks and sports which focuses on *The Summer King*, an opera about National Negro League player, Josh Gibson. It's designed to bring arts and sports together, which goes beyond the issue of, it happens to have a particular theme about Josh Gibson, but it's a step that we believe is attracting interest and participation which goes outside the arts community.

Torrie Allen also shared these insights relative to the work of opera leaders, and how it interfaces with audiences and communities:

So, when you're actually running the company, you've got to deal with boards and you've got to deal with the community. And when you start changing stuff, you have to have mentors who are there to say to you, "Look. It's okay to change. You're gonna get some pushback. That's okay. Don't get scared. Keep going." And if there is not enough of those kind of mentors, that can prepare people, change mentors, that can make people feel comfortable. Fear and stasis will prevail. I've learned that it is possible to negotiate this change. If one embraces the diplomatic mindset and related techniques, it may take a little bit longer and require more patience, but you can take people and communities from A to B. Grow to understand the links between ADEI, relevance, and greater economic impact. Apply ADEI filters to all aspects of the business, not just for what's happening on stage or for show.

Speaking explicitly about casting, Linda Jackson commented, "When I was at Chautauqua I was very conscious about how we handled colorblind casting and all of those issues. It is not as though I have gone out and done anything major or important in terms of wanting to change the nature of how the field works." Also, this as one of the then leaders of Connecticut Opera, a non-Black opera company:

> I am assuming we are hearing from more singers of color than a lot of other places are in terms of wanting to audition for us and everything, which is sort of a blessing and a curse, because I think there is also some expectation that we are going to be more accepting. A bad singer is a bad singer no matter what color they are. You know, it is sort of an awkward kind of position to be in.

Willie Anthony Waters shared a story that demonstrated his knowledge of singers and casting and its importance in distinguishing himself in his career:

> At the time, Mr. Adler was casting *Flying Dutchman*, and it didn't have a Senta. We are sitting there; Richard Rezinski was my predecessor, they would go over the names and everything. He gave me two sets of cards. One was the artist and the other was the role, so Senta and all the people who sang the role. He told me to look at the card, and he said, "Who are some of the people who are not listed on that card?" I came up with two names, one of which was Gwyneth Jones. He called Richard and said that Gwyneth was not on this card. They both looked at each other, and they were really shocked. That was one of the things that clinched it because he said later, "You have the most encyclopedic knowledge of opera and opera singers of any young person that I have ever met." I lived, ate, slept, drank opera and still do.

In their advocacy for racial justice, Black opera leaders must also have a sophisticated understanding of how artistic programming, casting, hiring, community engagement, and audience development work together to yield an audience for Black opera, another often neglected population in definitions of Black opera. Relative to a Black opera leader's advocacy for racial justice, Torrie Allen said the following:

> I'm passionate about the arts. I also believe my way to change the world, to manifest Martin Luther King Jr.'s dream is through the

arts. That's how I do it. When it comes to our species and how we interact with each other, I want a world where we value curiosity above fear. So many beautiful opportunities are missed when you don't reflect all of humanity.

Wayne Brown expressed the following statement in response to a prompt that I provided regarding the lack of progress and change in opera and the creative sector broadly relative to racial access, diversity, equity, and inclusion (ADEI):

> I would say I've seen significant change. Even with OPERA America. The conversation that took place about diversity in 2005, and conversations taking place now, worlds apart. That does not underscore the fact that there's so much to be done. I think the leadership role being played by OPERA America as being more that the leadership continues to evolve and therefore the leadership can tend to assert itself a little more. It's a different place. And that's a good thing. Sometimes those reactions are identical because one's experience tends to be contained and when it's contained you're going to have similar kinds of results. So one needs a little altitude. Sometimes all of us don't always allow ourselves to pull back a little bit.

Mr Brown also maintained that he would prefer to talk about career development on a one on one basis versus just with a group of Black people. Though, he did not oppose the idea. On the other hand, Linda Jackson, expressed the statement below as evidence of her racial identity development:

> I am honestly glad I did not grow up White. It is not because I was necessarily a big, out-there, Black pro-whatever. It is just that I don't think I would have the opportunities or the sensitivity that I have if I had been raised as something comfortable. I mean I think the challenges that have been presented to me because I am a woman and because I am Black have made me a better person. I am not sure I would have had those same challenges if I had just been raised a White male, upper middle class, or something else. I am not sure I would have the same humility.

As evidence of his racial identity development, her colleague at Connecticut Opera at the time, Willie Anthony Waters, commented:

> A lot of the Black singers in New York look at me as a hope for them. A few of them have said this, "You should bring all these Black singers to Connecticut, and you could cast an all-Black *Don Giovanni*. I could cast an all-Black anything, but I am not going to do it because that to me is not what I am here for."

Audiences, Black Opera Leaders, and Black Opera: A Theory

When their advocacy for racial justice informs their integrative leadership and management of artistic programming, casting, hiring, community engagement, and audience development Black opera not only yields a broad audience for Black opera, but also a Black audience for Black opera. Relative to Theodore Drury Company's production of *Aida* at the 14th Street Theater in 1906, one New York Times review, stated, "The opera company, the programme says, is made up of some 100 people, and they are negroes. A good part of the audience was colored, too, and the boxes were filled by the leaders of New York's colored society." Linda Jackson relayed the following story in support of my observation:

> She said, "Opera North will do a production of Marriage of Figaro, and they will sell lots of tickets, and they will have all these Black audience members there, but they don't go see productions at the Opera Company of Philadelphia or Pennsylvania Opera Theatre." I told her that they go because they see themselves reflected on the stage. It has nothing to do with the quality of the opera. They are not coming to see your shows because if there are all White singers up there, no one will be interested, and they won't care.

Willie Anthony Waters shared the following about attracting Black opera audiences:

> When Angela Brown and Mark Rucker made their Met debuts, there was a noticeable bump in African Americans attending the Met. Now Black people go to the Met all the time because it is New York, but this was very different. Part of it was an orchestrated thing, because Angela was the first Black singer in a long time to make her debut there doing *Aïda*, and she had developed herself to a point where people were really watching her and watching her development and all. I mean, there were rows and rows and rows of Black people in the orchestra section. Now the Met ain't giving out no tickets. These people bought expensive tickets to see this sister sing *Aïda*. And the same thing with Mark Rucker.

Maestro Waters articulated what he thought compelled Black opera audiences uniquely to attend the MET, but based on the opposition he expressed to casting an all-Black *Don Giovanni*; his racial identity development did not allow him to make the connection between artistic programming, casting choices, and the potential development of a Black opera audience for Connecticut Opera.

In his review of *Fire Shut Up in My Bones* Tommasini (2021) wrote, "it was exhilarating to see them cheered on by an almost entirely Black cast, chorus and dance troupe, as well as by an audience with notably more people of color than

Fig. 3.1.   A Theory of Black Opera Leader's Process.

usual at a Met opening." I have also observed this phenomenon since 2004 at productions of Davis' *Just Above My Head*, Thompson's *The Snowy Day*, Davis' *X*, Giddens and Abels' *Omar*, and Menefield's *Fierce*. As Fig. 3.1 shows, Black opera leaders embolden the phenomenon of social identification by using Black opera to attract and maintain a broad audience for Black opera, but especially a Black audience for Black opera. However, the Black opera leader's racial identity development suggests that their orientation to racial justice advocacy must inform their process of strategically leading the integration of artistic programming, casting, hiring, community engagement, and audience development.

Conclusion

In this chapter, I explored the research question, what is the role of Black opera leaders in Black opera? Clearly, Black opera leaders have a role to play in Black opera because their unique professional positionalities afford them decision-making power to impact change. However, Black opera leaders' racial identity development remains of critical importance because Black people are not a monolith, and thus they will not share the same vision or strategy for achieving racial justice and progress in opera. Similar to the Civil Rights movement in the United States, and now the #BlackLivesMatter movement, an inability to unite in racial solidarity may hinder and undermine racial justice in opera. Still, the Black Opera Alliance and the Black Administrators of Opera have achieved consensus about what opera can do to ingratiate itself to Black artistic and leadership personnel, and thereby audiences (Cuyler, 2022, 2023) even if the exact how remains subject to the brilliance, creativity, ingenuity, and resilience of each opera company.

In this chapter, I also proposed a theory of the integrative dynamic process of artistic programming, casting, hiring, community engagement, and audience development that Black opera leaders use to enable the development of a broad audience for Black opera, and especially a Black audience for Black opera. Using this theory, future research could conduct comparative analyses to investigate which Black opera leaders, based on their proclivity toward advocacy for racial justice, more successfully develops audiences for Black opera. In addition, studies could explore this question, too, among non-Black opera leaders, as well as between Black and non-Black opera companies. One could hypothesize, for example, that Black opera companies more successfully develop, engage, and sustain Black opera audiences because of their proximity to the Black community. But, is this true, and how might knowing improve the creative sector's ability to understand audience development informed by social identification theory? Lastly, researchers should more deeply investigate the leadership philosophies and approaches of the elders of Black opera leaders and how they inform the missions of Black opera companies today. The field suffers because of Black opera companies' isolation and the lack of support they receive. In addition to oral histories, a future study should seek to assess how Black opera companies define success and sustain themselves.

References

André, N. (2018). *Black opera: History, power, engagement.* University of Illinois Press.

André, N. (2022). Black opera, looking back: A historical perspective. *Seattle Opera Blog.* https://www.seattleoperablog.com/2022/02/black-opera.html

Borwick, D. (2012). *Building communities, not audiences: The future of the arts in the United States.* ArtsEngaged.

Caplan, L. (2017). *The improbable rise of the first African American opera impresario.* Classical Voice. https://www.sfcv.org/articles/feature/improbable-rise-first-african-american-opera-impresario

Cheatham, W. (1997). *Dialogues on opera and the African American experience.* Scarecrow Press.

Crenshaw, K. (1989). Demarginalizing the intersection of race and sex: A Black feminist critique of antidiscrimination doctrine, feminist theory and antiracist politics. *University of Chicago Legal Forum, 1989*(1), 139–167.

Cuyler, A. (2021). *Access, diversity, equity, and inclusion in cultural organizations: Insights from the careers of executive opera managers of color in the US.* Routledge.

Cuyler, A. (2022). Moving beyond @operaisracist: Exploring blacktivism as a pathway to antiracism and creative justice in opera. In D. Abfalter & R. Reitsamer (Eds.), *Music as labour: Inequalities and activism in the past and present* (pp. 204–218). Routledge.

Cuyler, A. (2023). (Un)silencing blacktivism in opera: An interview with Quodesia Johnson about the letter to the opera field from Black administrators. In A. Bull & C. Scharff (Eds.), *Voices for change in the classical music profession* (pp. 255–266). Oxford University Press.

Floyd, Q., & Cuyler, A. (2023). The death of white supremacy in the US creative sector & implications for arts management: A critical race theory view. In Y. Jung, N. Vakharia, & M. Vecco (Eds.), *The Oxford handbook of arts and cultural management*. Oxford University Press.

Gilmore, N. (2019). *America's first Black opera composer left behind a rich untapped archive*. https://www.saturdayeveningpost.com/2019/10/americas-first-black-opera-composer-left-behind-a-rich-untapped-archive/

Hamerlinck, J. (2022). Community outreach vs community engagement. https://leadingdifferently.com/2019/06/06/community-outreach-vs-community-engagement/

Miller, C. (2019). Mary Caldwell Dawson: First lady of opera. https://blogs.loc.gov/music/2019/03/mary-cardwell-dawson-first-lady-of-opera/

Miller, C. (2023). Mary Caldwell Dawson: Upcoming lecture at the Library of Congress. https://blogs.loc.gov/music/2023/01/mary-cardwell-dawson-upcoming-lecture-at-the-library-of-congress/

New York Times. (1906, May 29). Colored opera stars produce Verdi's 'Aida'; The Theodore Drury Company opens at 14th ST. Theater. A study in color schemes some good singing among the principals – Chorus made up in action what they lacked in voice. *New York Times*. https://www.nytimes.com/1906/05/29/archives/colored-opera-stars-produce-verdis-aida-the-theodore-drury-company.html

OPERAAmerica. (2022). *Field-wide opera demographic report 2021*. https://www.operaamerica.org/media/afsfdynw/demographicsreport_final_6-21-22.pdf

Palmer, C. (1998). *Defining and studying the modern African diaspora*. https://www.historians.org/research-and-publications/perspectives-on-history/september-1998/defining-and-studying-the-modern-african-diaspora

Riley, S. (2023, April 11). Cast members of 'Porgy and Bess' opera hope to inspire more diversity in Raleigh show. https://spectrumlocalnews.com/nc/charlotte/news/2023/04/11/stage-director-of-porgy-and-bess-aims-to-inspire-more-minorities-to-pursue-careers-in-opera#:~:text=According%20to%20the%20U.S.%20Bureau,than%2010%2025%20are%20African%20American

Rustin, B. (1970 August/September). *The role of artists in the freedom struggle* (pp. 260–263). The Crisis.

Saha, A. (2018). *Race and the cultural industries*. Polity.

Schmidt, J., & Schroeder, M. (1999). *Aida's brothers and sisters [Film]*. Arthaus.

Smith, E. (1994). *Blacks in opera: An encyclopedia of people and companies, 1873–1993*. McFarland Press.

Southern, E. (1997). *The music of Black Americans: A history*. W.W. Norton and Company.

Story, R. (1990). *And so I sing: African American divas of opera and concert*. Warner Books Inc.

Tommasini, A. (2021, October 19). Review: 'Fire' brings a Black composer to the met, finally. *New York Times*. https://www.nytimes.com/2021/09/28/arts/music/fire-blanchard-met-opera.html

Turner, K. (2015). Class, race, and uplift in the opera house: Theodore Drury and his company cross the color line. *Journal of Musicological Research, 34*(4), 320–351.

U. S. Census Bureau. (2023). *Quick facts.* https://www.census.gov/quickfacts/fact/table/US/PST045222

Walker-Kuhne, D. (2005). *Invitation to the party: Building bridges to the arts, culture, and community.* Theatre Communications Group.

Watkins, M. (2019). *Universal child: The Emmett till story.* https://marydwatkins.com/operas/emmett-till-the-opera/

Chapter 4

Performing Arts in a Francophone Minority Context: A Case Study of *L'Association la Girandole d'Edmonton*

Srilata Ravi[a] and Olivia Leclair[b]

[a]University of Alberta, Canada
[b]L'Association La Girandole d'Edmonton, Canada

Abstract

In Canada today, Francophone minority communities (FMCs) outside Québec exist in every province and territory and cross all sectors of Canadian Francophonie (French-Canadians, Francophone immigrants, Francophone Métis as well as Francophile anglophones). Besides their linguistic immersion in primary, secondary, and postsecondary educational institutions, these Francophones living outside Quebec counter linguistic assimilation and affirm their place in Canada's bilingual and multicultural society through their cultural productions (music, theatre, dance, cuisine, literature). In this study, we take up the case of *L'Association, La Girandole d'Edmonton*, a cultural association dedicated to the teaching and promotion of French-Canadian dance in Edmonton (Alberta) to examine the multiple challenges such organizations face despite the crucial role they play in ensuring the vitality of linguistic minority communities in Canada.

Keywords: French-Canadian; folk dance; L'Association la Girandole d'Edmonton; linguistic minority; Franco-albertain; identity

Introduction

Anglophone and Francophones compromised to build Canadian federalism. Notwithstanding the fact that this compromise has been enshrined in the Canadian Charter of Rights and freedoms (1982) and the Official Languages Act (1988), tensions continue to persist between these two historically established linguistic

---

Accessibility, Diversity, Equity and Inclusion in the Cultural Sector, 47–65
Copyright © 2024 Srilata Ravi and Olivia Leclair
Published under exclusive licence by Emerald Publishing Limited
doi:10.1108/978-1-83753-034-220241008

communities, especially outside Quebec. From around 1840 to 1960, Francophone communities outside Quebec, whose members were mainly descendants of French colonizers that founded Acadia and Québec City in the 17th century, identified themselves as part of the nation *canadienne-française* whose political project was to unite all French-Canadians. Following the 1967 Estates General that recognized a Québécois nation, French Canada as a "coast to coast" political concept came to an end. The breakup forced a redefinition of Canadian Francophonie along both provincial and national lines. Francophone minority communities (FMCs) outside Québec exist in every province and territory and cross all sectors of Canadian Francophonie (French-Canadians, Francophone immigrants, Francophone Métis as well as Francophile anglophones). French-Canadians have now become *Franco-Ontariens, Franco-Manitobains, Fransaskois, Franco-Albertains, Franco-Colombiens, Franco-Yukonnais, Franco-Ténois, and Franco-Nunavois* (Iacovino & Léger, 2013). In today's Canada, Francophonie outside Québec finds itself in a vulnerable situation. The latest census indicates a decline in the number of French speakers while changing demographics also show that there are more allophones than Francophones. Even if this has encouraged those who do not support official bilingualism to question the validity of Canada's language regime, the passing of Bill C-13 modernizing the Official Languages Act (2023) with an emphasis on protecting and promoting French and encouraging Francophone immigration to ensure the survival of Francophone minority communities, has been perceived by FMCs as a step in the right direction to protect French in Canada.[1]

That being said, members of linguistic minority communities like the FMCs are not merely political or social actors; they are also cultural agents producing and consuming cultural products which contribute significantly to the resilience and vitality of these communities. Besides their linguistic immersion in primary, secondary, and postsecondary educational institutions, it is through their cultural expressions (music, theater, dance, cuisine, literature), that the Francophones living outside Quebec find opportunities to counter linguistic assimilation and affirm their place in Canada's bilingual and multicultural society (Fauchon, 1993; Labrecque, 2018). Cultural productions in FMCs are dependent on provincial and federal sources of funding for their growth and survival.[2] Not only do they constitute crucial sites of resistance and affirmation of a minority identity but they also aspire to become spaces of innovation reaching out to other sections of Canadian society. In this study we take up the case of *L'Association la Girandole d'Edmonton*, a cultural association dedicated to the promotion of French-Canadian dance in Edmonton (Alberta), to examine the

---

[1] It must be noted here, that following the growing demands for the recognition of Indigenous languages, the federal Indigenous languages Act was finally adopted in 2019.
[2] Following the enactment of the 1969 Official Languages Act and its subsequent passage of the 1988 Official Languages Act, French-language community-based organizations and institutions that offered cultural programming and services started receiving funds from the federal government.

challenges such organizations face despite the crucial role they play in ensuring the vitality of official linguistic minority communities in Canada.[3]

In Alberta more than 418,000 (or 10.5%) of Albertans are of French or French-Canadian heritage. Seven percent of the population (264,720 people) can speak both English and French.[4] From 2011 to 2016, there was an increase of 22% of people whose mother tongue is French.[5] Following a rapid growth in immigration from Francophone African countries in the last few decades, this community has also become increasingly diversified.[6] Music (singing is very popular in Francophone schools and in the community with many adult choirs including that of Collège St Jean, now Campus Saint-Jean of the University of Alberta) and theater have always been the primary manifestations of Francophone culture in Alberta.[7] Furthermore, several forums and activities throughout the year showcase Francophone cultural traditions in the province. In February, the *Flying Canoë Volant* festival presents the culture and traditions of the First Nations, French-Canadian, and Métis peoples and celebrates the beauty of the Mill Creek ravine and Edmonton's French quarter. In March, every year, the *Rendez-Vous de la Francophonie* is celebrated across Alberta and includes Franco-Albertan flag-raising ceremonies, community gatherings, multicultural meetings, concerts, performances, educational opportunities, and more. In July, the *Fête Franco-albertaine* brings together Francophones of all ages from across the province. Besides these events, there is also a range of other cultural festivals targeting Francophone youth like *Edmonton Chante, Le Galala, La Chicane*, etc. In Alberta, the city of Edmonton has the largest number of Francophone cultural associations, *La Girandole* being one of them.

Dallaire and Denis (2000), in their study of the Francophone Games, have shown that identity and belonging form a complex issue in linguistic minority communities outside of Quebec. They note that it is because of the lack of consensus on the nature of "cultural truths" in the discourses producing Francophone identity outside Quebec besides the ability to speak French. This, they argue, often results in a confused representation of events, practices, and activities

---

[3]This study is a community engaged research initiative that engages ethically and respectfully with community members and supports transformative social change. We wish to thank local artists and pioneers, specially, Isabelle Laurin, Gilbert Parent, and Olivia Leclair for being generous with their time and for sharing their memories and experiences.

[4]It is outside the scope of this article to delve into the history of Albertan Francophonie. See Kermoal (2005) for a history of Francophones in Alberta. See also, Bonjour Alberta (2023). *Francophone heritage in Alberta*. Government of Alberta. https://www.alberta.ca/francophone-heritage.aspx#jumplinks-1

[5]Government of Alberta (2018, November 1). *The Francophonie in Alberta: strong and vibrant (2018)*. Alberta Government. https://open.alberta.ca/publications/9781460141731

[6]Twenty-four percent% of the Francophones in Alberta were born abroad. Fifty percent of the immigrants are from Francophone Africa. Commissariat aux langues officielles (2023) *Présence francophone en Alberta*. Commissariat aux langues officielles. https://www.clo-ocol.gc.ca/fr/statistiques/infographiques/presence-francophone-alberta

[7]For a history of Francophone theater in Alberta see Godbout et al. (2013).

carried out in French. Similarly, cultural associations are caught between national discourses and minority discourses on Francophonie. On the one hand, they originate from and contribute to a pan Canadian Francophone community (and to a global Francophonie as immigration changes the ethnic demographics of this population), and at the same time, they are committed to strengthening and visibilizing a minority and provincial francophone identity. This conundrum is the gravest challenge faced by most small community associations like *La Girandole* in linguistic minority settings in Canada.

L'Association la Girandole d'Edmonton: The Beginnings

L'Association la Girandole d'Edmonton, first started like most theater and music associations in Alberta, in the heart of the minority community, as a dance class catering to French-Canadians. Gilbert Parent, a local dancer and performer was asked to teach a French-Canadian dance class in the context of a continuing education program at the French-Immersion school J.H Picard in 1979–1980. As this activity became increasingly popular, inspiring other such French-Canadian dance classes around Edmonton, Parent was also asked to teach a folk dance class to students at the Faculté Saint-Jean (See Fig. 4.1).

Fig. 4.1.   Gilbert Parent's Group Presenting a Traditional Dance During a Sugar Shack Performance in Edmonton in 1981.

In a recent interview, Parent recalls having traveled around Alberta from his hometown of Falher to St Paul, spending a year with the folk group *Les Blés d'Or* before traveling to Québec and spending an intensive week to revitalize the repertoire he taught in Alberta.[8] As a member of the already existing *Gigue Électrique*, a three-member student band, Parent encouraged his students to perform folk dance with the band at local shows in and around Edmonton. Following the growing popularity of dance as a collective cultural expression of Francophone identity, *L'Association la Girandole d'Edmonton* was officially founded in 1980 as a not-for-profit organization under the artistic direction of Suzanne Foizy and Ronald Boivin.[9]

The enactment of the 1969 Official Languages Act and the adoption of the Charter of Rights and Freedoms in 1982 encouraged Francophones living outside of Quebec to express their collective identities and aspire for institutional completeness (Breton, 1964). As the enthusiasm for expressing a Franco-Albertan identity grew, parents became keen to instill Francophone culture in their children. From 1979 to 1982, the Association created three new dance groups for children: *les Arcs-en-ciel* (12–17 years), *les Alouettes* (9–11 years), and *les Étincelles* (6–8 years), alongside the adult performing group *la Girandole*. Increasing demand for such classes brought about the creation of other classes like *les Crépuscules* in Saint-Albert (7–10 years) and *les Jeunes Adultes* in Edmonton's studios as well as *les Lucioles* for younger children (4–5 years) in 1995. The need and demand for performances of folk dance were also growing, giving dancers of all ages the opportunity to perform on the local stage. The dancers of *La Girandole* saw themselves quickly being sought out on the provincial and international stage with various tours – in Alberta (1983, 1989), in Ireland (1983, 1987, 1990), and in the Maritimes (1993). Many of these dancers continued in teaching and administrative positions later on (See Fig. 4.2).

Starting out, at first, as a place of exchange for *Franco-albertains* wanting to revisit tradition and to celebrate their French-Canadian culture on the local stage through dance, *L'Association la Girandole* then encouraged dancers to pursue their interests in becoming teachers themselves and taking administrative roles within the organization so as to ensure a viable and sustainable future for the Association and its members. At the time, *La Girandole's* day-to-day operation costs were funded by provincial bodies like Alberta Foundation for the Arts, Alberta Lotteries, and Alberta Community Development under the provincial government's goal to promote bilingualism and multiculturalism. As its visibility and popularity in the community grew, the Association saw a more traditional non-for-profit structure with a board of directors, employees, and dance teachers (Dumoulin et al., 2020. p. 113). This reflected the growing number of students and instructors as well as the expanding vision of the association which was moving

---

[8]Interview with Gilbert Parent, 4 Jan 2023.
[9]Gilbert Parent moved *away from teaching classes to starting his own performing company Les Bûcherons While the activities of Les Bûcherons* focused on children in local schools, *La Girandole* developed programs meant for people of all ages: children, teenagers, and adults. See https://lesbucherons.com/about-us/

Fig. 4.2.   La Girandole Dance Troupe (1981). *Source:* Archives of la
Girandole.

away from a simple forum to teach dance to training professionals to becoming
the strongest voice for French-Canadian dance in the West.[10]

It is quite difficult to define "French-Canadian" dance. Like many other types of
traditional and folk art, dance is not immune to the challenges that researchers face
when attempting to retrace the exact time, place or people that first started the folk
art. Lack of a universal typology and record keeping system, just like differences
between regions and local rituals, are all factors that need to be recognized when
explaining the origins of folk dance (Lessard, 1999, p. 68). In French Canada's case
however, colonialism and the cultures of the countries of origin of the first European
settlers who arrived in Canada, such as France, Scotland, Ireland, and England, have
had a clear influence on French-Canadian dance. These influences are still present
today in various ways: the types of formations present in social dances, the types of
music and musical phrases used, the types of steps used during social dances, as well
as the percussive dance or step dancing (*gigue*). Jean-Pierre Joyal (1999) explained
the key musical differences between a "reel" (native of Scotland), the "gigue or jig"
(representing either a 2/4 measure or that of an Irish 6/8), the "galop" (native of

---

[10]Although *L'Association la Girandole d'Edmonton* isn't the only dance association in
Alberta – with *Les Blés d'Or* in St Paul, Alberta and *Les Plein Soleil* in Peace River – it
remains to this day one of the strongest voice of French-Canadian dance in Western
Canada, being able to marry tradition with modernism, attracting youth and adults alike.

France), the "hornpipe" (native of England), the "Grande gigue simple" or "Grondeuse," as well as the "Brandy" (both originated from Québec). Each variation has its place in French-Canadian dance and step dance, now understood and studied as the origins of French-Canadian dance. What is most interesting, however, is how French-Canadian dance has evolved from the first years of colonialism; firstly, in Eastern Canada with Québec and Ontario developing regional stylizations that are recognized today and further accentuated with costumes in the 1970s, and, secondly, in Western Canada, the prairies have adapted and reappropriated their own particular styles and identities. Notably, the *Grande gigue simple* now danced by Métis step-dancers or jiggers as "Gigue de la Rivière-Rouge" (Joyal, 1999, p. 15).

As *La Girandole* became a leader of French-Canadian dance in Edmonton, the Association needed a greater access to both professional development opportunities and archival resources. In 1997, la Girandole invited two of their artistic directors to visit folk dance schools in Québec as well as the music and dance documentation center in the hope of creating the first French-Canadian dance, music, and cultural resource center in Western Canada. With developing relationships involving multiple artists and dance schools in Québec came opportunities of exchange through folk dance workshops. *La Girandole*, in collaboration with other folk ensembles across Western Canada, organized several cultural workshops with dance and musical artists from Québec. These workshops ensured professional development and also provided ways to reunite folk artists in the West and create new collaborations across cities.[11] And so, with the turn of the millennium came new ideas and bigger dreams to found a semi-professional dance troupe: *Zéphyr*. Isabelle Laurin was headhunted to lead this project in 2002.[12]

Zéphyr: Breathing New Life Into the Association

Until then *La Girandole* was primarily funded by provincial organizations committed to the promotion of diversity in the arts. In order to attract federal funding from *Heritage Canada*, the organization had to devise a new strategy. *Heritage Canada* does not generally support classes, and workshops which target individuals. It however promotes activities that reflect community identity and heritage activities. The creation of *Zephyr*, a professional dance troupe, was a strategic way to attract

---

[11]In 2020, the Association put in place a new project for the resource center: *Historique des troupes franco-albertaines*, which would be a document detailing the history of French-Canadian dance troupes in Alberta, notably that of the *Blés d'or, the Plein Soleil and la Girandole*. Although useful for this study, this project was commissioned without a clear objective that would serve the Association's vision, and was quickly forgotten about once written. It also remains unfinished, as a mural of photographs was supposed to accompany the project, and unfortunately pushed back due to a sewage backup in the *Cité francophone* building in May 2022.
[12]Isabelle first took the artistic director position of the Association in 2002, then the executive artistic director position of the Association in 2004. In 2007, she took over the artistic direction of *Zéphyr* until December of 2009. In 2013, she came back to take up the artistic direction of *Zéphyr* until 2017.

federal funding as well as to build the ultimate marketing and promotional tool for the Association. Changes were made within the association to reflect this shift: The *Arcs-en-ciel* group was changed to *Zéphyr Junior*, and the adult group *La Girandole* was transformed into a recreational dance class as opposed to the newly formed semi-professional activity that *Zéphyr* promoted. In 2004, new jobs were created to better serve the Association's new vision (Dumoulin et al., 2020). The following quote provides a useful distinction to talk about French-Canadian folk dance in Edmonton as it evolved with the creation of *Zéphyr*:

> La distribution géographique des danses traditionnelles demeure toujours un sujet délicat à traiter, la culture populaire ne coïncide pas toujours avec les structures administratives ou politiques. Certaines recherches européennes procèdent à une construction de modèles régionaux ou "zones ethnochorégraphiques". On y retrouve d'une part des 'zones conservatrices' où la communauté, plus fermée sur elle-même, impose des caractéristiques et assimile les danses provenant d'ailleurs ; et d'autre part des 'zones de transition', où la population, plus ouverte, adopte le répertoire étranger, sans l'altérer.[13] (Lessard, 1999, p. 68)

At the outset, as a "zone conservatrice," *La Girandole* was primarily interested in keeping, recording and sharing a traditional repertoire of French-Canadian dances for its members, all inspired directly from Québec or folk dances already taught in St Paul or Peace River, historical areas of Francophone settlement in Alberta. Choreographies rarely diverged from the repertoire and left almost no room for creativity, opting for a more traditional and even historical represen-tation on stage of dance through costumes, gendered dance and positions, types of dances as well as the songs used. These dances were recorded and kept in the Association's resource center for all local and provincial members to consult and use. However, in the early 2000s, with the arrival of Isabelle Laurin came a new vision for the Association as a space for creativity offering the chance for a new approach to French-Canadian dance and most importantly a more localized French-Canadian identity. Isabelle Laurin recalls being corrected upon her arrival in Alberta to use the term French-Canadian dance rather than Québécois dance, regardless of their common origins.[14] Laurin wanted to take folk dance from a *zone conservatrice* to a *zone de transition*. In Alberta, she saw an opportunity, a "carte blanche," for French-Canadian dance; the freedom to create, to

---

[13]"The geographical distribution of traditional dances remains a delicate matter for discussion as popular culture does not always coincide with administrative or political structures. Some European researchers propose regional models or 'ethnochoreohraphic' zones. Within this model, there are, on one hand, 'conservative zones' where communities closed-in on themselves, impose characteristics and assimilate dances coming from other regions; and on the other hand, there are 'transition zones' where more open-minded populations adopt outsider repertoire, without altering it" (Our translation).
[14]Interview with Isabelle Laurin, 05 January 2023.

collaborate, and to push the art form outside of traditional boundaries and stricter curricula seen in Québec.[15]

For the Franco-Albertan members of *Zephyr* the idea of pushing the constraints of traditional dance and allowing for collaborations, exploration of style, and percussive dance, as well as the merging and fusion of dance styles, was something exciting and much needed. As stated earlier the only consensus on identity within the francophone minority community in Canada was language and expressing identity through dance was novel and refreshing.

Here is how *L'Association la Girandole* promoted *Zephyr*:

> Zéphyr is the performance troupe of *L'Association la Girandole based in Edmonton*, Alberta. The company acquires its repertoire from traditional French-Canadian dance and of all the cultures that formed this province. Combining traditional and modern elements, Zéphyr will amaze you with their energy and professionalism.[16]

Zéphyr created a total of seven productions: Par Train (2003), FuZion (2005), Au rythme du monde et de nos vies (2008), Petits rêves (2011), Pot Pourri (2014), Destination: France (2015), and SaiZons (2017), each catering to and pushing the boundaries of what is French-Canadian dance in Alberta. As Laurin explained:

> Je savais que la gigue de haut niveau c'était ça qui était au cœur de Zéphyr, mais présenté dans une perspective contemporaine. [...] On vous a montré la danse traditionnelle mais on l'a tiré dans plein de niveaux pour montrer toute l'étendue de ce qu'on peut faire avec. On l'a fait avec la danse contemporaine; C'était un chorégraphe qu'on a fait venir [de Québec], et c'était assez funky. C'était aussi les balbutiements de la gigue contemporaine au Québec. On l'a fait avec du Gumboot ou le Gum-gigue, justement pour démontrer qu'en alliant d'autres traditions, d'autres communautés culturelles, on est tellement plus forts parce qu'on a tellement plus d'opportunités [sonores et percussives].[17] On l'a fait avec du Hip hop. [...] Une des raisons pour lesquelles je faisais venir des chorégraphes du Québec,

---

[15] These changes, or rather the opening of folk dance in Québec took a longer time to happen. Many of her colleagues from the dance group *Les Sortilèges* created the new professional dance troupe *Zogma* in 2001, defined as "Collectif de folklore urbain," meshing French-Canadian step dance, percussion and contemporary dance. But these changes were not in the folk dance schools, but rather on a professional level (Interview with Isabelle Laurin, January 5, 2023).

[16] *La Girandole* archives.

[17] Rain boots typically used for Gumboot were cut so that dancers could wear their step dancing shoes. A fusion of the two styles was created allowing for twice as many percussive rhythms and choreography.

c'était aussi pour l'inspiration, ça aidait mes danseurs, mais ça m'aidait moi aussi.[18]

See Fig. 4.3.

The spirit of going beyond tradition was also reflected in broadening the dance classes to offer a wider variety of dance styles: Kangourous (2–3 yrs), Ballet, Jazz, Hip-hop, Salsa, Gumboot and Musical Theater styles. In 2008, as the association added more members to the team, new dance classes such as

Fig. 4.3.   Zéphyr's Second Production: FuZion (2006). *Source:* Archives of la Girandole.

---

[18]"I knew that high level step-dancing was at the core of Zéphyr, but presented in a contemporary perspective. We showcased traditional dance but extended it to all kinds of levels to demonstrate just how far it can go. We did it with contemporary dance with a choreographer from Québec and it was funky. That was at the start of contemporary step-dancing in Québec. We did it with Gumboot or Gum-gigue, to showcase that the combination of other traditions and other cultural communities make us stronger as there are so many more opportunities (both percussive and auditory). We did it with Hip-hop. One of the reasons why I brought choreographers from Québec was also for inspiration, it helped my dancers but it also helped me" (Our translation).

Swing, Rwandese, and Burundi dances were offered to reflect the growing ethnic diversity of the French-Canadian community.[19] However, it was important that *L'Association la Girandole* maintain a balance between tradition and modernity since the members of the main group supporting *Zéphyr* were those who were also keen to retain Franco-Albertanity as a political identity. As much as Isabelle Laurin innovated with *Zéphyr*, she still understood that she had an ethnographical role in providing knowledge to the association's dance teachers and maintaining a basic traditional repertoire from which to modernize from. There was a demand for such traditional fare during *Cabane à sucre* events and in front of Anglophone crowds curious to learn about French-Canadian heritage. This repertoire was also provided to other troupes in Alberta as part of the resource center initiative and later, as the Association added a provincial mandate to their vision under Laurin's direction. Dancers were tasked by the management to visit other Franco-Albertan troupes and share repertoire as well as organize weekend workshops for professional development. This initiative ended in 2008, although today, the Association is working toward reestablishing their provincial mandate.

An Ongoing Challenge: Maintaining a Fine Balance Between Multiple Mandates

All in all, *Zéphyr's* growing presence as a professional troupe and the diverse repertoire of dance classes offered by the association resulted in a record-breaking number of new and returning clientele to la Girandole.[20] For the next 10 years, *La Girandole's* classes and performance stayed mostly the same – finding a wide range of styles that interested children and adults alike, while maintaining the core folk roots that it had developed since the beginning. After 2010, the association saw a noticeable drop in popularity and waning of community interest. Management was forced to substitute or cancel classes due to lack of enrollment or simply the lack of teachers. There is evidence to say that this coincides with the move from its location in Center 82 to the newly constructed *la Cité Francophone* in Bonnie Doon. Despite the attractive venue, which basically created a Francophone village regrouping all the different cultural organizations into one space, the move came with a huge financial risk for smaller units like *La Girandole*. The revenues of *Zéphyr* alone could not guarantee to cover the space costs on a long-term basis. Although many members and administrators were excited by the move to a closer location and to be nested in the heart of the francophone cultural sector, the cost of renting and the administrative fees soon became a huge

---

[19]Dusablon (2016) *La Girandole au rythme des danses traditionnelles du Burundi.*
[20]Interview with Isabelle Laurin, 05 Jan 2023.

financial stress that had a negative impact on artistic projects.[21,22] Indeed, *Zéphyr* had to cancel its anticipated tour of France in 2017 due to financial reasons, and subsequently resulted in Isabelle Laurin's final departure from the Association.[23] The initial deficit following the move to *la Cité* was $78,865 which took approximately 10 years to recover, and it was only in 2020 that the debt was paid off in its entirety.[24] It must be said that the stagnation and eventual drop in popularity was also a result of a lack of a unified artistic direction for *Zéphyr* and for the association as a whole. As Laurin recalled about her return to the artistic director's position in 2013:

> Je suis revenue après Casey Edmunds qui lui avait pris le relai après Aline Dupuis. Il s'est passé quelque chose et on m'a demandé de revenir. Puis, d'un point de vue artistique, je sentais que c'était un peu perdu. Je pense en partie à un manque de connaissances d'un répertoire assez large. Ça tournait autour des mêmes choses et ça a pris une certaine fin; Et je pense que c'est du fait de juste circuler ici, dans l'Ouest. Quand je suis arrivée de l'Est, je suis arrivée avec tout un autre bagage que personne ne connaissait ici. [...] Moi, j'ai quitté Zéphyr parce que je me demandais 'qu'est-ce que j'apporte de nouveau?'. Un, j'étais très occupée, je venais de prendre la direction générale à l'ACFA et c'était juste trop, et deux, je n'avais plus cet espace de ressourcement qui est fondamental. Je pense que la vision de c'est quoi la direction artistique de Zéphyr c'était devenu aussi un rôle de coordination de spectacle, et il y avait un écart entre mes attentes de ce que l'administration de la Girandole aurait dû faire et de ce que le conseil d'administration aurait dû faire. Quand moi j'étais là avant, il y avait comme un alignement entre la vision artistique de Zéphyr, la vision artistique de la Girandole dans son ensemble

---

[21]Archives (2010, June 9) *Bientôt la fin des travaux d'agrandissement.* Radio-Canada https:// ici.radio-canada.ca/nouvelle/476316/cite-francophone
[22]Antonine Bergeron, former president of the Association, is quoted in a testimonial that the move to the Cité francophone was one of the achievements she was most proud of: "Pendant toutes mes années à la Girandole, c'est du déménagement du studio dans la Cité francophone dont je suis le plus fière. Ma collègue et moi avons conçu et aménagé le nouveau studio, supervisé sa construction et vu à tous les détails, y compris les garde-robes." Dumoulin et al. (2020) ("During all my years at *La Girandole*, I am most proud of our move into the Cité francophone. My colleague and I, we designed the new studio, supervised its construction and oversaw all the details, including the wardrobes" (Our translation).
[23]Dusablon (2017, February 23) *Zéphyr signe SaiZons et le départ d'Isabelle Laurin.* Radio-Canada   https://ici.radio-canada.ca/nouvelle/1018612/zephyr-danse-traditionelle-alberta-saizons-isabelle-laurin
[24]Financial records for the year ending 30 April 2010. *La Girandole* archives.

et la vision des besoins administratifs. Quand ça s'est dissocié, on a
perdu beaucoup.[25]

Two factors contributed to the confused mandate of the association: firstly,
that the Board of Directors and the artistic direction did not agree on a
common mission for the association. Secondly, that the Board of Directors
lacked knowledge and understanding of the context surrounding folk dance in
Alberta. The Board being solely made of parents of children enrolled in the
classes offered by the Association seems to have a one-dimensional understanding of the Association's roles and mission. It has often times resulted in
conflict of interest with parents advocating cheaper costs for dance classes
instead of considering the association's wider interests, both on a day-to-day
level and on a broader one of elaborating mid- and long-term strategic plans.[26]
There is also no clear tracking system of members and therefore, we can guess
that there are around 40 members within the Association for the 2022–2023
year.[27] Annual meetings are oftentimes very poor in participation, barely
meeting the ten-member quorum. Very clearly, a greater political and strategic
investment in the association is required for ensuring that the association
maintains the vision that the creation of *Zéphyr* defined 20 years ago. The
association is a far cry of what it was once in 2002 when it dreamed of being

---

[25]"I came back after Casey Edmunds had taken over from Aline Depuis. Something
happened and they asked me to come back. From an artistic perspective, I felt that they
were a little lost. I think it might have been from a lack of knowledge of a very vast
repertoire. They were circling around the same things and it had come to an end; and I
think it's mostly because they were just circling here, in the West. When I first arrived from
the East, I came with a lot of knowledge that no one had here. When I left Zéphyr, I had
asked myself, 'what is left to give that's new?'. One, I was very busy professionally, as I had
just started as Executive director of the ACFA, and it was just too much, and two, I didn't
have the artistic development space that is fundamental. I think the vision of Zéphyr's
artistic director became that of a performance coordinator, and there was a gap between
my expectations of what la Girandole's administration should be doing and what the board
of directors should be doing. When I was there before, there was this alignment between
Zéphyr's artistic vision, la Girandole's artistic vision as a whole and the vision of
administrative needs. When that ended, we lost a lot" (Our translation).
[26]*La Girandole*, being a nonprofit organization, mandates that the administrative council be
members of the association voted into the board during annual general meetings, by other
members. To become a member of the association, a 25-dollar fee is asked. One of the
Association's policies is that all families wanting to register for classes with *La Girandole*
need to pay either an individual 25 dollar or a family 40-dollar fee. Members then have
access to discounted prices, access to the resource center and free events.
[27]Roughly the number of parents and children above the age of 16, as well as other
members who have paid this year.

the first professional French-Canadian company in Western Canada.[28] Today, *Zéphyr* and *La Girandole* face many structural challenges. If the creation of *Zéphyr* was to give credibility and to distinguish the *L'Association la Girandole* from communal dance schools by taking the dance form outside of the community and into the greater social context of Alberta, then the Francophone community as a whole, represented by the Board of *L'Association la Girandole*, must do much more to continue to support this goal. The COVID-19 pandemic, and a sewage backup in the physical studio space in *La Cité francophone* in May 2022 have only exacerbated the situation.[29]

Lessons Learned

Cultural associations in Francophone minority communities are still trying to build a path that would reconcile them with a more cosmopolitan idea of Francophonie as well as integrate them within the political institutions of their respective provinces and territories. This result in ambivalent expressions of identity and belonging as we see in the confusion of terms used to describe folk dance of French-Canadian origin in Alberta-Francophone, Franco-Albertan, and French-Canadian. Each of these terms refer to a different way of defining culture-from a more ethnicist perspective (French-Canadian) to a politically charged minority identity (Franco-Albertan) and finally to a more nebulous one (Francophone) that appears inclusive and diverse but remains vague on the ground. The reality of FMCs in Alberta is that of professional dancers like Olivia Leclair who herald new ways to apprehend the complexity of being "Francophone" in Alberta. Olivia Leclair identifies herself as a Franco-Albertan and considers the French-Canadian culture her "adopted culture." Her maternal family is from France and Slovenia while her paternal side hails from Ireland and Germany, as well as Ontario. She has danced with the *L'Association la Girandole* since 2012, and joined *the Zéphyr* troupe in 2013. She also dances with the Lebanese folk ensemble, Al-Jabal Dance, since 2014. Young professionals like Olivia Leclair capture the complexities of the FMCs in 21st century Canada and both community leaders and academics can learn much from *La Girandole's* story:

Firstly, openness to embracing change and artistic innovations that take into consideration the diversity of the community that they serve, like *Zéphyr*, are crucial for the growth of these cultural producers. Olivia Leclair noted:

---

[28] *La Girandole* is currently rebuilding the value of this art form post-COVID-19. There is an even greater demand for folk dance and interest in sharing it on a wider scale. Digital delivery of performances and concerts was on one hand a way to cope with the isolation, but on the other hand, the ease of which the art was shared tended to devalue the art itself. Dance is already a minoritized art form, and folk dance as doubly minoritized, suffered in that sense. The rebuilding process is a crucial one for both artists and audience to participate in in-person events as it creates an understanding and attaches a tangible value to the art form.

[29] Reduced to four-membered troupe from an original group of 12–16 dancers, *Zéphyr* continues to maintain traditional dance as the heart of their choreographies while exploring percussive dance through multiple avenues: accessories, choice of music, types of styles, and costumes.

As folk-dance teachers in *la Girandole*, the chance to create new and exciting choreographies adapted to students' interests and modern influences is more and more favoured, rather than recycling and re-doing the same traditional dances from a time and historically-fixed repertoire. It is not about re-enacting a museum piece on stage, but rather expressing a cultural identity through folk dance that interests me. Although recognizing a traditional and folkloric curriculum is needed to ensure that the heritage is shared with students, choreographies can be altered and re-purposed to define the Franco-Albertan identity as it is today.[30]

Isabelle Laurin also pointed out to the importance of embracing diversity for the vitality of francophone communities:

La francophonie n'appartient pas au canadien-français, plus maintenant. Patrimoine Canadien devrait soutenir le studio, mais le studio devrait être embrassé par toutes les cultures, qui forment la mosaïque de la francophonie albertaine, et ouvrir les portes à tous ces gens-là. Quand je suis arrivée, l'immigration africaine commençait à peine, et tout de suite en 2005, on a fait venir Dominic Desrochers, un chorégraphe qui faisait du Gumboot. C'était important pour moi d'avoir quelque chose d'africain dans notre répertoire, je ne connaissais pas d'autre personne qui faisait un métissage. Le Gumboot vient de l'Afrique du Sud, qui n'est pas de l'Afrique francophone. Mais au moins, les gens vont se retrouver avec ça, ça va être une façon de tendre la main. Il y avait même un monsieur rwandais qui avait dit 'Tu viens d'expliquer dans treize minutes ce que nous on essaye d'expliquer depuis des années,' Ça sert à ça la danse.[31]

---

[30]Ideas expressed here are Olivia Leclair's and do not represent those of the Association. Resistance to innovation in folk dance stems mostly from an older generation of dancers, Olivia Leclair recalled a conversation she had with an older dancer from Saint Paul in 2014, explaining that he did not really like the modern take *Zéphyr* brought to folk dance; he was more interested in keeping traditions alive through dance.

[31]Interview with Isabelle Laurin, January 05, 2023. "Francophonie doesn't belong only to French-Canadians anymore. Canadian Heritage funded the dance studio, but the dance studio should be embraced by all the cultures that form the Albertan Francophone mosaic and should open its doors to these people. When I first arrived, African immigration had just started and immediately in 2005, we invited Dominic Desrochers, a Gumboot choreographer. It was important for me to add something African in our repertoire, I didn't know anyone that had tried that combination. Even though Gumboot comes from South Africa, which isn't part of Francophone Africa, it was something that people could identify with, it was a way to welcome them. There was a Rwandese man that came after a performance and said 'You just explained in 13 minutes what we have tried to explain in years,' That's what dance does" (Our translation).

Secondly, sustaining community spirit through intergenerational membership has been vital for the survival of the Association. *La Girandole* plays a significant role as a cultural player as it is not only a dance association, but a contributing member and active community forum, where relations and romances have produced a new generation of dancers wanting to follow in their parents' footsteps. Indeed, *La Girandole's* current director, Julianna Damer noted that: "Une des choses les plus spéciales avec La Girandole, c'est d'avoir un aspect multigénérationnel."[32]

Thirdly, *L'Association la Girandole* has the potential to not only contribute to a living heritage for many Francophones in Edmonton, it also collaborates and expands its reach to other folk dance groups in Alberta and creates new partnerships with Québec and the rest of the Francophone world. This vision needs to be at the core of the Association's strategic plan but it requires delicate navigating between varying definitions of French-Canadian dance and varying mission statements. Take for example, les *Bûcherons*, Gilbert Parent's performing company for schools in and around Alberta. Its vision, since 1982, is "Sharing Canadian History and traditional French Canadian Culture using Song, Stories, and Dance."[33] Shaped by a conventional idea of "French-Canadian" culture, *Les Bûcherons* is interested in traditional teachings, gendered roles in dance and folk tales that share Canadian history without contextualizing it from a contemporary perspective. This perspective is attractive to some members of the community. Franco-Albertan artists have worked under Gilbert Parent and *Les Bûcherons*, notably, Roger Dallaire and Daniel Gervais who formed their own musical duo Trad'badour in 2008, and are recognized individually and together for their performances in schools and other festivals in Western Canada such as the Flying Canoë Volant Festival, Deep Freeze Festival, to name a few.[34] Gilbert Parent is optimistic for the future of dance as a folk art in Edmonton and even envisages a collaboration with *La Girandole* but he also perceived it as a challenge mostly because of the Association's continuing attempt to maintain a more evolving definition of this art form which is different from his own vision:

> L'avenir, je ne suis pas sûr pour les autres troupes en Alberta. Mais
> à Edmonton, il y a une bonne base avec la Girandole. S'il y a un

---

[32]"One of the most special things about *La Girandole* is its multigenerational aspect" (Our translation), Lafond (2021, November 18). *Quand la passion pour la danse se transmet de génération en génération*. Radio-Canada https://ici.radio-canada.ca/nouvelle/1840686/arts-studio-danse-ballet-tradition-spectacle

[33]Les bûcherons (2019) About us. https://lesbucherons.com/about-us/

[34]Musician, storyteller, puppeteer, and folklorist Roger Dallaire has been performing in schools all across Canada since 2000. He has also performed with Daniel Gervais in their duo "Trad'badour." Gervais is an accomplished violinist currently teaches as sessional faculty at MacEwan University in the jazz and popular music program. Daniel has toured with Zéphyr, a French-Canadian dance group, performing at the Smithsonian Folklife Festival in Washington, D.C., Mondial des cultures in Drummondville, PQ, the Folkmoot USA Festival in North Carolina, and Festival Interfolk in France. Gervais & Dallaire (2023) Bio. http://www.troubadours.ca/bio.html

défi à surmonter à la Girandole, c'est de trouver une façon
d'amalgamer les ressources des *Bûcherons* et les ressources de *la
Girandole* pour créer quelque chose qui accroche les professeurs et
même les sixièmes années pour qu'eux-autres soient les leaders de
la danse.[35]

Conclusion

The tension between the desire to reclaim an authentic and fixed identity and the need
to develop a more dynamic idea of cultural heritage that is continually evolving is
reflected in the differing visions between the Board of *L'Association la Girandole* and
the artistic direction. This conflict prevails within FMC in Alberta and elsewhere in
Canada. Community stakeholders cannot understate the importance of having an
artistic director/leader that understands this tension and is willing to fight for a better
representation of this art form within and outside the traditional FMC on a political
level. This requires a better understanding of the systems and structures put in place
at both the provincial and federal levels. Furthermore, it also requires active and
innovative collaboration with local commercial enterprises to promote French-
Canadian dance in the wider community. In 2015, the Association rethought the
adult folk dance classes and opened them up as kitchen parties (*veillées*) in the locale
of Café Bicyclette, conveniently located in the Cité francophone. Not only did it
make the dance form more accessible to a wider public but it was also a great promotional tool for both the Association and the Café Bicyclette. Traditional *veillées* or
kitchen parties are an important social component to French-Canadian dance, as a
space to come together, meet other French-Canadians, and dance traditional dances
to live music. A *câlleur* or a lead is present to guide dancers through each formation.
Bricault (2014) explained "La veillée de danse est un rassemblement festif …un
élément du patrimoine culturel et une composante de l'identité québécoise et
francophone."[36] A report by Radio-Canada (2015) compared this type of event as
reminiscent of the *Soirée canadienne* TV series, an event that transported dancers and
musicians alike back to a small rural town in Québec.[37] Indeed, there is this risk of
stereotyping "French-Canadianness" and reducing it to a quaint folk culture when

---

[35]Interview with Gilbert Parent, January 4th, 2023. "I am not sure what will become of
other dance troupes in Alberta. But in Edmonton, there is a good foundation at *la
Girandole*. If there is one challenge to overcome at la Girandole, it will be to combine
the resources of *Les Bûcherons* and those of la Girandole create something that really
engages teachers and might convince sixth graders to become leaders in dance" (Our
translation).
[36]Patrimoine culturel, désignations, patrimoines immatériels. (2023, February 15) *Veillées
de danse*, Conseil du patrimoine culturel. Retrieved February 15, 2023, from https://
cpcq.gouv.qc.ca/patrimoine-culturel/designations/patrimoine-immateriel/veille-de-danse/
[37]Dusablon and Roy (2015, December 4) *Les veillées de la Girandole: une tradition qui fait
bouger*. Radio-Canada. https://ici.radio-canada.ca/nouvelle/753484/veillees-girandole-
tradition-danse-musique-canadienne-marie-eve-dusablon-brent-roy

such community events are commercialized. As both Olivia Leclair and Isabelle Laurin have noted, attempts have been made to mix traditional dance styles and create unique choreographies that showcase this cultural *métissage*. Both have expressed the view that *L'Association la Girandole* must find new strategies to encourage children and adults from other ethnic backgrounds within and outside the traditional Francophone communities, to learn French-Canadian dance as a form of cultural activity performed in French. Eventually, exchange and collaboration will reduce the risk of folklorizing culture. Furthermore, in Alberta, the wider Francophone community cannot ignore the cultural contribution of a growing population of African Francophone immigrants to the vitality of FMCs and such exchanges are already in place in other cultural sectors like music.[38] The attempts at collaborating within FMCs reveals that it is a fine balancing act between responding to the needs of a diversified community while still contributing to an identity-driven art such as folk dance. Despite the challenges it faces, *L'Association la Girandole*, continues to contribute actively to promoting Francophone minority identity, culture, and heritage in Alberta through dance as both an art form and also an expression of "Francophoneness" and its ambiguities. It also recognizes the potential role it could play in taking Francophone cultural heritage to a larger audience beyond traditional FMCs and becoming a space where people from diverse backgrounds meet socially and learn about other cultural traditions.

References

Archives. (2010, June 9). *Bientôt la fin des travaux d'agrandissement*. Radio-Canada. https://ici.radio-canada.ca/nouvelle/476316/cite-francophone

Bonjour Alberta. (2023). *Francophone heritage in Alberta*. Government of Alberta. https://www.alberta.ca/francophone-heritage.aspx#jumplinks-1

Breton, R. (1964). Institutional completeness of ethnic communities and the personal relations of immigrants. *American Journal of Sociology, 70*(2), 193–205.

Commissariat aux langues officielles. (2023). *Présence francophone en Alberta*. Commissariat aux langues officielles. https://www.clo-ocol.gc.ca/fr/statistiques/infographiques/presence-francophone-alberta

Dallaire, C., & Denis, C. (2000). "If you don't speak French, you're out": Don Cherry, the Alberta Francophone games, and the discursive construction of Canada's Francophones. *The Canadian Journal of Sociology/Cahiers Canadiens de Sociologie, 25*(4), 415–440. https://doi.org/10.2307/3341607

---

[38]See *Patrimoines en devenir: Langue, Mémoire, Éducation* (IMELDA-Loft Prod 2021). Available online on the audiovisual platform of University of Alberta. https://ualberta.aviaryplatform.com/collections/1778/collection_resources/59017. It must be noted here that despite the commonality of language, many Francophone African immigrants find themselves doubly minoritized through language and race (Madibbo, 2016) in Canadian society. Furthermore, for French speaking African immigrants, cultural identification in the diaspora is also expressed through African languages and practices as is evidenced by the presence of several African community organizations founded along nationalist lines.

Dumoulin, M., Perreaux, D., & Levasseur-Ouimet, F. (2020, October 15). *Historique des troupes de danse folkloriques franco-albertaine.* L'Association la Girandole d'ed-monton. https://www.lagirandole.com/_files/ugd/c0d9cd_5a32126fe1e54bc99e3f609 6700967c6.pdf. Accessed on February 15, 2023.

Dusablon, M.-È. (2016, November 6). *La Girandole au rythme des danses traditionnelles du Burundi.* Radio-Canada. https://ici.radio-canada.ca/nouvelle/812850/danse-burundaise-traditionelle-girandole-francais-burundi-leila?depuisRecherche=true

Dusablon, M.-È. (2017, February 23). *Zéphyr signe SaiZons et le départ d'Isabelle Laurin.* Radio-Canada. https://ici.radio-canada.ca/nouvelle/1018612/zephyr-danse-traditionelle-alberta-saizons-isabelle-laurin

Dusablon, M.-È., & Roy, B. (2015, December 4). *Les veillées de la Girandole: une tradition qui fait bouger.* Radio-Canada. https://ici.radio-canada.ca/nouvelle/753484/veillees-girandole-tradition-danse-musique-canadienne-marie-eve-dusablon-brent-roy

Fauchon, A. (1993, October 14–16). *La production culturelle en milieu minoritaire (Conference session).* 13e colloque du Centre d'études franco-canadiennes de l'Ouest, Collège Universitaire de Saint-Boniface. https://ustboniface.ca/presses/file/actes-colloques/colloque13-ilovepdf-compressed.pdf

Gervais & Dallaire. (2023). Bio. http://www.troubadours.ca/bio.html

Godbout, L., Ladouceur, L., & Allaire, G. (2013). *Plus d'un siècle sur scène ! Histoire du théâtre francophone en Alberta de 1887 à 2008.* Institut pour le patrimoine de la francophonie de l'Ouest canadien. Campus Saint-Jean, Université de l'Alberta.

Government of Alberta. (2018, November 1). *The Francophonie in Alberta: strong and vibrant.* Alberta Government. https://open.alberta.ca/publications/9781460141731

Iacovino, R., & Léger, R. (2013). Francophone minority communities and immigrant integration in Canada: Rethinking the normative foundations. *Canadian Ethnic Studies Journal, 45*(1–2), 95–114. http://doi.org/10.1353/ces.2013.0034

Joyal, J.-P. (1999). Au-delà du reel: Introduction à la musique traditionnelle instru-mentale québécoise. In Les Cahiers Mnémo (Ed.), *Danse et musique traditionnelles du Québec* (pp. 9–21). Éditions Mnémo.

Kermoal, N. (2005). *Les Francophones de l'Alberta.* Éditions GID.

Labrecque, R. (2018). L'identité fransaskoise en pièces ou l'insoutenable angoisse de l'autre: tensions entre communautarisme et cosmopolitisme dans le théâtre fransas-kois. *Cahiers franco-canadiens de l'Ouest, 30*(1), 43–79. https://doi.org/10.7202/1045595ar

Lafond, I. (2021, November 18). *Quand la passion pour la danse se transmet de génération en génération.* Radio-Canada. https://ici.radio-canada.ca/nouvelle/1840686/arts-studio-danse-ballet-tradition-spectacle

Les Bûcherons. (2019). About us. https://lesbucherons.com/about-us/

Lessard, D. (1999). Recherche en danses traditionnelles: L'approche méthodologique de La danse traditionnelle dans l'est du Canada par Simonne Voyer. In Les Cahiers Mnémo (Ed.), *Danse et musique traditionnelles du Québec* (pp. 65–69). Éditions Mnémo.

Madibbo, A. (2016). The way forward: African francophone immigrants negotiate their multiple minority identities. *Journal of International Migration and Integra-tion, 17*(1), 853–866.

Patrimoine culturel, désignations, patrimoines immatériels. (2023, February 15). *Veillées de danse.* Conseil du patrimoine culturel. https://cpcq.gouv.qc.ca/patrimoine-culturel/designations/patrimoine-immateriel/veillee-de-danse/. Accessed on February 15, 2023.

Section 2

Music

Chapter 5

A Transformation of an Orchestra Through Gender Equity and Diversity

Sophie Galaise

Melbourne Symphony Orchestra, Australia

Abstract

Established in 1906, the Melbourne Symphony Orchestra (MSO) is a cornerstone of Victoria, Australia. Through the shared language of music, it creates meaningful experiences for its audiences, delivered to the highest possible standard. Considered one of Australia's preeminent cultural ambassadors, the MSO performs in Australia and internationally while attracting guest artists from around the world. Annually the MSO engages with more than 5 million people through live concerts, TV, radio and online broadcasts, international and regional tours, recordings, and education programs. In 2021, the MSO launched its digital platform MSO.LIVE engaging with an audience in 58 countries. The pandemic brought many challenges to the Orchestra but also some extraordinary opportunities. Pre-pandemic the MSO board, management, staff, and musicians worked to transform the Orchestra. The many lockdowns created the perfect occasion to redefine the vision. It became an opportunity to transform. Equity and diversity, in a world of classic music where traditionally white men dominate, were identified as the way forward. MSO aspires to lead the way for equality across its Board, staff, and musicians, and throughout its artistic programming. The MSO was the first professional Australian orchestra to join the Keychange movement in early 2020. The MSO is committed to promoting a culture that celebrates and supports the diversity of its people and community. Diversity in its people, its music, and its audience is a specific goal and a plan has been developed to achieve by 2024.

Keywords: Gender equity; cultural industries; performing arts; arts management; governance; orchestra; leadership

Accessibility, Diversity, Equity and Inclusion in the Cultural Sector, 69–82
Copyright © 2024 Sophie Galaise
Published under exclusive licence by Emerald Publishing Limited
doi:10.1108/978-1-83753-034-220241010

Introduction

The pandemic has accelerated a transformation of the Melbourne Symphony Orchestra (MSO). Equity and diversity, in the world of classic music where white men have dominated, present not only a challenge but also an opportunity. As the MSO believes this is fundamental to being relevant and vibrant, it has embarked on a journey toward achieving this.

MSO aspires to lead the way for equity across its Board, staff, and musicians, and throughout its artistic programming. First professional Australian orchestra to join the Keychange movement in early 2020, the Orchestra's journey toward achieving equity is related in this chapter.

For years the MSO unwaveringly supports a culture celebrating the diversity of its people and community. Diversity in its people, its music, and its audience are specific goals and the efforts to enable this are presented here.

Context

The nation's first professional orchestra, the MSO has been the sound of the city of Melbourne since 1906. The MSO is a vital presence, both onstage and in the community. It offers extraordinary symphonic music experiences in Melbourne, Victoria and the world. It is one of the major performing arts organizations in Australia. It employs a standard of 88 permanent musicians and more than 500 people per year (permanent, casuals, and contractuals).[1]

Internationally acclaimed, the Orchestra nurtures strong cultural partnerships throughout South-East Asia, Europe, and North America. In recent years, it has established multiyear agreements with the Ministry of Culture of the Special Region of Yogyakarta, Indonesia, the Singapore Symphony Orchestra, the Shanghai Philharmonic Orchestra, the National Centre for Performing arts in Beijing, the Sichuan Symphony Orchestra, the London Symphony Orchestra, and the Royal Academy of Music.

The MSO attracts great artists from around the globe while bringing Melbourne's finest musicians to the world through tours and collaboration agreements. The MSO is considered a cultural flagship of Australia. It started touring internationally in 1965 and became the first Australian orchestra to perform at Carnegie Hall in 1970. In the last 10 years, MSO has visited China, Indonesia, the United Kingdom, Europe, and the United States.

---

[1]The MSO Musicians Enterprise Agreement 2023, Clause 7.4 provides the following definitions:
A permanent musician is "A musician who has been appointed to a position of the Melbourne Symphony Orchestra"; A casual musician is a "musician who is neither a permanent nor a contract musician but has been engaged on a per call basis"; and a contract musician is a "musician who is not a permanent musician but has been engaged for some fixed period on a full-time basis".

In 2022, MSO appointed Spanish maestro, Jaime Martin, its 16th Chief conductor. With a goal to expand and enrich the artistic vision of the MSO, since 2016, the Orchestra has added to its artistic family.

These artists comprise influential conductors, composers, and soloists from Australia and abroad. They actively participate in setting MSO's artistic goals and programs. They represent a diverse spectrum of the finest musicians from diverse ages, cultural backgrounds, and gender. They have significantly contributed to the internal discussion on gender equity and diversity that has led to MSO's transformation.

They include:

- Chief Conductor, Jaime Martin (2022–present)
- Principal Guest Conductor, Xian Zhang (2020–2023)
- Principal Guest Conductor in Residence (Benjamin Northey, 2020–present)
- Cybec Assistant Conductor, Carlo Antonioli (2022–2023)
- MSO Chorus Director, Warren Trevelyan-Jones (2017–present)
- Soloist in Residence*, Siobhan Stagg (2023)
- Young Artist in Association, Christian Li (2020–present)
- Ensemble in Residence*, Gondwana Voices (2023)[2]
- Composer in Residence*, Mary Finsterer (2023)
- Cybec Young Composer in Residence*, Melissa Douglas (2023)
- First Nations Creative Chair, Dr Deborah Cheetham Fraillon AO (2020–2025)
- Learning and Engagement Creative Chair, Dr Anita Collins (2020–2025).

*Yearly program

In addition to this group, four honorary members: Conductor Laureate, Sir Andrew Davis CBE (who recently passed away on 20 April 2024); Life Member, Sir Elton John; two Artistic ambassadors Lu Siqing (violinist) and Tan Dun (composer and conductor) provide guidance to the orchestra. The MSO annually engages with more than 5 million people in Australia through some 150+ live concerts, TV, radio and online broadcasts, international and regional tours, recordings and education programs. In 2021, the MSO launched its new digital platform MSO.LIVE engaging with audiences from around the world – 58 countries in 2021 (Melbourne Symphony Orchestra, 2022).

Legal and Funding Structure

Like many orchestras around the world, the MSO is a "for purpose" (not-for-profit) organization with a board of directors (14 in 2022). As defined by the Australian Tax Office, it provides services to the community and does not operate to make a profit for its members (ATO, 2022). The Melbourne Symphony Orchestra Pty Ltd derives its revenues from three sources: earned, public, and private revenues. Ticket and subscription sales serve as its main source of revenue (50% +). Creative Australia, the Commonwealth Government's arts funding and

---

[2]It is a National Children's Choir founded by Lyn Williams AM.

advisory body, principally funds MSO; including support by the Victorian Government through Creative Victoria and the Department of Jobs, Precincts, and Regions (DJPR) and the City of Melbourne. The Principal Partner Emirates also funds MSO, as well as individual and corporate sponsors and donors.

Impact of a Global Pandemic – A Time for Survival and Innovation

The pandemic was a time of survival but also a time to reimagine. On March 13, 2020 (The Guardian, 2020) Scott Morrison, then Australian prime minister, announced that Australia would go into a nation-wide lockdown to respond to the threat of the new Coronavirus quickly spreading around the world. That lockdown was the first of many in Melbourne. Melbourne became the city sustaining the longest lockdown in the world: 8 months in 2020 and 6.5 months in 2021 (The Guardian, 2021).

The impact of the pandemic for the MSO, and a majority of arts organizations and artists around the world, was disruptive. Activities of the years 2020 and 2021 were significantly impacted. Highly dependent on earned revenues, and with small reserves, the MSO was faced with many challenges. Its own sustainability was at risk.

At the end of the second year of the pandemic, David Li, Chairman of the Board reported in MSO's 2021 annual report: "sadly, we were forced to cancel more than half of our annual season, and concerts that proceeded were impacted by density restrictions and the understandable reticence of anxious audiences. (…) The MSO canceled 77 of its planned mainstage performances. Resulting from these necessary event cancellations, MSO's earned revenue was $11M below pre-Covid levels achieved in 2019." (MSO, 2022).

The organization responded to these exceptional circumstances motivated by its values of being respectful, collaborative, innovative, and diverse. To quote the European Group on Ethics in Science and Technologies (EGE, 2022): "Values play an important role in how we understand, make sense of, and tackle crises. They influence how we frame the problems that crisis management is supposed to address and how we chose the instruments for that." The EGE reminds us of the importance of human dignity and solidarity being at the core of crisis management, with processes of deliberation that make values explicit (EGE, 2021).

Confronted with a lengthy period of lockdown leading to the inability to deliver its normal activities and generate earned revenues, the status quo was not an option. Board and management agreed to two priorities to respond to the crisis. The survival of the Orchestra and preservation of its people's employment was the first priority. The MSO made it a goal to retain all its people, the most precious asset of an orchestra. MSO achieved this goal. Management quickly designed a four-pillar strategy approved by the MSO board. It provided a way forward to ensure the Orchestra would survive and adapt to a new reality and a different future. The leadership team delivered this strategy aiming to:

- protect our people;
- keep the music going;

- respect our financial and legal obligations;
- and prepare for a different future.

To ensure it would respect its financial and legal obligations the MSO needed sufficient revenues. Faced with the loss of the majority of its earned revenues (subscriptions and tickets sales), MSO management and board decided to reach out and engage anew with its audience and community. MSO had been the sound of the city for more than 100 years. With the assistance of its musicians and administrative staff, MSO asked its audience, donors, and patrons to consider coming to the rescue of their beloved orchestra. The overwhelming and positive response was heartening.

Looking back at the end of 2020, Michael Ullmer, the then Chairman summarized the situation in the MSO annual report by stating: "Our priority had to be the future viability and sustainability of the Orchestra, and the wellbeing of our people. JobKeeper was a welcome relief and to maintain payments following the initial advice of the scheme's end, the Board pledged $1,000,000 to support musicians and staff, which was funded from personal donations by Board directors and reserves.[3] Additionally, the Board approved other measures to support our permanent and casual musicians and staff experiencing personal hardship, with these measures continuing to this day. As MSO emerged from this dark period united as an organisation, with its musicians and staff working seamlessly together to preserve our MSO, the achievements have been quite simply magnificent." (MSO, 2020).

To sustain the organization, Management advocated to governments for special funding. MSO's financial situation was assessed by the federal and state governments and considered dire. To support MSO's ongoing viability and resilience and assist with the impact of the pandemic a total of $9,500,000 was received from federal and state governments over 2021 and 2022. These sustainability grants (Office for the arts, 2022) were given with a condition that the MSO would better its financial situation, which it did.

A Challenge is an Opportunity

The second priority came out of necessity. This was the time to look forward, a luxury in normal times, and use this challenge as an opportunity to transform the orchestra. As was the case in many countries, artists and arts sector workers were declared "nonessential." This confronted our orchestra. For years MSO musicians had been playing in proximity to their colleagues, bringing artistic excellence to an appreciative audience. Because of the situation, they suddenly found themselves unable to deliver on their art and engage with the audience and

---

[3]Jobkeeper was a program designed by the federal government that helped keep Australians in their jobs and supported businesses affected by the significant economic impact of the COVID-19 pandemic. In the first phase of JobKeeper (30 March to 27 September 2020) eligible businesses and not-for-profits were able to receive $1,500 (before tax) per fortnight per employee to cover the cost of wages (Treasury, 2020).

community. The Orchestra's purpose was unexpectedly and profoundly challenged. It was the catalyst that led to the orchestra's transformation.

In response to the distress, a program that focused on mental health and wellbeing was put in place to ensure that the MSO employees would be supported. Training in mental health first aid was provided to 23 employees (management, administrative staff, and musicians) to assist their colleagues. Regular communications (weekly updates, company meetings, online activities, etc.) were offered. A focus on mental health is now well ingrained at the Orchestra.

A Tale of Transformation and Digital Innovation

At the end of 2020 the MSO leadership team had, in addition to managing the extraordinary circumstances brought about by the pandemic, progressed significantly in transforming the Orchestra. It continued implementing these strategic changes during 2021. Chairman Ullmer summarized in MSO's 2020 Annual Report: "Notwithstanding the existential threats, during 2020, we made significant progress on our strategic agenda. The team accelerated the implementation of our digital strategy, not only responding to the immediate challenge of closed venues but creating the platform for digital and live performance to coexist in the future. On other fronts, we approved the Keychange pledge for gender equality, our Commitment to Diversity statement, and Green Orchestra plan." (MSO, 2020).

The story of MSO's digital transformation started with a short-term goal to respond to MSO's situation during the pandemic. To "keep the music going" the leadership team reverted to a 2019 board approved digital strategy. This new strategy outlined a plan to deliver online content in addition to its offering of live concerts. Initially it would have been put in place over a 3-year period. Management decided to accelerate its delivery. A revised digital plan was adapted to achieve specific goals that would help the Orchestra engage with an international audience. MSO would do this through bespoke digital content (recording of live concerts and additional ancillary content) that would allow the Orchestra to generate and diversify its revenues.[4] The MSO digital strategy evolved from a first strategy to "keep the music going" which allowed the Orchestra to:

- remain engaged with its local audience and provide them with much needed music and
- provide opportunity for its musicians to create a musical offering either recorded from their own homes or, when allowed to rehearse and record, recorded in a studio with a small number of musicians in between periods of lockdown.

---

[4]In conversation events, round tables, master classes, etc., related to the theme of the digital program.

Recognized as an Australian cultural ambassador among major orchestras, the leadership team quickly realized that there was an opportunity to create long-term engagement with an international audience. A digital platform offered a way to provide music to a world that was desperately missing it and in need of it. Management developed a platform that allowed the Orchestra to engage with the audience from around the world, first via the establishment in 2020 of an MSO YouTube channel and, from 2021 onwards, through the creation of a new digital platform MSO.Live. This initiative was possible because of the multiyear support of the Ian Potter Foundation, Perpetual Foundation, and Alan (AGL) Shaw Endowment. It allowed the MSO to develop with partners the expertise to present online concerts and content on a fortnightly basis. It also allowed small music ensembles, such as the Bamboos and the Melbourne Ensemble, to be presented through this channel. At the end of 2021, MSO.Live offered subscriptions and pay per view to an audience based in 58 countries.

An Opportunity to Transform

The pandemic brought many challenges to the Orchestra but also some extraordinary opportunities. Pre-pandemic the MSO board, management, staff, and musicians had started to work on a cultural transformation of the Orchestra. The many lockdowns created the perfect occasion to redefine the vision for the organization. It became an opportunity to transform in more than one way. Gender equity and diversity, in the world of classic music where traditionally white male dominate, were identified as important for our future. MSO chose to focus on increasing its support of women in music, its engagement with First Nations artists and communities, a marginalized group in classic music, and its work with culturally diverse groups. The way forward was going to be different. MSO had the will, the skills, and the rigor to change what it is, what it does, and the way it leads.

Achieving Gender Equity

It started with a reflection on gender equity in the world of orchestras. According to the League of American Orchestras: "Women still make for less than half of the performers in professional orchestras throughout Europe and the United States (…) they account for less than 15% of orchestra conductors at all levels (youth and adult)." In February 2022, Laurie C. Williams writes: "In a recent global study by Utrecht University and Universitat Pompeu Fabra researchers, 98% of the music performed by major orchestras was written by male composers. Women represent just 20% or fewer of composers and songwriters." (MS Magazine, 2022) The journey toward gender equity and diversity started in

2016 with a board that was focused on a transformation of the Orchestra and ready to facilitate it. At that point the MSO had had a succession of managing directors and experienced some years of financial instability and cultural challenges.[5] In 2016, the board decided to restructure the administration and hired Dr Galaise, its first female Managing Director in 110 years of history.

With a mandate to innovate and transform the Orchestra, it was agreed to focus on increased artistic vibrancy that would lead to a stronger engagement with the community and financial stability. Artistic vibrancy is achieved with a transformation of the culture. To remain relevant in a changing world, achieving gender equity and diversity became goals to underpin this transformation. As Arthur Chan, the behavioral scientist and diversity, equity, and inclusion (DEI) strategist, stated: "Diversity is a fact. Equity is a choice. Inclusion is an action. Belonging is an outcome."[6] After discussion it was decided that, to achieve gender equity, specific targets were needed. As a step toward achieving this goal, the board agreed to make a pledge through Keychange. Keychange is supported by the Creative Europe Programme of the European Union and defines itself as "(...) a global network and movement working toward a total restructure of the music industry in reaching full gender equality. Keychange consists of partners collaborating from 12 different countries, working proactively to make this change. (...) Keychange is a movement fighting for a sustainable music industry. *(It)* supports talented but underrepresented artists and encourages organisations to take a pledge for gender equality. (...) Keychange champions statistics, achievements, and our roster of talent, allies and leaders."

MSO pledged to lead the way for equality across its people (Board, management, staff, musicians, and guest artists) and through its artistic programming. The MSO was the first professional Australian orchestra to join the Keychange movement in early 2020 (MSO, 2020).[7,8]

MSO pledged:

Our Statement

The Melbourne Symphony Orchestra is committed to promoting a culture that celebrates and supports the diversity of its people and community. We aspire to lead the way for equality across our Board, staff, and musicians, and throughout our artistic programming.

---

[5]In the previous 10 years four managing directors led the Orchestra. From Trevor Green (2007–2010); Matthew Van Besien (2010–2011); Andre Gremillet (2012–2015); Richard Evans (October 2015 to March 2016).

[6]General Assembly.

[7]It remains the only one at the time this is written.

[8]"Keychange is an international campaign which invests in emerging talent whilst encouraging music festivals, orchestras, conservatoires, broadcasters, concert halls, agents, record labels and all music organisations to sign up to a 50:50 gender balance pledge by 2022." (MSO, 2020).

Our Pledge

- *Maintain gender parity on the MSO Board and within the organization across the administration team and musicians.*
- *Work toward appropriate gender balance and representation in our concert seasons.*
- *Commit to equitable gender and cultural representation in our emerging artists programs.*
- *Commit to equitable gender and cultural representation in new work commissioned and presented.* (MSO, 2020)

Achieving gender equity became one of our annual strategic goals. It has now been achieved with MSO board and board committees, with the Leadership team and with our administrative staff and musicians. It is a constant challenge to aim to choose the right person for a job while taking into consideration ratios and being mindful of adverse discriminating. Like everything else in life, one needs to apply itself wholeheartedly and passionately to achieve a goal while keeping an open mind. The role of a leader is to guide and bring people on a journey while remaining kind to oneself and others. The biggest challenge for the Orchestra was to achieve gender equity among our guest artists (conductors, soloists) and in our programs. The artistic programming team has been leading an inclusive process to achieve changes. Seasons are built years in advance.[9] MSO 2021 Season had 27% of female artists in its core program. In Season 2022, it grew to 34% while 47% of commissions were written by women. Season 2023 saw 48% of female artists and 61% of commissions now written by women composers. The transformation and changes that have taken place at the MSO are noticed by our stakeholders (funding partners, corporate partners, patrons and donors, audiences, colleagues in the industry, and the media). Many have expressed their approval.

Yvonne Frindle wrote in the Australian Limelight, a magazine dedicated to performing arts: "Orchestras are also recognising they need to engage more deeply with their communities. (...) And the Melbourne Symphony Orchestra's season brochure again makes this explicit. It's a remarkable document that functions as a marketing tool while setting out artistic vision and institutional priorities, including the representation of women, the nurturing of new Australian music, and respectful partnerships with First Nations artists. What's impressive is that MSO programming walks the talk." (Limelight, December 2022).

Cultural Diversity

Australia is a vast and multicultural country. It is the "home to the world's oldest continuous cultures, as well as Australians who identify with more than 270 ancestries. Since 1947, almost seven million people have migrated to Australia."

---

[9]As a noticeable difference from the northern hemisphere, in the southern hemisphere artistic seasons go by calendar year.

(Australian government, 2022) Embracing cultural diversity in Australia is a must. The MSO is multicultural. The last 2019 voluntary survey of MSO employees showed that 31% employees were born outside of Australia representing 15 countries. Twelve percent had a first language that was not English.

Over the last few years, MSO has focused mostly on engaging with two communities where it could play a leadership role: First Nations and Asian communities. MSO has developed a First Nations Strategy (2022) and a First Nations Reconciliation Plan (in train) to ensure that it welcomes and embraces the extraordinary musical traditions of First Nations. It is based on a commitment to place First Nations artists and creators at the heart of what the MSO does. MSO's first Creative Chair First Nations, Deborah Cheetham Fraillon AO, with other First Nations artists have been guiding us on this journey. The MSO now offers a variety of programs to First Nations emerging artists (musicians, composers, and ensemble) to support their music. MSO's Season celebrates First Nations artists and their music.

MSO is one of the few orchestras to celebrate NAIDOC week with an offering of programs. The Australian government defines: "NAIDOC Week (National Aborigines and Islanders Day Observance Committee) occurs annually in July, and celebrates the history, culture and achievements of Aboriginal and Torres Strait Islander peoples. NAIDOC is celebrated not only in Indigenous communities, but by Australians all over the country and overseas." (DFAT, 2023) According to the US Census Bureau World Population Review (2022), the racial demographic of Melbourne shows that, after British or Irish ancestry and Australian ancestry, the third largest group is Asian. With approximately a fifth of Melbourne's population from Asia, a transformation of our programming to include a variety of Asian artists was a given. The MSO has been celebrating Chinese New Year for more than 10 years with a popular concert showcasing wonderful artists from Asia. Over the last 6 years, MSO has presented an East Meet West Series of concerts throughout the year.

Looking Around and Ahead

At MSO, curiosity, broadening of knowledge, and innovation is encouraged. A review of the literature on DEI in orchestras shows that the League of American Orchestras is by far the most advanced organization researching and reporting on gender equity and diversity in the world of orchestras.[10] From analysis of

---

[10]The biggest association of orchestras on a set territory, "The League of American Orchestras leads, supports, and champions America's orchestras and the vitality of the music they perform. Its diverse membership of more than 1,800 organizations and individuals across North America runs the gamut from world-renowned orchestras to community groups, from summer festivals to student and youth ensembles, from conservatories to libraries, from businesses serving orchestras to individuals who love symphonic music. A national organization dedicated solely to the orchestral experience, the League is a nexus of knowledge and innovation, advocacy, and leadership advancement." (League of American Orchestras, 2023).

orchestra repertoire in US orchestras (LAO, 2022) to a report specifically on racial and ethnic diversity within the orchestra field for both musicians and orchestra staff (LAO, 2023) they have inspired us. The League has been at the forefront, publishing regular reports on diversity and inclusivity (LAO, 2023). A new report (2022) produced by the Institute for Composer Diversity and the League of American Orchestras noted increased presentation of works by women and composers of color among professional orchestras. It noted that efforts still had to be made to encourage diversity among Music Directors and the inclusion of nonbinary people.

In Canada, we note that Cukier et al. (2022) have researched diversity in leadership roles in the performing arts and cultural institutions in Canada in "The state of diversity among leadership roles within Canada's largest arts and cultural institutions' and found that the leadership of major arts organisations in Canada does not reflect the diversity of Canada's population" (Cukier et al., 2022). The authors "offer strategic recommendations for the arts sector to challenge the status quo of leadership and to ensure diverse representation" (Cukier et al., 2022). The MSO in comparison benefits from its diversity.

The consultancy firm McKinsey & Company has been working with government and industry leaders for many decades, collating data from all around the world. In recent time, they collated extensive data on DEI presented in their Diversity, Equity and Inclusion Lighthouses 2023 Report (McKinsey & Company, 2023). They identified five success factors common across the DEI initiatives that yielded the most significant, scalable, quantifiable, and sustained impact for under-recognized groups. The success factors are: a nuanced understanding of the root causes; a meaningful definition of success; accountable and invested business leaders; a solution designed for its specific context; and rigorous tracking and course correction.

Using this model and looking back on our journey to achieve DEI:

- we started by understanding the fabric of our "milieu" and the history of our Orchestra;
- we defined success as "achieving gender parity within a certain timeframe";
- the leadership team and their teams became invested in achieving our goal;
- we agreed to put in place a mechanism that would allow us to achieve our goals. For example, tasking the Season design team to scout for female talents (conductors, soloists, composers);
- we track on a regular basis our progress and report to stakeholders on it.

How to Do It – Empowering Employees to Achieve Diversity, Equity, and Inclusion (DEI)

An orchestra is built of talented musicians, whose main role is to perform with their colleagues to diverse audiences, and dedicated administrative teams who are tasked with the delivery of programming, operations, marketing and sales, communications, finance, media, etc. As Covey (2004) said: "Strength lies in differences, not in similarities." MSO chose to empower teams to ensure they would participate in achieving DEI. Considering the size (500+ employees) and the collaborative nature of our Orchestra, management chose not to create a DEI Director's position to achieve results. We felt this should be a responsibility that is shared throughout the organization, starting at the top. Over the last few years, some programs were put in place to help develop MSO's people. The leadership team recognized that to transform our Orchestra they had to invest in our people.

While musicians are hired through an anonymous audition process, behind a black curtain, the MSO is pleased to note that the hiring process has led to parity within the Orchestra. On the administrative side, some programs were put in place to assist MSO's administrative employees with professional development. Having created succession plans for the different departments, management started defining second in command positions. It invested in providing these leaders with a better understanding of their own strengths and weaknesses (feedback through performance discussion and 360 evaluation). MSO has since offered them:

- group (for example, all senior managers) and individual mentoring;
- additional professional development;
- a buddy system where a new employee is paired with a seasoned employee from another department who will help the individual become familiar with the Orchestra;
- and have been creating awareness of conscious and unconscious bias.

When possible, the leadership team has gone back to basics and made MSO's people aware of verbal communication differences between genders. For example, they have noted that men in the organization tend to describe someone's good work with superlatives "amazing, superb, etc." while women tend to describe the same good work using words such as "good, very good." These verbal differences can have an impact on selection of employees to progress within the organization. In summary, to ensure we achieve and will keep gender equity we have:

- taken a pledge,
- put ratios in place for our people and our music,
- made people accountable (top down),
- and reported on it to our board and stakeholders.

Conclusion

Setting a goal, developing a strategy, analyzing, reporting results, and sharing this information with stakeholders is the way the MSO has progressed this over the last few years. The organization recognizes that constant efforts and actions need to be delivered to maintain a balanced position.

As MSO progressed on its transformation, it had to review the way it works. To be able to push its boundaries, MSO chose to work collaboratively with its people to define guiding principles. In designing its seasons and activities, more than ever it listens to its people and its audiences. The MSO strives to build connections that bring joy and validation. It creates welcoming experiences that showcase the beauty and wonder of its artistry. By combining individual strengths and celebrating its love of music, MSO works to foster better understanding, creating a sense of belonging.

As MSO makes sense of a world that is rapidly changing with climate change, a pandemic, and increased conflicts between nations, the Orchestra is focused on enriching lives through music. Its mission is more relevant than ever: through the shared language of music, MSO creates meaningful cultural experiences for audiences, delivered to the highest possible standard. The pursuit of gender equity and diversity among its people, its music, and its audiences will remain a major goal for years to come.

References

Australian Government, Department of Infrastructure, Transport, Regional Development, Communications and the Arts, Office for the Arts, Australia. (2022). https://www.arts.gov.au/departmental-news/arts-sustainability-fund-recipients-announced

Australian Taxation Office, Australia. (2022). https://www.ato.gov.au/Non-profit/Getting-started/Starting-an-NFP/

Covey, S. R. (2004). *The 7 habits of highly effective people: Restoring the character ethic* (Rev. ed.). Free Press.

Cukier, W., Lightwala, O., Wall-Andrews, C., & Wijesingha, R. (2022). The state of diversity among leadership roles within Canada's largest arts and cultural institutions. *Equality, Equality, Diversity and Inclusion: An International Journal, 41*(9), 30–46. https://www.emerald.com/insight/2040-7149.htm

Department of Foreign Affairs and Trade. (2023). *Naidoc Week.* https://www.dfat.gov.au/people-to-people/public-diplomacy/indigenous/naidoc-week

European Commission, Directorate-General for Research and Innovation, European Group on Ethics in Science and New Technologies. (2022). *Values in times of crisis: Strategic crisis management in the EU.* Publications Office of the European Union. https://data.europa.eu/doi/10.2777/79910

European Group on Ethics in science and new technologies. (2021). https://data.europa.eu/doi/10.2777/79910

Frindle, Y. (2022, December 23). Season preview 2023: Orchestras and Choirs. *Limelight Magazine.* https://www.limelight-arts.com.au

Keychange. https://www.keychange.eu

League of American Orchestras. (2022). https://americanorchestras.org/2022-orchestra-repertoire-report/

League of American Orchestras. (2023). https://americanorchestras.org/about-us/. https://americanorchestras.org/racial-ethnic-and-gender-diversity-in-the-orchestra-field-in-2023/. https://americanorchestras.org/learn/resources-data-and-research/

McKinsey & Company. (2023). *Diversity, equity and inclusion lighthouses 2023 report.* https://www.mckinsey.com/featured-insights/diversity-and-inclusion/diversity-equity-and-inclusion-lighthouses-2023

Melbourne Symphony Orchestra. (2020). https://www.mso.com.au/behind-the-music/about-us/keychange-pledge

Melbourne Symphony Orchestra. (2021). https://issuu.com/melbsymphony/docs/2020-mso-annual-report

Melbourne Symphony Orchestra. (2022). https://mso.com.au, https://issuu.com/melbsymphony/docs/2021-mso-annual-report

MS Magazine. (2022). https://msmagazine.com/2022/02/08/gender-equity-music-fine-arts-women/

MSO Musicians Enterprise Agreement 2023, Melbourne, Australia. (2023). https://www.google.com/search?sca_esv=7d7a298ed3e3445f&sca_upv=1&rlz=1C5CHFA_enAU1060AU1060&sxsrf=ADLYWIKAshSvbAxSFHI66rWD1R0WgfZBWA:1716105362968&q=Melbourne+symphony+orchestra+enterprise+agreement+2023+dates&sa=X&ved=2ahUKEwiD1rnUnpmGAxXC-DgGHXGbCoMQ1QJ6BAgqEAE&biw=1271&bih=668&dpr=2

The Guardian. (2020, May 2). https://www.theguardian.com/world/2020/may/02/australias-coronavirus-lockdown-the-first-50-days

The Guardian. (2021, October 20). *Melbourne readies to exit world's longest COVID-19 lockdown*. https://www.reuters.com/world/asia-pacific/melbourne-readies-exit-worlds-longest-covid-19-lockdowns-2021-10-20/

Treasury, Australia. (2020). https://treasury.gov.au/coronavirus/jobkeeper

US Census Bureau World Population Review. (2022). https://worldpopulationreview.com/world-cities/melbourne-population

Chapter 6

Navigating Gendered Spaces: Activists' Synergies in Montreal's Electronic Music Scene

Nancy Aumais and Coline Sénac

Université du Québec à Montréal, Canada

Abstract

Data from international journals show that woman* and other minorities continue to be drastically underrepresented in the music industry worldwide and in the electronic music industry in Europe, Canada, and Quebec. Recent work focusing on the contributions of female electronic music DJs and producers also testify to the intersectional difficulties they face. In this chapter, we examine the strategies they deploy daily to make a career in an overwhelmingly male environment by studying the case of the Montreal electronic music scene. To do so, we use qualitative interviews and observations using the shadowing technique and we deploy a gender-as-social-practice approach, which focuses on how people practice gender in everyday life by considering gender not as a stable state or characteristic of people, but as a dynamic process performed in interactions that produce difference. Our research, which runs from 2021 to 2025, aims to find explanations for the persistent underrepresentation of women* in the electronic music world. More specifically, our results highlight the strategies and coping mechanisms our participants mobilize to negotiate their place and identity in the electronic music industry, paying particular attention to the collective aspect of their mobilization and to their feminist practices, such as creating solidarity networks.
*People who identify as woman.

Keywords: Electronic music industry; feminist activism; gender practices; inequalities; solidarity; underrepresentation

Accessibility, Diversity, Equity and Inclusion in the Cultural Sector, 83–96
Copyright © 2024 Nancy Aumais and Coline Sénac
Published under exclusive licence by Emerald Publishing Limited
doi:10.1108/978-1-83753-034-220241014

Introduction

In 2018, Misstress Barbara, an electronic music DJ and producer from Montreal (Quebec, Canada), posted on her Facebook page about how far she had come since her mid-90s debut and mentioned that, throughout her career, she had frequently been told, "You're pretty good, for a girl." This sexist remark illustrates the challenges women* still face in the predominately men-dominated electronic music industry.[1] Farrugia and Olszanowski (2017) and Gadir (2017) present data from international journals indicating that women remain drastically underrepresented in the music industry at large, with specific details on the underrepresentation of women in the electronic music industry being notably scarce. Women electronic music DJs and producers remain underrepresented at festivals and events worldwide (Abtan, 2016; Gadir, 2017; Hesmondhalgh & Baker, 2015). For example, men comprised 71% of all festival acts between 2017 and 2019 (Female: Pressure, 2020). The inherently technological character of electronic music performance and production has led to this genre of music being a "predominantly male domain" (Parsley, 2022, p. 698). This chapter aims at highlighting the strategies and coping mechanisms our participants deploy to negotiate their place and identity in a mostly men-dominated cultural industry.

Women are also less visible in the professional media and production networks, which tend to focus on men (see, for example, Butler, 2006; Holmes, 2012; Kirn, 2011). In Montreal, the practical importance of this issue is highlighted by the many groups working to address it, such as MTL (Montreal) Women in Music, F*EM, female:pressure, AMPLIFY Digital Arts Initiative, Keychange, and shesaid.so Montreal. In Quebec, in 2016–2017, only 10% of people involved in festival programming overall were women (DIG, 2017). In 2019, women comprised 23% and 30%, respectively, of the artists playing at ILESONIQ and MUTEK electronic music festivals (Female: Pressure, 2020). Meanwhile, roughly equal numbers of women and men graduated with music degrees in 2015 (Statistics Institute of Quebec), and around 50% of singers and musicians in Canada are women (Hills Strategy Research, 2016; Nordicity, 2015). The underrepresentation of women in the Canadian electronic music scene is not unique to that country: In 2019, just under 13% of the musicians booked to appear at European electronic music nightclubs were women (A8M, 2019).

Although there has been an increase in the number of women involved in the electronic music scene since the 2000s (McRobbie, 1994), they remain underrepresented. More recent work focusing on the contributions of women electronic music DJs and producers also demonstrates the intersectional (at the intersection of various identities, such as ethnicity, gender, sexual orientation, age, and capacity) difficulties they face (Farrugia & Olszanowski, 2017). Our research, which runs from 2021 to 2025, aims to find explanations for this persistent

---

[1] *Woman/women: person/people who identify as woman/women. Man/men: person/people who identify as man/men. We acknowledge the fluidity and non-binarity of gender, but we mobilize the categories of "women" and "men" as operatives in this chapter because of their persistence and relevance to the people involved in this research.

underrepresentation and invisibilization. How do we explain this persistent underrepresentation of women in the electronic music world? What are the day-to-day consequences for women DJs and producers? What are the strategies they deploy daily to forge a career in such an environment? This chapter focuses specifically on the latter question and describes the strategies and coping mechanisms our participants mobilize to negotiate their place and identity in a mostly men-dominated cultural industry. We pay particular attention to the collective aspect of their mobilization and to their feminist practices, such as creating networks of solidarity.

Theoretical Approach and Objectives

To examine the underrepresentation of women in the electronic music scene, we mobilize a practice perspective. Organizational theory has undergone a "practice turn" in recent decades and organizational theorists have increasingly turned their attention to understanding organizations by studying the actual practices that take place within them, rather than solely focusing on abstract concepts, formal structures, or idealized models (Feldman & Orlikowski, 2011; Gherardi, 2012; Nicolini, 2009). This practice perspective, which stems from the work of sociologists such as Bourdieu and Schatzki, is also increasingly mobilized in the two theoretical fields that inform our project: entrepreneurship (Champenois et al., 2020; Steyaert, 2007; Thompson et al., 2020) and gender (Aumais, 2017, 2019; Martin, 2006). Thus, we use social practice – a set of activities that are both routine and unpredictable – as our unit of analysis (Nicolini & Monteiro, 2016; Schatzki, 2018; Schatzki et al., 2001).

Adopting a practice perspective means we consider both entrepreneurship and gender-as-social-practices. A gender-as-social-practice approach focuses on how people practice gender in their everyday lives by considering gender not as a stable state or characteristic, but as a dynamic process: A set of words, body postures, gestures, behaviors, and activities performed in interactions that produce difference (Aumais, 2017; Martin, 2006). The term "practice" does not simply refer to a conceptual category that includes everything actors think and do but also encompasses meaning-making, identity formation, and actions, which are situated in specific historical conditions (Nicolini, 2009).

Methodological Approach

We have established the gendered disparities in the Quebec electronic scene; however there is little material about how individuals experience these gender disparities in their daily lives and how these disparities are (re)produced daily. Such data could help us study the mechanisms underlying the underrepresentation and invisibilization of women in Quebec's electronic music industry and the obstacles that explain the persistence of inequities. Without these data, as we have explained, the main emphasis of this research is the daily emergence of social practices within interactions. As Ashcraft (2013) explains, the alignment of certain embodied social identities with particular occupational identities (the "glass slipper" that fits some feet and not others) is hard to capture. To access these social practices and rich details that normally escape our notice and that of our participants, we use the shadowing technique (Aumais & Germain, 2021; Aumais & Vàsquez, 2023; Czarniawska, 2014; Gill et al., 2014; Vásquez, 2013), an ethnography-inspired qualitative approach that entails closely following participants in their daily activities, which enables us to account for real-world interactions and to contextualize data. We gather participants' testimonies through a combination of unstructured, reflexive interviews (Alvesson & Sköldberg, 2010) and observations (shadowing) of the artist or programmer at work, using their equipment, sharing their personal history, and interacting with other artists, stakeholders, and the audience.

Since the project started in 2021, the research team (the authors of this chapter and a master's degree student) has conducted 12 interviews with DJs and other industry actors. We are currently shadowing three participants (two DJs and one venue booker/promoter) during their daily professional activities, such as performing DJ sets, recording sessions, negotiating, attending production meetings, and organizing events. During these shadowing sessions, we take notes of unfolding events, interactions, nonverbal cues, and dialogues. Shadowing also allows many informal discussions with our participants during which they openly share their interpretations of the events we witness. The transcripts, notes, and photographs (when authorized) are then transferred to NVivo.

This (growing) body of material goes through a first round of coding and collective analysis to identify recurring themes. This chapter mainly relies on the material collected between September 2021 and May 2023. We conducted and recorded our formal interviews online via Zoom, while informal conversations with participants took place in person during shadowing sessions. Despite being physically remote, the online interviews felt no less "real" than the later in-person observations and conversations. During these video interviews, we were able to establish a rapport and build connections that facilitated the observations-on-the-move phase of the project. We used pseudonyms to protect the identities of the participants in the following quotes.

From Individual Coping Strategies to Activist Synergy

Women continue to be underrepresented and marginalized in men-dominated tech-driven creative cultural industries (Eikhof, 2017) such as the electronic music industry (Parsley, 2022) in which the actors (DJs, programmers, agents, producers, and even audiences) are mostly men. To observe the effects of this underrepresentation context, we asked our participants to share their experiences and perspectives of Quebec's electronic music scene, and we heard their stories, interpretations, and views of the industry. The material we have collected up to this point allows us to report various experiences of marginalization, discrimination, and stigmatization.

Most participants shared their experiences of marginalization, understood here as a form of setting someone aside or pushing them to the margins of a group, which leads to invisibilization (Barel, 1982). For example:

> I think about the organizing side. It's like... we put DJs at the beginning [of the event]. But you know, that's not how the event was presented. I don't think it's really bad will from the organizers... but it gave me the impression that they were going for female DJs to add to the dudes' line-up that [was] going to be the main one. (Zoe)

In this example, Zoe is sharing her reaction to organizers offering her the opportunity to perform at an event before she realized, on arrival, that she was to open for the main (men) musician. Zoe felt she was being sidelined because she is a DJ. Thus, while the electronic music scene does offer visibility for women DJs performing on stage, in this situation, Zoe was invisibilized during her DJ set because playing first means playing to a mostly empty room.

Some participants reported experiences of discrimination. According to Gardner (1996), discrimination is a prejudice related to a lack of approval and acceptance from others. In reported experiences, this discrimination can translate into people experiencing situations in which they feel devalued, for example, because of their gender identity. This is the case in Claudie's reported experience of discrimination:

> You know, I was popular in Spain because I used to play super hard techno, and they are so [intense] out there that they need it [the music] to be really hard to be able to enjoy. But at some point, like everyone else around 2010, we all got a little softer. It was less techno, it was more minimal, electro... and I did the same, you know, when I went to Spain to play... I almost received empty beer bottles in the face... The people... were like... "Come on, let's gooooo!" (mimicking the screaming) ... they were acting like animals in front of me saying, "Come on, go ahead!" "Harder, harder, harder!" And I thought to myself, "Damn, you would not do that to a man, eh?" (Claudie)

During one of her Spanish tours, Claudie's audience shouted at her, demanding she play harder rhythms (hard techno), thus implying that her music was not sufficiently techno. Discrimination here translates into Claudie feeling that women DJs were having experiences that were not shared by their men counterparts. Claudie did not feel accepted as being on an equal footing with men DJs and felt her performance skills as a DJ were devalued.

Finally, some participants shared their experiences of stigmatization. This happens when assessments of identities and competencies are based on gender, which can have the effect of devaluing experiences, skills, and expertise (Goffman, 1963). This is the case in Joanie's experience of stigmatization:

Yeah, it was just this interesting thing, like people kept [saying]...
"Oh, you're the hipster rapper." You know, I don't love that label,
like you've identified me as THE one in this category means that...
maybe [it means] I shouldn't be here. (laughs)... I didn't feel
negatively about it. It was more about like, OK, ... this is where
I am... It's just always challenging if you're in a space where you
don't have peers there with you. So, if they were like, "Oh, you're
one of the many hipster rappers here," [...] But when it's like, "I'm
identifying you as THE one and you're an outsider," that feel[s]...
I mean, anytime you're excluded, even in a subtle way, it's like,
you know that feels a certain way. (Joanie)

At an event designed to showcase her work, Joanie was labeled as a "hipster
rapper," which differentiates her from other rappers. By labeling her in this way,
the audience member was implying that she is not really a rapper. Joanie felt
categorizing her in this manner was a tacit way of excluding her. Stigmatization in
this context can thus be viewed as an attempt to exclude women DJs.

These experiences of marginalization, discrimination, and stigmatization often
stem from stereotypes and prejudices related to women's relationship with technology, their technical skills, and their musical talent. Such experiences tend to
reinforce the dominance of the majority (white men) actors. This is due to a lack
of recognition and legitimacy. These effects can be linked to the patriarchal
culture embedded in the electronic music scene, which, according to Delvaux
(2020), is akin to a boys' club. The following conversation, recorded during an
interview with two DJs, Lili and Zoe, highlights this boys' club phenomena:

Lili: It's so much just dudes. It's like really there's a bro culture... in
this business... that I'm so excited to like throw myself in there and be
like, "Move over..."

Zoe: I remember the guy... from behind [saying] like, "Oh yeah, you
do it like that," whereas we [women] are like, "Oh yeah, check this
out," (laughs)... a bit more uninhibited. There, it's really like an
attitude of proving yourself... not proving yourself by the way you
talk... It's a way, it's like... you say stuff just to prove that you know
something.

Lili: Yeah, yeah, it was really... it was like, "Ah, you mix this key here
with this key there?" And I had never asked myself about these keys.
Yes, it's stupid, but from that moment on, just that comment there, I
was like, "I'm going to go do some research on the internet about
keys..." (laughs)

During their tour, Lili and Zoe met men DJs who questioned their technical
skills to the extent that they wondered if they were mixing properly. They later
explained that women* DJs have a different way of discussing their activities with

each other, and they think that men tend to show off their knowledge just to prove themselves. In doing so, however, they create power relationships in which women are seen as less capable than men at producing and creating music.

All these experiences show the effects of the underrepresentation context in the electronic music industry. Sometimes, it is difficult to identify and interpret these effects as situations often raise questions of representativeness, credibility, and prioritization. The situations demonstrate, however, that women artists are treated differently than their men counterparts. In these experiences, we see that the electronic music scene has recently tried to include more women to counter-balance gender-based inequities. Nevertheless, in the experiences described, women continue to be underrepresented and feel their expertise is devalued. They are marginalized, discriminated against, and stigmatized in their daily lives while performing activities that demonstrate their ability to produce, create, and evolve in a men-dominated boy's club environment.

Given the persistent underrepresentation of women in the electronic music scene and the lack of research on the obstacles that explain the persistence of inequities, it seems crucial to better understand the workings of this phenomenon. We now highlight the individual and collective strategies women deploy and how they adapt to navigate this field. Individually, they adjust their behavior to counteract marginalization, such as that exhibited through stereotypical and negative representations of women DJs. Collectively, they develop close rela-tionships and show strong solidarity. For example, organizing women DJ parties, networking, and joining forces when problems arise are ways to unite as a marginalized group.

During our interviews, women DJs often used the term "strategy" to refer to the need to take action from a certain perspective. For example, on the recom-mendation of her therapist, one of the women DJs mobilizes the notion of strategy when she needs to define goals to pursue her career. Another mobilizes the concept with her agent to establish her branding and place in the music industry. Both women seek to project themselves and carve out a place in the environment in which they operate as women DJs.

Fighting Stereotypes: Avoiding Labels and Changing Names

The women in our study adopt strategies to combat the stereotypical and negative representations of women DJs. Stereotypes tend to reinforce biased representa-tions of them, which can have concrete implications for experiences and practices.

As one participant said, "I have better strategies for navigating complex sit-uations and I am less likely to allow these people to attack my privacy and then interfere with my work," one of these individual strategies was to change her name to avoid discrimination. Claudie, for example, thought of changing her name a male one to be recognized for the music she creates and not for the "women DJ" she embodies. She is still hesitant to do so to promote her music without risking gender-based discrimination:

(...) I wanted to [use] a guy's name so that my music, from the start, would be heard for itself... and not... for who I am... If it wasn't me, would [it] not be good?... One thing I must confess, I've been thinking about changing my name for a long time. And I think to myself, "Oh, it's going to be a mess because I've made... blunders in my career, but, at the same time, if... I had to do it again, I'd do it the same [way]." I'll give you an example. When I made my albums that were not techno, I decided to release them under [the name] Bob Smith because I had the mentality. I still have it. If you are an artist, you have the right to do what you want, according to the moment, and people must understand, then I will release my albums [as] Bob Smith. (Claudie)

In this example, stereotypical ideas about women are deflected by using a male name that prevents such discrimination.

One participant questioned the appropriateness of mentioning that she is a feminist in her biography. She then described the pros and cons of labeling herself as such:

I tried to include in my artist bio..., beyond productions that I've done and my artistic journey, [to include] how my feminist approach informs my... in fact, [how] my feminism informs my approach ... I did [include it] a little, then, after that, there are places where it is interesting to mention it because I feel that it is directly linked to my art. ... You know, I talk about feminism, ... even intersectional feminism at times... I'm in the early stages of applying that, but I still have reflexes of inclusion and expanded awareness... and battles to be fought... I open so many doors when I answer your questions... they are such big questions! I tell myself that a feminist tag can prevent me from having certain contracts because it can be frightening to some ... who might think, "Hmm, this will not be an easy production" .... I don't know... I'm not sure I've integrated it. (Roxanne)

One individual strategy is to constantly try to detect the psychological profiles of individuals encountered to better understand the situation and to try to anticipate potential problems. During the interviews, a women DJ told us about a problematic situation with a technician who would not set up the machines she needed to do her DJ set. She felt devalued by this technician, who did not take her requests seriously. She adopted strategies so that she could do her job properly and reduce the psychological impact and the marginalization she experienced:

I think of personalities that are less compatible with mine, [where] the communication, my requests, my needs are [not] taken into account... I could feel that my expectations were [considered] too big, that it didn't make sense... that I was being overprotective of my material, etc. Having been around people like that two, three, four times, I now manage to... tell myself, "OK, this is that type of situation..." I [have learned] to detect more quickly the type of person in front of me to try to become less fragile and [more] motivated to express my requests clearly... my needs, to talk to the right people, to tell myself, "OK, I'm going to choose my battles," and ... in relation to my personal life, it affects me less ... and I want to continue to meet people with complex temperaments. (Roxanne)

Women DJs adopt these individual strategies to protect themselves from adversity and to navigate an environment known to be traditionally masculine. They also develop collective strategies to form a group that comes together to resist marginalizing practices. For example, they organize events where only women DJs are booked, defend themselves in cases of difficulties with men, and share contacts to promote their work. Some women DJs show solidarity by involving each other in collective music projects. One participant works on a collective project called "Feminism for men: A little survival guide."

I think most of the time, we end up with music that is composed by men who... But no... it's a big statement that isn't clear... But I know that to go and look for women who make music in the music industry, you have to make an effort because they have perhaps less exposure. Uh... I think this group is a gem. The mutual support, there are always people who are like, "Hey, I'm looking for someone to come and make a video, I'm looking for someone to record in the studio, I'm looking for someone..." People suggest women or non-binary people or at least people not associated with... the male gender. Hmmm... and I think these are really concrete gestures... for the advancement of women. (Roxanne)

Another collective strategy is to create a union or association to establish a pricing scale to avoid gender inequity in terms of pay:

Creating an association [is] like contacting the whole group of women DJs. Let's get the gang together ... We'll work together. People want us as women DJs... They want us as a women DJ because it sounds good, because it's fair. But it's also because it shows that they're, like, open to go[ing] into something that is a natural reflex from a men-dominated environment. Well, OK girls, we don't accept gigs under $300 any more... (Roxanne)

In the following example, Anouk decided to use the collective she had launched in order to gain control over her own career to help others:

I quickly realized that I was being asked to work *for* them and not *with* them. And besides, I saw them collaborating on the same event I'd been offered to work on... But they were men, so they were giving each other opportunities. So I realized very quickly that I had to work much harder so I decided to launch my collective... Then I wanted to generate a kind of local economy, redistribute to the artists. So, I decided to register as a non-for-profit organization and organize live streams, so [I] started inviting artists into my living room... (Anouk)

Discussion: Activists' Synergies in the Montreal Electronic Music Scene

Our investigation enabled us to observe the experiences and to access the sense-making practices of women DJs and producers who operate at the margins of Quebec's electronic music scene. Through their situated experience (Haraway, 1988), we have learned how they experience and interact with the social norms and relational dynamics that support intersectional inequities. They have spoken about experiencing marginalization, discrimination, and stigmatization in their working lives; about the discomfort and pressure they undergo; and about the strategies and coping mechanisms they mobilize to negotiate their place and identity in a mostly men-dominated cultural industry. Our preliminary results also highlight feminist practices, such as establishing networks of solidarity and support. Faced with an organized system that marginalizes, stigmatizes, and underestimates women, we find that our participants mobilize activist strategies. We call them "activists" because all our participants not only try to survive but also strive to change the system. We organize their strategies into four main interrelated categories of social practice:

(1) Creating their own business
   Almost all our research participants, after some time in the business, recognize the challenges of being marginalized and feel the need to organize. They have launched their own businesses or not-for-profit organizations. This has empowered them to help not only themselves but also others, which most of them do by organizing events that book women DJs; sharing resources, equipment, and technical knowledge; playing a mentoring role or acting as a role model; and sharing advice and guidance on career progression and navigating obstacles. Taking on leadership roles has empowered them to eventually shape culture, policies, and practices; influence positive change; promote inclusivity; and create opportunities for other women.
(2) Increasing their visibility
   Our participants need to increase their visibility in order not only to promote themselves as artists or promoters (e.g., by associating their names with prominent venues or events) but also to advocate for themselves and other

individuals and causes around specific needs, goals, and successes. This in turn enables collective organization and creates an online following, which, ultimately, puts them in an improved position to negotiate better opportunities, promotion, and equal pay, as well as to voice their opinions and ideas. Increasing visibility can help promote storytelling and shared narratives in order to create emotional connections and foster shared understanding. This is often achieved through digital platforms.

(3) Branding
Branding is crucial for all DJs and promoters, regardless of gender, in order to establish a distinct identity, build a fan base, and differentiate themselves. Our participants also identify branding as a way of coping, making a place for themselves, helping others, and contributing to political change. They are concerned about authenticity, breaking stereotypes, and standing out from the crowd. They need to highlight their skills, expertise, and distinctive qualities (in a world that undervalues them), while promoting diversity, equity, and inclusion (DEI). Our participants pay close attention to their use of labels such as "feminist" and sometimes consider changing their names in order to be recognized for their art rather than their gender.

(4) Creating affective circuits of solidarity
Affective circuits of solidarity practices combine concepts from affective and social solidarity. "Affective circuits" refers to experiencing and mobilizing emotions, empathy, and compassion, and a sense of belonging, while "solidarity" refers to a sense of unity, support, and cooperation among individuals or groups. We find that in their public relations (PR) activities, our participants rely a lot on emotional connections that foster and strengthen bonds of solidarity between the various stakeholders (e.g., colleagues and audiences).

We also note that our participants seem to have been shifting relatively quickly from individual coping strategies to collective strategies and solidarity.

Conclusion

This chapter aims to contribute to existing knowledge of the electronic music scene in Quebec by exploring the experiences of women DJs and producers of electronic music. In so doing, we bring out salient issues and challenges and identify the relational dynamics and practices that people deploy in the face of gendered norms. We find that the various strategies our participants deploy – creating their own business, increasing visibility, paying attention to their branding, and creating affective circuits of solidarity – create a synergy in the sense that combining resources, power, and relationships achieves more for everyone involved than would be achieved through pursuing one individual element.

This work helps us to better comprehend the gender norms and preconceptions that still pervade social interactions, and which translate into a subordinate position for women in the electronic music sector. It also gives us a deeper understanding of the issue of women underrepresentation in this environment. As a result, this research will help current and future marginalized cultural entrepreneurs who actively contribute to the growth of a thriving cultural sector in Montreal, as demonstrated by the success of electronic festivals and events that were developed in the city and then exported, such as Piknic Électronik, Igloofest, and MUTEK.

These findings will eventually lead to recommendations for better representation of DEI so that marginalized groups can thrive socially and economically from their entrepreneurship. This research also advances our understanding of gender-based discrimination in the electronic music scene, which forms part of a larger discussion on the effects of these disparities in similar contexts. On a practical level, it answers the call of various organizations to give more consideration to gender DEI, which entails expanding our knowledge of the daily practices contributing to social, economic, and artistic barriers that account for the enduring underrepresentation of women in this field. By promoting greater visibility and inclusion of women DJs and producers, this work will also contribute to the search for practical applications to (re)establish the technical, artistic, and intellectual contributions of women DJs and producers in electronic music.

References

A8M. (2019). *Female artists representation within the electronic music industry – A preliminary study.* https://femalepressure.files.wordpress.com/2019/10/a8m-datareview-finale-version-v3.pdf

Abtan, F. (2016). Where is she? Finding the women in electronic music culture, contemporary. *The Music Review, 35*(1), 53–60. https://doi.org/10.1080/07494467.2016.1176764

Alvesson, M., & Sköldberg, K. (2010). *Reflexive methodology – New vistas for qualitative research* (2nd ed.). SAGE Publications Ltd.

Ashcraft, K. (2013). The glass slipper: 'Incorporating' occupational identities in management studies. *Academy of Management Review, 38*(1), 6–31. http://www.jstor.org/stable/23416300

Aumais, N. (2017). Studying the doing and undoing of gender in organisations – Promises and challenges. *International Journal of Work Innovation, 2*(2/3), 216–230. https://doi.org/10.1504/IJWI.2017.10012528

Aumais, N. (2019). Parce qu'une ombre demeure visible. In J.-L. Moriceau & R. Soparnot (Eds.), *Recherche qualitative en sciences sociales – S'exposer, cheminer, réfléchir ou l'art de composer sa méthode* (pp. 275–279). Éditions management et société.

Aumais, N., & Vàsquez, C. (2023). Tisser des relations: Dialogue autour de la pratique de shadowing. *Recherches Qualitatives, 42*(1), 1–24. http://dx.doi.org/10.7202/1100246ar

Aumais, N., & Germain, O. (2021). Shadowing as a liminal space: A relational view. In A. S. Risberg (Ed.), *The Routledge companion to organizational diversity research methods* (pp. 147–161). Routledge. https://doi.org/10.4324/9780429265716

Barel, Y. (1982). *La marginalité sociale*. Presses Universitaires de France. https://doi. org/10.3917/puf.barel.1982.01

Butler, M. J. (2006). *Unlocking the groove: Rhythm, meter, and musical design in electronic dance music*. Indiana University Press.

Champenois, C., Lefebvre, V., & Ronteau, S. (2020). Entrepreneurship as practice: Systematic literature review of a nascent field. *Entrepreneurship & Regional Development, 32*(3–4), 281–312. https://doi.org/10.1080/08985626.2019.1641975

Czarniawska, B. (2014). *Observation on the move: Shadowing*. Sage Publications.

Delvaux, M. (2020). *Le Boys club*. Éditions Remue Ménage.

DIG (Groupe de recherche sur les différences et inégalités de genre dans la musique du Québec). (2017). https://www.digmusiquequebec.ca/

Eikhof, D. (2017). Analysing decisions on diversity and opportunity in the cultural and creative industries: A new framework. *Organization, 24*(3), 289–307. https:// doi.org/10.1177/13505084166877

Farrugia, R., & Olszanowski, M. (2017). Women and electronic dance music culture. *Dancecult: Journal of Electronic Dance Music Culture, 9*(1). https://doi.org/10. 12801/1947-5403.2017.09.01.00

Feldman, M. S., & Orlikowski, W. J. (2011). Theorizing practice and practicing theory. *Organization Science, 22*(5), 1240–1253. https://www.jstor.org/stable/ 41303116

Female: Pressure. (2020). *The female pressure: Facts survey*. https://femalepressure. wordpress.com/

Gadir, T. (2017). Forty-seven DJs, four women: Meritocracy, talent, and postfeminist politics. *Dancecult: Journal of Electronic Dance Music Culture, 9*(1), 50–72. https:// doi.org/10.12801/1947-5403.2017.09.01.03

Gardner, J. (1996). Discrimination as injustice. *Oxford Journal of Legal Studies, 16*(3), 353–367. https://doi.org/10.1093/ojls/16.3.353

Gherardi, S. (2012). *How to conduct a practice-based study*. Edward Elgar Publishing.

Gill, R., Barbour, J., & Marleah, D. (2014). Shadowing in/as work: Ten recommendations for shadowing fieldwork practice. *Qualitative Research in Organizations and Management, 9*(1), 69–89. https://doi.org/10.1108/QROM-09-2012-1100

Goffman, E. (1963). *Stigma: Notes on the management of spoiled identity*. Prentice Hall.

Haraway, D. (1988). Situated knowledges: The science question in feminism and the privilege of partial perspective. *Feminist Studies, 14*(3), 575–599. https://doi.org/10. 2307/3178066

Hesmondhalgh, D., & Baker, S. (2015). Sex, gender, and work segregation in the cultural industries. *The Sociological Review, 63*(1), 23–36. https://doi.org/10.1111/ 1467-954X.12

Hills Strategy Research. (2016). *Profil statistique des artistes au Canada en 2016*. https://hillstrategies.com/resource/profil-statistique-des-artistes-au-canada-en-2016/ ?lang=fr

Holmes, T. (2012). *Electronic and experimental music*. Routledge.

Kirn, P. (2011). *The evolution of electronic dance music*. Backbeat Books.

Martin, P. Y. (2006). Practising gender at work: Further thoughts on reflexivity. *Gender, Work and Organization, 13*(3), 254–276. https://doi.org/10.1111/j.1468-0432.2006.00307.x

McRobbie, A. (1994). *Postmodernism and popular culture*. Routledge.

Nicolini, D. (2009). Zooming in and out: Practices by switching theoretical lenses and trailing connections. *Organization Studies, 30*(12), 1391–1418. https://doi.org/10.1177/0170840609349875

Nicolini, D., & Monteiro, P. (2016). The practice approach: For a praxeology of organisational and management studies. In A. Langley & H. Tsoukas (Eds.), *SAGE handbook of process organization studies*. Sage Publishing.

Nordicity. (2015). *A profile of women working in Ontario's music industry*. https://www.womeninmusic.ca/images/PDF/A+Profile+of+Women+Working+in+the+ON+Music+Industry.pdf

Parsley, S. (2022). Feeling your way as an occupational minority: The gendered sensilisation of women electronic music artists. *Management Learning, 53*(4), 697–717. https://doi.org/10.1177/13505076221091625

Schatzki, T. (2018). On practice theory, or what's practices got to do (got to do) with it. In C. Edwards-Groves, P. Grootenboer, & J. Wilkinson (Eds.), *Education in an era of schooling. Critical perspectives of educational practice and action research* (pp. 151–165). Springer.

Schatzki, T., Knorr-Cetina, K., & von Savigny, E. (Eds.). (2001). *The practice turn in contemporary theory*. Routledge.

Steyaert, C. (2007). 'Entrepreneuring' as a conceptual attractor? A review of process theories in 20 years of entrepreneurship studies. *Entrepreneurship & Regional Development, 19*(6), 453–477. https://doi.org/10.1080/08985620701671759

Thompson, N., Verduijn, K., & Gartner, W. (2020). Entrepreneurship-as-practice: Grounding contemporary theories of practice into entrepreneurship studies. *Entrepreneurship & Regional Development, 32*(3–4), 247–256. https://doi.org/10.1080/08985626.2019.1641978

Vásquez, C. (2013). Devenir l'ombre de soi-même et de l'autre: réflexions sur le shadowing pour suivre à la trace le travail d'organisation. In T. Dans Dijk (van) (Ed.), *Discourse as social interaction* (Vol. 2). SAGE Publications.

Chapter 7

The Expanding Economic Borders of South African Musicians: A Policy Effect

Akhona Ndzuta

University of South Africa, South Africa

Abstract

While referring to the inability of South Africa (SA) to absorb the large number of new musicians produced by SA universities each year and how South African music practitioners find limited employment opportunities for themselves in SA's cultural sector, a panel member at a musicology symposium in 2011 stated that "we are creating exiles." The panel member made the statement during dialogue on the state of national higher education level music curricula, whether they were transformed to mirror the needs of the country or not, and what this meant for a contemporary music performance career in SA. Exile is the point of departure of this chapter, where conditions of public and institutional policy during and after apartheid are framed as encouraging the expanded borders of SA musicians. The emphasis is on how exile is a desired economic result especially among Black musicians who have a scarcity-prone SA music marketplace. This chapter also engages with multilevel policy-led interventions of inclusion and diversity that attempt to grow the SA Black music market.

Keywords: South African musicians; cultural policy; institutional policy; exile; markets

Introduction

The pre-COVID-19 geographical concentration of frequent performances by South African music acts of different genres deemed successful in mainstream South African media tends to be more outside of the country than within the borders of South Africa (SA). The artists include Ladysmith Black Mambazo, Goldfish, Abdullah Ibrahim, Black Coffee, Vusi Mahlasela, Mahotella Queens,

Accessibility, Diversity, Equity and Inclusion in the Cultural Sector, 97–116

Copyright © 2024 Akhona Ndzuta

Published under exclusive licence by Emerald Publishing Limited

doi:10.1108/978-1-83753-034-220241016

Derrick Gripper, the late Hugh Masekela, the late Johnny Clegg, Die Antwoord, Freshlyground, and Wouter Kellerman. Their gigs listings suggested that they predominantly performed in the Global North.[1] Of course, there is demand in Global North cultural markets for this music and enough disposable income to attract SA acts to these shores. Even so, this scarcity of SA gigs for these musicians within the country, and therefore their absence from home, poses a problem. It may suggest that there is not as much demand in SA for their talents. As the media have often reported, "many [SA] artists struggle to make a living from the industry and are enticed either to perform their arts abroad where opportunities seem abundant or find an alternative industry to make a living from" (Bizcommunity, 2015).

In this chapter, I propose that the prevalence of these performances abroad is an expansion of borders and a type of exile. It is an exile caused by complex political circumstances, public and institutional level policies, and factors that act against the sustainable development of music careers in SA, but especially so among Black performers. I discuss how some of these complexities influence Black or non-white people, who have been economically and otherwise historically disadvantaged on various levels during apartheid and its ongoing legacy, including how these complexities hinder the economic inclusion of this group in the cultural sector.[2] Through a qualitative exploration of the idea of an economic exile, I posit that by Black SA musicians performing abroad so frequently, they in fact become economic exiles to compensate for the scarcity of music markets at home. To partly avoid economic exile, their inclusion in broader SA-culture-and-diversity-friendly programming across SA cultural institutions is necessary. Such an approach to cultural programming is gradually manifesting across the country. It has, however, been slow, owing to the stagnant pace at which cultural institutions have been ready to transform to meet postapartheid demands (Maree, 2005). SA society has also been conditioned by apartheid to be outward-looking, to prize non-South African music, and to benchmark the cultural norms of the West and the Global North (Ansell, 2022a; DSAC, 2020; Maree, 2005).

---

[1]The Global North is a contentious construct but a term embraced in the social sciences to represent the hierarchical location of global development and political power. It refers to a metaphorical area of the world, involving the West and Asia, where most of the robust economies are located. The Global North stands in direct contrast to the Global South, which is homogenized as underdeveloped or emerging. The Global South is mainly imagined as countries in Africa, South America, Southeast Asia, etc. (Mignolo, 2011; Sud & Sánchez-Ancochea, 2022).

[2]Apartheid was a white supremacy-based system of separate development implemented in South Africa (SA) between 1948 and 1994. It was institutionalized and enforced by various arms of state through violent and other means. Among other injustices, apartheid intentionally underdeveloped Black people and those deemed non-white in SA. These include people of mixed racial and cultural heritage, called "Colored," immigrants from Asia, and those whose descendants were brought over as slaves from Asia. The system exploited Black labor, criminalized racial mixing, and systematically erased progressive Black and brown people's histories. (Magubane, 1996).

To make these arguments, I elaborate on what I mean by the expansion of borders, exile, and an economic exile. I then outline the political, cultural, and material conditions during apartheid that shaped this economic exile. Next, I discuss the conditions of public and institutional policy that also influence this exile during the democratic dispensation. Finally, I document a few policy-led interventions that expand SA music markets and address social diversity and inclusion. Essentially, this chapter answers these research questions: Why is there not enough demand for SA music? What are the consequences of this absence? Which cultural policy interventions counter this absence?

The Expansion of Borders and the Definition of Exile

My point of departure is an utterance by a musicologist at the Mozart Festival's Music and Exile Symposium in 2011 that "we are creating exiles."[3] This utterance came at the realization that SA at the time had insufficient capacity to absorb the large number of new music practitioners produced by SA universities each year. The context for this statement was a discussion about the limitations of untransformed SA university music curricula for students whose skills had to be relevant to the needs of contemporary times. The discussion revealed that SA music practitioners found limited job opportunities for themselves in SA's cultural sector and were compelled to seek such opportunities elsewhere in the world. As such, the problem was identified and labeled "exile."

I expand on this idea and suggest that the problem is not just "exile" but a labor-related, market-related, and economy-related type of exile. The problem is not that South African musicians are going abroad at all. Ordinarily, going abroad to perform or explore would be a worthwhile opportunity for any musician. It would be a chance for artistic experiments, testing new markets, etc. In this case, however, the lack of choice toward a prolonged absence from home is caused by the domestic scarcity of music-related employment and conditions that do not favor a stream of music-centered employment. SA musicians are in this way catapulted into a status of exile while they maintain employment abroad for periods of three to six months or more in a year even when those periods are not consecutive. This status affects Black SA musicians more due to their current disadvantaged socioeconomic reality and a history where they were excluded from the music industry and its "decision-making processes" (Walters, 2011, p. 41).

Of course, many factors contribute to SA music performers seeking employment in music-related ventures abroad (Ndzuta, 2013). Like performers from other countries, SA artists also seek thriving European, North American, and Australian summer festivals and similar spaces, to grow their audience base, artistic impact, and to network for other opportunities (Jansson & Nilsson, 2016;

---

[3]Many years later, the musicologist in question did not remember making this statement and specifically asked not to be associated with this utterance; hence, their identity is not revealed as part of this reference.

Ndzuta, 2019). From the gig listings of these performers, however, performances away have happened regularly over several years. Research among musicians has, however, also corroborated that the South African cultural sector in fact does not have enough capacity to absorb new SA music graduates (Ndzuta, 2013). For at least a decade, there have not been enough music-related opportunities to sustain local music performance careers (Ndzuta, 2013).

Some of the factors that contribute to this inability to keep musicians in SA relate to national cultural policy, the struggling SA economy which is unable to create disposable income to support cultural activities, access to digital resources, education at school and university levels that does not positively impact the music community, infrastructure inadequacies, etc (Ndzuta, 2021b; Oyekunle & Sirayi, 2018). In the Western Cape province of SA specifically, inadequate sector infrastructure was found to be a large contributor to limitations to the career growth of musicians (Ansell et al., 2007). There have also consistently been few live music venues around the country, which means that there is no real music circuit (Ansell, 2023; Ansell & Barnard, 2013; Coplan, 2007). Insufficient live venues mean there is not enough space to earn a living for musicians (Ansell, 2023; Ndzuta, 2013; Shaw & Rodell, 2009). This shortage of venues also does not encourage demand for local music (Ndzuta, 2013).

Under such conditions, SA musicians pursue greener pastures abroad. They do so not only to expand their audience reach but to have earnings which sustain their music careers as a matter of necessity (Ndzuta, 2013). In working abroad for protracted periods, however, these musicians also go into a self-imposed exile for economic reasons and become economic exiles.

Economic Exile

The idea of exile in this context is understood not as expulsion or banishment from one's country of origin by some form of authority but as a site of diverse experiences and "strategies of struggle" which "are played out in a range of social relationships, all diffused with power" (De Sas Kropiwnicki, 2014, p. 36). This context regards exile as estrangement from one's place of origin because of structural circumstances at political–economic–historical level. Exile here is based on the idea of a migrant worker or "a person who is to be engaged, is engaged or has been engaged in a remunerated activity in a State of which he or she is not a national" (IOM, 2023). This form of exile also means that there is no complete severing of ties between the individual leaving and their country of origin, but there is a "sense of betweenness" or "relationality" (Vos, 2016, p. 11). The individual does not necessarily move permanently from their place of origin to another country but does so in desperate need of a labor market there and other structural conditions that enable continual employment. It is a mobility that reveals structural dysfunction and a mobility forced by restrictive conditions even though it is self-imposed (Hackl, 2017).

In this sense, musicians, as economic exiles, are like other economic and political migrants who are produced by structural collapse or dysfunction and so remain in a different country for prolonged periods under restricted conditions which have to be legally authorized through mechanisms such as visas and taxation, for example (Gamlen, 2015). These exiles do not simply emigrate to better their socioeconomic position but are "forced by economic need" caused by problems with political roots (Forsdyke, 2005; Gamlen, 2015, p. 309).

The musicians are catapulted into a nomadic existence which challenges the idea of where home should be.[4] As Vos (2016, p. 63) explained about the condition of migrancy, home becomes "forever the place of migration." The condition of returning home, however, does not depend on what the exiles achieve in the country in which they briefly settle. So, even though the extraction of oneself from home is self-imposed, it is not clear when it might end because that depends on whether the structural circumstances in the country of origin change or not. For economic exiles, therefore, the condition of return is determined by their country of origin and not the country in which they settle (Hackl, 2017).

Simultaneously, the status of exile here is not only concerned with material conditions. It also means that the musician is separated from their artistic community of origin (Forsdyke, 2005). This is a community in which the musician's heritage is shared or commonly understood. So, removal from this community also has ramifications. By leaving SA, they not only become economic exiles but also exile the immediate reach of SA heritage. They live in musical displacement as Vos (2016) has suggested of the political exile of prominent SA musicians during apartheid.[5]

Conditions Perpetuating Economic Exile

As mentioned earlier, the insufficient capacity for SA to absorb its musicians drives economic exile. This capacity is affected by complex developmental issues before and during the democratic period starting in 1994. In this section, I explain the political, cultural, and material conditions that shape this exile in apartheid. I also explain the conditions that influence this exile in democratic SA. The latter are conditions of cultural, educational, and infrastructural policy.

Conditions During Apartheid

SA is a country with a majority Black population. The country has been unjustly occupied by the Dutch, French, Portuguese, and English since the 1600s

---

[4]This nomadism is different to musicians traditionally performing on tours. This nomadic existence also does not prove that we live in a smaller globalized world but is a site of struggle and desperation. Musicians could tour between towns in one country but others employed in SA cultural and creative industries currently cannot because of lack of disposable income due to a depressed economy, high rates on unemployment to support culture, lack of the development of culture, etc. (Ndzuta, 2021b; Van Graan, 2019).
[5]By this displacement, I am not suggesting that cultural confluence should not be enabled by musicians of different places coming together. What I am highlighting is that heritage sharing is not a one-way street, it follows many directions.

(Magubane, 1996). Due to this colonization and impact of the slave trade on the African continent and its routes between Asia and Europe, the country is multicultural. Nonetheless, Black people are still a large majority. After colonization, the National Party government instituted apartheid between 1948 and 1994.

During apartheid, Black people were laborers or had limited professions available to them such as lawyers, doctors, teachers, social workers, and nurses as dictated by state machinery (Bonnin & Ruggunan, 2016). Black people and others deemed non-white by the state were situated in areas called townships located on the outskirts of cities and serving SA's gold mining industry and commercial interests related to it.[6] Black people could not be self-employed or easily be artists as such cultural participation was perceived as a political act, unless used within an ethnicity-based framework approved by the state (Ansell, 2005; Coplan, 2007; Olwage, 2008). As such, Black people were not fully integrated in cultural work without struggle (Nawa, 2021). They were excluded in the state narrative of what SA culture constituted, but many Black artists resisted and defied such exclusion within the country through various successful and unsuccessful strategies and through financial support from anti-apartheid foreign donors (Nawa, 2021; Peterson, 1990). Others had to leave SA to continue to contribute to its diverse cultural heritage and stand against government propaganda (Ansell, 2005; Coplan, 2007; Nawa, 2021). These political exiles impacted the footprint of SA music and other art forms in, especially, Europe and North America (Ansell, 2005; Coplan, 2007; Nawa, 2021).

The apartheid government was also culturally outward-looking. It looked to European culture as the standard for cultural aesthetics to reinforce its propaganda about the superiority of the white race and its Christian-centric dominion over those indigenous to Africa (Hamm, 1991). Western forms of art such as opera, ballet, classical music, etc., performed by white artists were sponsored by the state, as well as visual art, theater, and film that were neutral or embraced the propaganda of the state (Maree, 2005; Peterson, 1990). Forms of art with origins of racial intermingling were banned, cautiously monitored, and barred from distribution within the country (Hamm, 1991; Olwage, 2008). Even though there was a burgeoning jazz, rock, and popular music culture based on the popular music genres of the United States in different communities around SA, most forms of SA media were censored to drive the nationalist propaganda (Ansell, 2005; Coplan, 2007; Hamm, 1991; Olwage, 2008). Black radio was divided according to ethnic group lines, broadcasting music which separated Blackness from modernity, urbanity, intellectual life, and sophistication (Coplan, 2007; Hamm, 1991).

As Black urbanization increased due to labor required in growing cities and more radio stations began playing popular music that was monitored and was

---

[6]Townships are suburbs that were designated for Black and brown people due to apartheid segregationist town planning. These areas are still underdeveloped and underserved after apartheid.

within state ideology, different genres of music reached wider multicultural audiences. By the 1970s and 1980s, however, after a political miscalculation by the apartheid government where "homelands," or ethnically defined areas within the country, were given independence to reinforce the glories of separate ethnic development, these areas were also accorded independent radio stations. These stations did away with playing much censored music, and instead broadcast music of different cultural origins from different parts of the world. They used radio programming formats from predominantly the United States and the United Kingdom, which proved very popular across SA since the transmission signals went over the borders (Hamm, 1991).[7]

As more independent stations multiplied due to demand for different formats, "a new generation Black township audience with some buying power" was also emerging (Baines, 1998, p. 70). In 1986, Metro FM, an English language radio station targeted at Black audiences, was established, but it did away with music based along ethnic lines (Baines, 1998; Hamm, 1991). Its brand embraced Black modernity in an urban setting, and like the other independent radio stations, it looked to the West for its playlists (Baines, 1998; Hamm, 1991). While these were signs of the SA population responding to a long cultural repression, this trajectory of SA radio station programming was dominated by Western and non-South African music. Such programming was perceived as more sophisticated and has prevailed in SA media postapartheid. For a long time, SA radio has inadvertently furthered and prioritized cultural trends from foreign societies (Baines, 1998; Mkhombo, 2019; SOS Coalition, 2015). Western music has, thus, been standardized, creating little space for the development of music produced in SA. As such, the development of SA music markets and their audiences have been negatively impacted. This has more of an imprint on Black music and is caused by reasons grounded in cultural policy, education policy, and policies related to infrastructure, which I detail below.

Conditions of the Democratic Dispensation

Cultural Policy

One of the forms of public policy that has contributed to the status of economic exile of SA musicians is cultural policy after apartheid. Drafted in 1996 and revised in 2020, SA cultural policy has pushed SA culture outside of SA's borders, for skills development, as well as accessing and competing with new markets. In SA cultural policy, the state's role in national culture is a facilitative one in the development, preservation, and promotion of SA culture and heritage, within and outside the country's borders. The government has as such tried to implement cultural programs directly or indirectly or fund programs to achieve goals of

---

[7]This popularity was also driven by the agenda of "multinational recording companies" that "foreign western music content [was] more significant than locally produced products" (Baines, 1998; Walters, 2011, p. 44). These companies also did not invest enough in music produced in SA (Baines, 1998; Walters, 2011).

development, preservation, and promotion, as stipulated in the 1996 White Paper on Arts, Culture and Heritage (WPACH-1996). One of the programs in this document addresses "Cultural Development and International Cooperation," for improving "economic and other development opportunities for South African arts and culture, nationally and globally, through mutually beneficial partnerships, thereby ensuring the sustainability of the sector" (DAC, 2009, p. 7). For this program, often government-to-government ventures have been instituted; however, its goals have been more aggressively addressed by the 2011 neo-liberal Mzansi Golden Economy (MGE) cultural policy strategy.

MGE embraces both the concept of the creative industries, which positions culture within the framework of production-for-consumption, as well as the cultural sector's role in social transformation and development (Ndzuta, 2019). As such, the strategy focuses less on larger government-to-government projects to achieve cross-border cultural interchange but supports smaller initiatives by artists to achieve cross-border cultural interchange. MGE is more concerned with enhancing "job creation and productivity," increasing "the sector's global competitiveness," to "stimulate demand," "develop audiences for the creative and cultural industries" and increase their consumption, foster "human capacity development," and to develop cultural entrepreneurs (DAC, 2017a, 2017b, pp. 5–6).

The strategy also funds artists who align with its objectives, funding them to create jobs while working anywhere abroad and creating demand for the SA music product. As such, MGE unintentionally encourages local musicians into exile as a desired outcome and as an acknowledgment of the inadequate mechanisms of the state in developing and promoting the cultural sector in the country for self-sufficiency and abroad so that there is demand for SA culture. One of the ways MGE has endeavored to create demand abroad has been to invest in festivals, where musicians considered familiar in specific regions, like the USA, are put on the bill and where other lesser known musicians are put in a position where they incorporate music that is palatable to audience in the regions to which they perform (Ndzuta, 2019). In this way, MGE is an internationalization type of policy, internationalizing SA cultural market and products (Ndzuta, 2019). The risk, however, is that such internationalizing policies have the capacity to weaken domestic policies (UNCTAD in Oyekunle & Sirayi, 2018).

Another example for how cultural policy encourages cultural sector workers to be outward-looking is that in the WPACH-1996, cultural workers like musicians were encouraged to engage in the kind of domestic-based cultural diplomacy that was designed to upskill them, expose them to international cultural sector workforce practices, and reintegrate them with the rest of the world after the isolation of apartheid (DACST, 1996; Ndzuta, 2019). The underlying goals, however, were political network-building for the government (Ndzuta, 2019). Later cultural policy strategies, like MGE, also incentivized SA cultural workers to seek international markets to contribute to economic development, not necessarily for the growth of their careers but for the sector's contribution to growing the gross domestic product (GDP) (DAC, 2017b; Ndzuta, 2019).

A further policy example is the 2020 parliament-approved decoloniality-conscious revised version of the White Paper on Cultural Policy and Heritage (WPACH-2020) built on the WPACH-1996. One of the WPACH-1996 stipulations encourages the establishment of orchestras and orchestra companies, while the WPACH-2020 puts more emphasis on cultural diplomacy (DSAC, 2017). The WPACH-2020 catalyzed the formation of a traditionally Western-art music orchestra that would be an engine for cultural diplomacy and would drive the creation of jobs among SA orchestras and social transformation by diversifying orchestra personnel (Ansell, 2022a; Tembe, 2022). The orchestra has a generous budget, is supposed to have a non-South African conductor, and performs domestically and abroad (Ansell, 2022a; Tembe, 2022). This initiative, however, risks not investing as much in or giving prominence to other large ensemble-based music genres that originate in SA when it comes to international cultural diplomacy platforms and employment opportunities. The initiative also risks further representing SA art forms as benchmarked on Western art forms even in its intentions of rectifying the exclusion of people of color in SA orchestras and presenting a commonly shared art form for international cultural diplomacy best practices.[8]

As mentioned earlier, SA music radio broadcasting is dominated by music from outside of SA. So, SA media audiences have consumed more international music than SA music for decades. Broadcasting policies post-1994 have addressed the privileging of international music on radio and television, but mainly through the implementation of a quota system that still disadvantages SA music (Baines, 1998; SOS Coalition, 2015). In the WPACH-2020, a fund has also been set up to incentivize radio stations to have more SA content (DSAC, 2020). Even with such interventions, the demand for SA music is only very slowly being boosted. SA musicians produce more Western-derived music like jazz, classical or Western-art music, hip-hop, etc., for instance. These genres vie for airplay along with music produced in the Global North, negatively impacting the GDP since less SA music airplay means less revenue from royalties goes to local artists, adversely affecting the diversity of the cultural sector and harming national identity. Music which was encouraged by the apartheid state on apartheid radio due to its emphasis on its origins from SA ethnic groups is now also marketed as World Music abroad (Baines, 1998; Ndzuta, 2019). As such, even the standardization of music genres is also based on Western norms.

Education Policies

The other drivers of economic exile among SA musicians are education policies that narrow the positionality of culture. Below, I discuss how the narrowness of these policies counters the generative social value of culture by focusing on a science, technology, engineering, and maths (STEM) framework and by excluding arts management courses in SA university arts curricula. There is also inadequate

---

[8]See Sikes et al. (2006) on the best practices of international cultural exchange programs.

integration of music in the curricula of primary and secondary education levels, some of which has to do with the privileging of STEM subjects in school curricula (Vermeulen, 2009). The WPACH-2020 also frames the irregular presence of arts-culture subjects in the curricula of primary and secondary education levels as a problem that hinders broader sustainable development (DSAC, 2020). This uneven distribution of arts subjects, and particularly music, in schools also has a direct impact on the development of future arts audiences since future audiences and arts participation are nurtured through institutions like those of education, in social groups and other cultural contexts (Hargreaves et al., 2003). Future music audiences, or music consumers, understand the aesthetic and social value of music from some form of participation in music (Beeching, 2016; Hargreaves et al., 2003).

The second education-related influence driving musicians seeking opportunities elsewhere is the marginalization of arts management courses within SA arts curricula in higher education (Sirayi & Nawa, 2014). The implication is that those who study music, for example, are limited in terms of the career trajectory they can follow post leaving university and do not smoothly transition into roles of music management if they have such an interest. As such, when these new music graduates enter the cultural and creative industries, they learn certain necessary skills like those of management on the job and join an already large pool of struggling musicians in the country trying to diversify their income sources (Ndzuta, 2013; Sirayi & Nawa, 2014). This situation renders SA with reduced capacity in the expansive area of arts management. Musicians in such circumstances have more chances of finding agents who have unique managerial expertise outside of the country, expertise that can promote their music for music labor conditions in SA and abroad. The jazz drummer Kesivan Naidoo, for instance, worked with the manager of the globally recognized trumpeter Hugh Masekela for a performance at Carnegie Hall in New York (Ndzuta, 2019). Similarly, a slew of SA musicians have been represented by the New-York-city-based manager Thomas Rome (Rome, 2018).

Infrastructure Challenges

Along with the policies above, public policies concerning infrastructure also create a barrier to musicians accessing potential music audiences and music markets. Challenges are brought on by inadequate infrastructure policies on transport and digital access, and this infrastructure negatively impacts the growth of music markets among Black communities. For instance, public policies on transport infrastructure do not sufficiently address crime (Eagle & Kwele, 2021; Vanderschuren et al., 2019). Public transport is mainly used by Black South Africans (Eagle & Kwele, 2021; Vanderschuren et al., 2019). This has meant that in urban and peri-urban areas, there are safety issues on public transportation like trains, buses, and minibus taxis (Eagle & Kwele, 2021; Vanderschuren et al., 2019). It also means that due to safety concerns affecting the public, potential music audiences are reduced for live night-time music events. Mainly, audiences that travel in private cars can easily attend music shows. Such audiences though, or audiences who often support the arts, irrespective of their race tend to be concentrated in historically white middle- and upper-income areas and not in townships where Black people still predominantly reside (Snowball, 2005). Meanwhile, due to not enough investment dedicated to rural development, an area which is also largely Black, live music circuits are not a staple in such areas (Malan et al., 2019). There is also not enough information on rural arts audiences that would support a supply of live music beyond the odd rural festival (Malan et al., 2019). In summary, Black arts audiences are small in rural, peri-urban, and urban contexts, with negative market implications for Black musicians.

Also, in terms of income, SA musicians make the bulk of their earnings from live music and not from digital sales (Ansell, 2022b). Unlike in countries in the Global North, where digital music sales have been commonplace for over a decade, in SA, such sales are complicated by a large digital divide (Ansell, 2022b; Ndzuta, 2021b). As much as the general SA population has phones and computers, SA is a country with the largest economic gap between the rich and the poor, where mainly middle- and upper-income homes have regular large-scale access to the internet and digital facilities where digital commerce is an everyday occurrence (Azionya & Nhedzi, 2021). Middle- and upper-income homes whose disposable income supports cultural ventures are also in the minority in the country, however, meaning that there are severe limitations to the flourishing of digital music markets and thus income for musicians. Digital access is expensive due to communication and technology-related public policies that do not position it as a public necessity (Ndzuta, 2021b). Access to digital life is also made more unreliable by regular electricity-infrastructure-related power outages that adversely affects the general consumption of music (Ansell, 2023).[9] This market is, thus, also miniscule for Black SA musicians.

Interventions of Diversity and Inclusion

Interventions of diversity and inclusion in SA at festivals, performing arts complexes, and music expos are evident. Changes were necessary in democracy to rid SA of the injustices of apartheid, including contesting the distribution and accessibility of resources within the creative industries. Such changes have mirrored power struggles in other areas of SA life concerning the dismantling of the ways in which apartheid reproduced, normalized, and racialized inequality (Madlingozi, 2007; Maree, 2005). For instance, there still needs to be a wider recognition, acknowledgment, and redress of the problems that compound each other to make the participation of Black people in the creative industries after apartheid not the same as other groups (Ndzuta, 2021a). Immediately after apartheid, Black people had to build their own professional sectoral networks because in apartheid, they were not invited to sit on white institutional boards and participate on white managerial platforms (Maree, 2005). A few Black people gradually found their way onto institutional boards and management platforms, etc. (Maree, 2005; Ndzuta, 2021a). There was a great need for structural change in the sector.

---

[9]Since 2008, SA has experienced scheduled and sometimes unscheduled power outages related to inadequate electricity infrastructure, its maintenance, and management.

The WPACH-1996 gave treatment to some of the inequalities caused by apartheid, resulting in the inaccessibility of the arts for the Black population. Clause 51 is about infrastructure, for example, and states

> The primary need for infrastructure is in rural and Black urban areas, close to where people live. The establishment of urban and peri-urban townships as dormitories, without proper facilities for recreation and leisure, is a feature of apartheid. This deprivation cannot be continued in the new dispensation which is concerned with improving the quality of people's lives at a local level. Such improvement must include the development of facilities to educate, nurture, promote, and enable the enjoyment of the arts, film, music, visual art, dance, theater, and literature.

Clause 16 also positions that:

> ... performing arts work and exhibition opportunities for Black artists at publicity-funded arts institutions were limited. With limited job opportunities, training in the arts was not pursued with the same vigour by Black people as other areas

Some initiatives aimed at creating more opportunities for SA musicians of color have manifested across the country, given impetus by institutional policy and the WPACH-1996. The impact of these initiatives has not yet been measured, but they contribute toward lessening scarcity in domestic music markets. These programs are conscious of SA cultural diversity and address the inclusion of Black artists who have historically been excluded from mainstream platforms of the cultural sector. The initiatives have a particularly Black-culture-friendly approach. Below, I detail platforms like festivals, performing arts complexes, and music expos.

Festivals

The first initiative involves the government's intentional sponsoring of festivals across the country. Festivals that drive the government agenda of demonstrating SA's social and cultural diversity are publicly funded, as per WPACH-1996 legislation. The Department of Sports, Arts, and Culture (DSAC) employs festivals as policy instruments, as highlighted in the 5-year strategic plan for 2011–2016 which recognized festivals as tools for promoting social cohesion, portraying the diversity of SA's cultural heritage, and promoting the cultural industries within our borders (DAC, 2016, pp. 12–19).[10] Festivals, therefore, have

---

[10]The department is also SA's Cultural Ministry. It has had various acronyms in the past due to how its two name changes since 1994. These include the Department of Arts, Culture, Science and Technology (DACST), then the Department of Arts and Culture (DAC).

been the means through which the government could redress the exclusion of Black identity in the apartheid national cultural narrative while creating a narrative about a multicultural democracy (Ndzuta, 2019).

As an intervention to expand music markets, festivals also address the need for quality performance work among Black and brown musicians who would not ordinarily have been hired on a festival circuit during apartheid and in early democracy. So, festivals that receive this funding and meet these objectives have grown across the country (Ndzuta, 2019). At surface level, the number of these festivals give the impression that Black musicians have many opportunities, since they are predominantly hired to perform there. In reality, these events cannot provide fully for SA musicians. They usually take place annually, sporadically, or are time-specific (Drummond et al., 2021). They also make up a fraction of overall festivals around the country, some of which are privately sponsored and do not actively promote cultural diversity (Hauptfleisch, 2006).

Performing Arts Complexes

The second initiative is the cultural programming at performing arts complexes across the country. An example is The Playhouse Company, in the city of Durban, which is a state-owned entity and agency of the DSAC. On a webinar hosted by the University of South Africa's Chief Albert Luthuli Research Chair, it came to light that the chief executive officer and artistic director of The Playhouse Company, Ms. Lynda Bukhosini, has addressed cultural diversity and "nation-building" within programming at The Playhouse Company (UnisaVideos, 2022).[11] She has, thus, actively pursued principles in national cultural policy by showcasing SA's cultural and artistic diversity but also making this part of institutional policy at The Playhouse.

While at the helm, Ms Bukhosini enriched programming by including traditional music genres such as the Zulu guitar-based *Maskandi* whose origins are of the province of KwaZulu-Natal.[12] She included orchestral music, poetry, religious music, jazz, popular music of different cultural origins, and music of Indian heritage reflecting the large population of people of Indian descent in Durban (Playhouse Company, 2022b). During her tenure, theater and dance of various cultural origins, conversations for creative industries capacity building, education-driven events are part of programming (Playhouse Company, 2022a). The programming is aimed at people of "all walks of life" in Durban and the province of KwaZulu-Natal (Playhouse Company, 2022a). Quantitatively, from The Playhouse Company's 2021–2022 annual report, the programming showcases a majority of Black culture (Playhouse Company, 2022a, p. 3). Not only does the programming represent the province's populace but also integrates the cultural diversity of the province. These are narratives that were shunned during apartheid.

---

[11]The webinar was titled "Music in South African Cities" and was part of *MusoCulture: A Music and Public Policy Series.*

[12]KwaZulu-Natal is one of SA's nine provinces. It is located on the eastern coast of SA, and Durban is its largest city.

Other SA performing arts centers have also grappled with changing their programming, but it has taken a long time (Maree, 2005).[13] Black SA culture, and music specifically, was not commonplace at these venues, nor was the Black management which now makes up most of the personnel in the governance structures.[14] It is important then to consider that due to few digital audiences, festival platforms, and other music venues for Black musicians, venues such as performance arts center are essential for boosting SA music markets and mainstreaming Black SA culture. Traditional SA music, for instance, is still rarely featured on highly billed SA music festivals, similarly to the fate of other traditional arts in the development initiatives of the cultural sector (Oyekunle, 2020). The inclusion of traditional music at performing arts centers is, thus, a milestone in embracing another aspect of SA's national identity apart from providing jobs.

A further example of the inclusion of musical cultures and people pushed to the cultural margins is the integration of the *Amapiano* music genre in the artistic programming of The Market Theatre in the city of Johannesburg. *Amapiano* is an electronic SA Black dance music genre which has become very popular among Black youth. It has also found resonance in the African diaspora audiences of the United Kingdom and the United States (BBC News Africa, 2022; Tsumele, 2022). The Market Theatre's *raison d'etre* is theater, but it has also often hosted SA jazz concerts. The inclusion of dance music embraces a new market bracket, and a Black youth dance market often shunned by cultural institutions (Long-Innes, 2022; Tsumele, 2022). This step also plays a role in transforming public perceptions of this music from the margins to the mainstream, generating more music employment opportunities within SA.

Music Expos

A third intervention is the presence of music expositions (expos). The Moshito Music Conference and Exhibition was the first such annual expo. Its necessity was highlighted in WPACH-1996 and then outlined in subsequent national cultural policy strategies.[15] The conference has provided discussion among multi-sector

---

[13]This includes Artscape in the city of Cape Town in the Western Cape province, the Performing Arts Centre of the Free State the city of Bloemfontein which is in the Free State province, and the State Theatre in the city of Pretoria in the Gauteng province.

[14]See the council members of each performing arts center. For The Playhouse Company, see https://playhousecompany.com/?page_id=1652 For Artscape, see https://www.artscape.co.za/council-members/ For the Pacofs in Bloemfontein, see http://pacofs.co.za/wp/?page_id=15961 For the State Theater, see https://statetheatre.co.za/about-us-page/

[15]See the WPACH-1996 topics of "building new audiences [and] developing new markets" as well as public–private partnerships in "private sector," in clauses 59–60 as well as 66–71, respectively. (DACST, 1996). Also see Shaw & Rodell (2009), Walters (2011), and Ndzuta (2019, pp. 164, 169) regarding the reports and strategies, like the Creative Industry Grown Strategy, that concretized the music necessity of a music expo and its funding by government to create music markets, be a bridge to tourism, develop the value chain of the SA music.

stakeholders, catalyzed the Global-South-to-Global-South and Global-North-to-Global-South creation of collaborative music networks and markets (Walters, 2011). Its driving values are to "broaden the business intelligence of music industry professionals in Africa, strengthen business networks for participants and inform delegates, traders and the public about the multifaceted and dynamic nature of the global music industry" (moshito.co.za). Moshito provides information about "new markets," "live music," "industry challenges (e.g., piracy)," "social economic development and technology" (Walters, 2011, p. 50). Since its establishment as a conference and expo in 2004, other music industry expos have been founded through public and private initiatives. Examples are The Music Imbizo in the city of Durban, the Breathe Music Sunshine Conference in the city of Cape Town, Live Music Conference (Limusico) in the township of Soweto outside of Johannesburg, and the Africa Rising Music Conference in Johannesburg.

These conferences and expos have varying commitments to demographic inclusivity and diversity but essentially address imbalances in the SA music industry. All of them have distinct offerings though. These offerings include presenting capacity-building workshops, having panel discussions about issues in the production and performance of music, and providing paid performance opportunities for artists. Each of them has a specific emphasis and takes a different approach to representation in the music industry.

The Music Imbizo, for example, distributes needed resources to another geographic area, since it is located away from the music industry clusters of Cape Town and Johannesburg, where the SA music industry is mostly concentrated (O'Connor, 2015; Shaw & Rodell, 2009). The Breathe Sunshine Music Conference pledged to upskill African music practitioners and highlighted the plight of independent artists on important music industry platforms (Herimbi, 2013). Limusico attempted to host a conference in 2022 in the underserved township of Soweto, where Black music practitioners have limited resources to shape music careers and make a significant impact in the music industry.[16,17] It recognizes that they need to make a "decent living" from music performance careers.[18] The Africa Rising Music Conference (ARMC) was established with the recognition that women in the music industry are not sufficiently represented. In fact, ARMC is an arm of Women in Music, a larger global umbrella body that focuses on the agenda to "advance the awareness, equality, diversity, heritage, opportunities, and cultural aspects of women in the musical arts through education, support, empowerment, and recognition" (Women in Music, 2022). So, these expos remedy exclusions in the music industry while driving their motivations for professionalization, commercialization, and internationalization.

---

[16]The expo was canceled.

[17]The music industry has historically and globally been primarily white and male dominated (Kofsky, 1998; Mitchell, 1993; Negus, 1999; Wolfe, 2019).

[18]See LIMUSICO at https://limusico-live-music-conference.yolasite.com/

Conclusion

It is absurd to be considering diversity and the inclusion of Black people in a Black majority country. This inability to recognize Black people as full humans, however, is a legacy of apartheid and colonialism and has found its way in contemporary parlance on equality. And so, the public and institutional policy conditions that excluded Black musicians in creative sector participation during apartheid influence the slow pace of sector transformation that has brought about their work scarcity, resource shortages, reduced markets, and therefore self-imposed economic exile. Policies of exclusion and inclusion during apartheid as well as after it have pushed and pulled Black SA musicians within and outside of SA borders. I have suggested that if the frameworks of cultural policy, educational policy, and infrastructural policy do not converge in addressing inequality and slow social and institutional transformation, then among other social problems, Black musicians will perpetually be in a state of economic exile.

In this chapter, I have also discussed how economic exile is encouraged by policies from multiple sectors. For instance, in relation to cultural policy, broadcasting norms and music genre categories reinforce the message that SA Black musicians are more part of the Global North than SA because they sell mainly genres that have found a home in the West. Education and infrastructure development policies are also not nuanced enough to effectively tackle scarce resources and inequality, and this has implications on Black audience development. So, there is a constant theme of not prioritizing local audiences, of looking away from SA culture for solutions to grow SA culture, and of not providing opportunities for SA music practitioners.

That said, however, cultural institutions such as festivals, performing arts centers, and music expos are some of the platforms that drive sector transformation and the economic inclusion of a large demographic of the population. These are public and private policy-driven initiatives addressing issues of diversity and inclusion. Although they may be long overdue, they do have the potential to meaningfully expand SA music markets and hopefully contribute toward reducing the imperatives of economic exile for Black SA musicians.

References

Ansell, G. (2005). *Soweto blues: Jazz, popular music and politics in South Africa*. The Continuum International.

Ansell, G. (2022a, July 12). Do we need a Mzansi National Philharmonic Orchestra? [Blog post]. https://sisgwenjazz.wordpress.com/2022/07/12/do-we-need-a-mzansi-national-philharmonic-orchestra/

Ansell, G. (2022b, December 6). Music streaming in South Africa – New survey reveals musicians get a raw deal. *The Conversation*. https://theconversation.com/music-streaming-in-south-africa-new-survey-reveals-musicians-get-a-raw-deal-194087?utm_source=whatsapp&utm_medium=bylinewhatsappbutton&fbclid=IwAR2xhlEYmD lhCQg-woPHdJ0gL8vGahWhdWT1OBK-7YM8TS4qwc2gdGdD2O8

Ansell, G. (2023, January 29). The second wave of closedowns: Live jazz fighting for survival. [Blog post]. https://sisgwenjazz.wordpress.com/2023/01/29/the-second-wave-of-closedowns-live-jazz-fighting-for-survival/

Ansell, G., & Barnard, H. (2013). Working small, acting big: Sources of, and strategies for, business innovation among South African Jazz musicians. *South African Journal of Musicology, 33*(1), 11–29.

Ansell, G., Barnard, H., & Barnard, P. (2007). *Report on the micro-economic development strategy for the music industry in the Western Cape.* Department of Economic Development and Tourism, Western Cape Provincial Government.

Artscape. (2022). Council members. https://www.artscape.co.za/council-members/

Azionya, C. M., & Nhedzi, A. (2021). The digital divide and higher education challenge with emergency online learning: Analysis of tweets in the wake of the COVID-19 lockdown. *The Turkish Online Journal of Distance Education, 22*(4), 164–182.

Baines, G. (1998). Catalyst or detonator? Local music quotas and the current South African music 'explosion'. *Social Dynamics, 24*(1), 66–87.

BBC News Africa. (2022, August 20). 'This is Amapiano' (Documentary): Director's cut BBC Africa. [Video file]. https://www.youtube.com/watch?v=ou0luMrf1mU

Beeching, A. M. (2016). Who is audience? *Arts and Humanities in Higher Education, 15*(3–4), 395–400.

Bizcommunity. (2015, August 18). Breathe Sunshine African Music Conference urges industry to come together. *Bizcommunity.* https://www.bizcommunity.com/Article/196/480/133221.html

Bonnin, D., & Ruggunan, S. (2016). Professions and professionalism in emerging economies. In M. Dent, I. Bourgeault, J. Denis, & E. Kuhlman (Eds.), *The Routledge companion to the professions and professionalism* (pp. 251–264). Routledge.

Coplan, D. (2007). *In township tonight: South Africa's Black city music and theatre.* Jacana Media.

De Sas Kropiwnicki, Z. (2014). Childhood in exile: The agency of second-generation exiles seeking refuge from apartheid. *Refuge: Canada's Journal on Refugees, 30*(1), 35–46.

Department of Arts and Culture (DAC). (2009). *Medium term strategic framework: 1 April 2009–31 March 2012.* http://www.dac.gov.za/sites/default/files/Strategy%20Plan%202009-2012.pdf

Department of Arts and Culture (DAC). (2016). *Strategic plan 2011–2016.* http://www.dac.gov.za/sites/default/files/2011-2016.pdf

Department of Arts and Culture (DAC). (2017a). *Annual report 2016–2017: The year of Oliver Reginald Tambo.* http://www.dac.gov.za/sites/default/files/Annual%20Report%202016-17.pdf

Department of Arts and Culture (DAC). (2017b). *Mzansi golden economy (MGE): Guidelines: Criteria, eligibility, processes & systems, 2016/2017, Version 1.0.* http://www.dac.gov.za/sites/default/files/eForms/2016-17-guidelines-for-mzansi-golden-economy-1-0-final.pdf

Department of Arts, Culture, Science and Technology (DACST). (1996). *White paper on arts, culture and heritage.* http://www.dac.gov.za/content/white-paper-arts-culture-and-heritage

Department of Sports, Arts, Culture (DSAC). (2020). *Revised white paper on arts, culture and heritage (4th draft)*. http://www.dac.gov.za/content/revised-white-paper-arts-culture-and-heritage-fourth-draft-0

Drummond, J. H., Snowball, J., Antrobus, G., & Drummond, F. J. (2021). The role of cultural festivals in regional economic development: A case study of Mahika Mahikeng. In K. Scherf (Ed.), *Creative tourism in smaller communities: Place, culture, and local representation* (pp. 79–107).

Eagle, G., & Kwele, K. (2021). "You just come to school, if you made it, its grace": Young Black women's experiences of violence in utilizing public "Minibus Taxi" transport in Johannesburg, South Africa. *Journal of Interpersonal Violence, 36*(15–16).

Forsdyke, S. (2005). *Exile, ostracism, and democracy: The politics of expulsion in ancient Greece*. Princeton.

Gamlen, A. (2015). 'An inborn restlessness': Migration and exile in a turbulent world. *Migration Studies, 3*(3), 307–314.

Hackl, A. (2017). Key figure of mobility: The exile. *Social Anthropology, 25*, 55–68.

Hamm, C. (1991). 'The constant companion of man': Separate development, radio bantu and music. *Popular Music, 10*(2), 147–173.

Hargreaves, D. J., Marshall, N. A., & North, A. C. (2003). Music education in the twenty-first century: A psychological perspective. *British Journal of Music Education, 20*(2), 147–163.

Hauptfleisch, T. (2006). Eventifying identity: Festivals in South Africa and the search for cultural identity. *New Theatre Quarterly, 22*(2), 181–198.

Herimbi, H. (2013, March 20). Changing perspectives on music. *IOL*. https://www.iol.co.za/entertainment/music/changing-perspectives-on-music-1489354

Jansson, J., & Nilsson, J. (2016). Musicians and temporary spaces: The case of music festivals in Sweden. In B. Hracs, M. Seman, & T. Virani (Eds.), *The production and consumption of music in the digital age* (pp. 144–160). Routledge.

Kofsky, F. (1998). *Black music, white business: Illuminating the history and political economy of Jazz*. Pathfinder Press.

Live Music Conference (LIMUSICO). (2022). About. https://limusico-live-music-conference.yolasite.com/

Long-Innes, D. (2022). *Bottom-up culture production: The growth of local music scenes in the digital age: A case study of the Amapiano music scene in the South African music industry*. MSc thesis, Copenhagen Business School.

Madlingozi, T. (2007). Post-apartheid social movements and the quest for the elusive 'new' South Africa. *Journal of Law and Society, 34*(1), 77–98.

Magubane, B. (1996). *The making of a racist state: British imperialism and the Union of South Africa, 1875–1910*. Africa World Press.

Malan, S. F., Dzansi, D., & Strydom, A. J. (2019). 'Musiconomy': A framework for the socio-economic development of a rural South African context. *African Journal of Hospitality, Tourism and Leisure, 8*(2), 1–18.

Maree, L. (2005). State of the arts. In J. Daniel, R. Southall, & J. Lutchman (Eds.), *State of the nation: South Africa 2004–2005* (pp. 287–312). HSRC Press.

Mignolo, W. D. (2011). The global south and world dis/order. *Journal of Anthropological Research, 67*(2), 165–188.

Mitchell, T. (1993). World music and the popular music industry: An Australian view. *Ethnomusicology, 37*(3), 309–338.

Mkhombo, S. M. (2019). *The status of indigenous music in the South African school curriculum with special reference to IsiZulu*. PhD Dissertation, University of South Africa. http://uir.unisa.ac.za/bitstream/handle/10500/25896/thesis_mkhombo_sm.pdf

L. Nawa (Ed.). (2021). *Culture and liberation struggle in South Africa: From colonialism to post-apartheid*. Ssali Publishing House.

Ndzuta, A. (2013). *Performing management: How ten Jazz musicians approach career organisation*. Masters' Research Report, University of the Witwatersrand.

Ndzuta, A. (2019). *South African festivals in the USA: An expression of policy, power and networks*. PhD dissertation, The Ohio State University.

Ndzuta, A. (2021). Rupture and power struggles in South African national cultural policy discourse. In L. Nawa (Ed.), *Culture and liberation struggle in South Africa: From colonialism to post-apartheid* (pp. 530–551). Ssali Publishing House.

Ndzuta, A. (2021b, December 6). The growth of South Africa's cultural industries depends on broader state policies. *The Conversation*. https://theconversation.com/the-growth-of-south-africas-cultural-industries-depends-on-broader-state-policies-171242

Negus, K. (1999). The music business and rap: Between the street and the executive suite. *Cultural Studies, 13*(3), 488–508.

O'Connor, E. (2015). *Johannesburg live music audiences: Motivations for, and barriers to, 18-to-25 year-old audiences attending and consuming live music in Johannesburg venues*. MA Research Report, University of Witwatersrand.

Olwage, G. (2008). *Composing apartheid: Music for and against apartheid*. Wits University.

Oyekunle, O. A. (2020). The contribution of creative industries to sustainable urban development in South Africa. Science, technology and innovation in BRICS countries special issue. *African Journal of Science, Technology, Innovation and Development, 9*(5), 104–113.

Oyekunle, O. A., & Sirayi, M. (2018). The role of creative industries as a driver for a sustainable economy: A case of South Africa. *Creative Industries Journal, 11*(3), 225–244.

Performing Arts Center of the Free State (PACOFS). (2022). Council members. http://pacofs.co.za/wp/?page_id=15961

Peterson, B. (1990). Apartheid and the political imagination in Black South African theatre. *Journal of Southern African Studies, 16*(2), 229–245.

Playhouse Company. (2022a). *Council members*. https://playhousecompany.com/?page_id=1652

Playhouse Company. (2022b). *Love Africa, love theatre*. https://playhousecompany.com/?page_id=970

Shaw, J., & Rodell, R. (2009). Music strategic framework (Final Report). Gauteng Sports, Arts, Culture and Recreation, Johannesburg: Gauteng Provincial Government. http://www.gauteng.gov.za/government/departments/sport/Documents/Provincial%20Strategies/Gauteng%20Music%20Strategic%20Framework%20%20FINAL%20DRAFT.pdf

Sikes, M., Campbell-Zopf, M., Goldstein, J., & Lawson, W. (2006). *The appreciative journey: A guide to developing international cultural exchanges*. Columbus Arts Council.

Sirayi, M., & Nawa, L. (2014). Cultural policy and arts management curriculum in South Africa's education system: Lessons for good governance. *South African Journal of Higher Education, 28*(5), 1643–1662.

Snowball, J. D. (2005). Art for the masses? Justification for the public support of the arts in developing countries–two arts festivals in South Africa. *Journal of Cultural Economics, 29*, 107–125.

SOS Support Public Broadcasting (SOS Coalition). (2015, June 18). *Written representations by the SOS: Support public broadcasting coalition on the ICASA position paper: Review of regulation on South African local content: Radio and television and ICASA draft South African music content regulations and ICASA draft South African television content regulations.* https://www.icasa.org.za/uploads/files/SOS_170406_053119.pdf. Accessed on June 18, 2015.

State Theatre. (2022). Council & executives. https://statetheatre.co.za/about-us-page/

Sud, N., & Sánchez-Ancochea, D. (2022). Southern discomfort: Interrogating the category of the global South. *Development and Change, 53*(6), 1123–1150.

Tembe, B. (2022, July 13). Mzansi National Philharmonic Orchestra will be a national asset that should be applauded. *Daily Maverick.* https://www.dailymaverick.co.za/opinionista/2022-07-13-mzansi-national-philharmonic-orchestra-will-be-a-national-asset-that-should-be-applauded/

The International Organization for Migration (IOM). (2023). Key migration terms. https://www.iom.int/key-migration-terms. Accessed on January 15, 2023.

Thomas Rome. (2018). Biography. https://thomasrome.com/biography. Accessed on January 29, 2023.

Tsumele, E. (2022, November 25). Viva Amapiano!: It makes its debut at market theatre, replacing popular annual jazz programme, potentially forcing sitting rearrangement. *City Life Arts.* https://citylifearts.co.za/viva-amapiano-it-makes-its-debut-at-market-theatre-replacing-popular-annual-jazz-programme-potentially-forcing-sitting-rearrangement/?fbclid=IwAR0Ui7jj2G8xLKg9Zox2rSFXQIX97JmRhGfjMpUOL jmMAjNcivnlSM60-aA

UnisaVideos. (2022, April 11). Music in South African cities. [Video file]. https://www.youtube.com/watch?v=fPtA6Z63r00&list=PLEvmG7KulyAUOGhbRCWRVoFS_swZMdg7Q&index=3

Van Graan, M. (2019, May 14). *On the creative industries in the South African context.* Future Africa Seminar [PowerPoint slides]. University of Pretoria.

Vanderschuren, M. J., Phayane, S. R., & Gwynne-Evans, A. J. (2019). Perceptions of gender, mobility, and personal safety: South Africa moving forward. *Transportation Research Record, 2673*(11), 616–627.

Vermeulen, D. (2009). *Implementing music in an integrated arts curriculum for South African primary schools.* DMus Thesis, University of Pretoria.

Vos, S. (2016). *South African Jazz and exile in the 1960s: Theories, discourses and lived experiences.* Doctoral Thesis, University of London.

Walters, L. (2011). *Moshito and small enterprise development.* DMus Thesis, MA Research Report. University of the Witwatersrand.

Wolfe, P. (2019). Women in the studio: Creativity. In *Control and gender in popular music sound production.* Routledge.

Women in Music. (2022). Our Story. https://www.womeninmusic.org/our-story

Chapter 8

To Understand Solidarity Through Hip-Hop Culture in Haiti

Sandy Larose

Université Laval, Canada

Abstract

Since its inception in the 1980s, solidarity has been one of the structuring elements of Haitian hip-hop. In this sense, what an artist could not do on his own for lack of financial means, peer groups enable him to achieve. Given Haiti's precarious socioeconomic context, the possibility of mobilizing more friends and colleagues makes it easier to cope with financial worries and other difficulties. Drawing on material from 36 in-depth semi-structured interviews, this chapter examines practices of solidarity and mutual aid in the world of hip-hop in Port-au-Prince. Drawing on Becker's theory of the art world and Soulet's theory of solidarity, this chapter analyzes the artistic practices through which rappers develop forms of solidarity and mutual aid to cope with various financial and social difficulties. I seek to understand the way rappers organize themselves, which can be likened to the Haitian *konbit*, a form of solidarity that emerged in the aftermath of independence and continues to this day. This study shows that hip-hop strengthens the social bonds between rappers in working-class neighborhoods, where lifestyles are based on solidarity and mutual aid.

Keywords: Hip-hop; solidarity; working-class; Haiti; youth

Introduction

Since 1982, across Haiti, hip-hop music has become a channel for expressing the social demands of young people challenged by the critical conditions of society, as well as a space for building solidarity. This chapter aims to show the potentiality of hip-hop culture as a space of solidarity creation. First, I will focus on hip-hop culture, its emergence in Haiti, and the different elements that make up this

Accessibility, Diversity, Equity and Inclusion in the Cultural Sector, 117–131
Published under exclusive licence by Emerald Publishing Limited
doi:10.1108/978-1-83753-034-220241018

movement as a space to express solidarity. Several rappers have put in place strategies to face the financial challenges and precariousness of daily life in Haiti. Second, I seek to understand how solidarity impacts the practice of hip-hop. This chapter stems from both participant observations and semi-structured interviews, to answer the following question: to what extent is solidarity important to Haitian rappers within the context of poverty?

Hip-hop emerged at an important period in Haiti's social and political history. This period was marked by crises in which the Haitian people expressed new social and political aspirations: the desire to end the Duvalier dictatorship and establish democracy. One of the first Haitian hip-hop songs, *Sispann* (1986), exemplifies the democratic aspirations of the time. In this song, George Lys Herard (a.k.a. Master Dji) played an excerpt from Pope John Paul II's 1983 speech during his visit to Haiti on a loop: "Something has to change!" Starting from that point, Hip-hop beginning is doubly marked by its ability to convey popular demands and evoke feelings of belonging. Sociopolitical discourse was often at the heart of Haitian hip-hop. The songs of Master Dji and the group Haiti *Rap and Ragga* show the sociopolitical character of the first period of this art in this country. These songs inaugurated the beginning of the movement in Haiti, and hip-hop became a space of solidarity.

Haitian hip-hop is not only characterized by the freedom of expression, but also by the political nature of the messages it conveys, which have also found their way into artistic practice. In this trend, some artists present themselves as committed to the cause of the weakest, denouncing social injustices of all kinds. This is by no means a new fact in Haitian music. Therefore, hip-hop was perceived by young people, especially from working-class neighborhoods, as a protest movement that incorporates Haitian cultural forms and shows a real sensitivity to the needs and desires of the lower class people (Faustin, 2020; Jean-Pierre, 2019; Larose et al., 2022; Lizaire, 2018; Price, 2006). Within this culture, the artist communicates and exposes his sociopolitical vision, but he also decodes the illogic, paradoxes, and realities to make them comprehensible through an exercise of consciousness inherent to his cultural and artistic practice. In this context, Jean-Pierre believes:

> Rap music, represented mainly by Master Dji and the Les Frères Parent, surprised many young people. The success of Politik Pam by Master Dji and Gade Kandida by the Parent Brothers attracted many fans of this music. They waited for the decade of the '90s for this music to become one of the masters in this field. (Jean-Pierre, 2002, p. 120)

In Haiti, art and politics often go hand in hand to pave the way for the emancipation of the people. Prior to the 1990s, during the early 1960s, there existed a movement known as "engaged songs," whose objective was to defeat the Duvalier dictatorship (Averill & Bouyssou, 2000). Even before that, music in Haiti was often seen as a political act to revive profound national issues. This explains why Haitian music is so thematically rich. Merceron summed this up in

1978 when he said, "Haitian music sings of hope, revolt, protest, irony; it is a music that criticizes social injustices but remains, despite everything, a music of love and beauty" (cited in Dauphin, 2014, p. 179).

This chapter is divided into four distinct sections. In the first section, I will explain what hip-hop is and introduce the framework I will use to understand the interviews. In the second section, I will explain the methodology of the research. The third section will describe the evolution of Haitian hip-hop in the context of post-dictatorship. Finally, the fourth section concerns the findings of the research.

Hip-Hop as Youth Culture of the Ghettos

Hip-hop describes a new emerging culture in the ghettos (Fernando, 2004). It referred to neighborhood parties (commonly known as block parties) that were often impromptu and had a double aspect of celebration and protest, which was expressed in the motto of hip-hop that has since become popular: "Peace, Love, Unity, and Having Fun." The 1970s marked a very important turning point in the history of US popular culture and music. For some, it was a Cultural Revolution, as popular music of the time was an expression of the social change that Western societies were undergoing (Askin & Mauskapf, 2017; Largey, 2006; McAlister, 2002). Hip-hop contributed to this revolution in many ways, combining a political aspect with an impetus for community engagement. Since its emergence in New York's South Bronx in the early 1970s, it has been a vehicle for self-expression, self-affirmation, and a space to reclaim rights for young Black Americans.

In the 1970s, the initiators of this movement stressed the need for the youth of the ghettos to unite to defend their rights. In this sense, hip-hop was born from the awareness of the marginalization of a part of the US population, especially Black people, who used it to make their voices heard. The Black man, "determined to become visible and gain the rights he was entitled to, had no choice but to leave the ghettos and take to the stage to make his voice heard". In this context, hip-hop expresses a discomfort felt by underprivileged people. Zidani thinks:

> The Bronx, the famous neighborhood in New York, was the scene of the birth of this movement. After the deindustrialization in the '70s, this part of the city became a real ghetto, where violence and drugs reign and most of the inhabitants are unemployed. This poorest population is mainly composed of African Americans and Mexicans. At the same time, President John Kennedy and Malcolm X had just been assassinated, and the Vietnam War and its collateral damage were at their peak. Thus, African American youth organized in the ghettos and gave rise to a protest movement: the Black Panthers. (Zidani, 2019, p. 18)

In the same way, another author reported:

> I always had an understanding of teachers such as the honorable
> Elijah Muhammad, Minister Louis Farrakhan and in the '60s
> watching the Black Panthers, Martin Luther King, Jr. and the
> rest of our great leaders that were doing a strong knowledge thing.
> So, by pulling all factions together we made this whole cultural
> movement called hip-hop. (Woods, 2010, pp. 38–39)

Nowadays, hip-hop is an immense phenomenon not only because of its diversity, its artistic practices, its geographical distribution, but above all because of the place it occupies in the daily life of young people (Atsena-Abogo, 2016; Béthune, 2004; Fernando, 2004). Béthune defined hip-hop as "an attitude, a way of thinking, a feeling, a worldview" (2004, p. 43). Hip-hop is a lifestyle in the sense of Giddens (1990). It is a way of life for many young people around the world. People who practice hip-hop differ in the way they talk, walk, sing, etc. In short, hip-hop allows people to see life in different ways, and live a freedom based only on their own experiences. Forthemore, Giddens' (1990) definition of "lifestyle" intersects with the evidence of solidarity in Haitian Hip-Hop, namely "the individual [rapper]'s constant concern to make the choices he or she makes in different areas" of social life. As a space of identity building, Hip-hop allows young people to carry out their own biographical development in an environment that has become more uncertain and riskier, like Haiti. For this reason, most youth who engage in hip-hop are often considered deviants (Giddens, 1990), but they live according to some rules of solidarity.

Theory Framework to Understand the Solidarity in the Hip-Hop

For the Marxist movement, "Solidarity derives from the consciousness of a common condition of oppression and a common possibility of emancipation" (Sebastiani, 2004, p. 21 in Soulet, 2004). Durkheim distinguished two forms of solidarity, the "mechanical solidarity" is "observed between individuals linked by their similarities (same beliefs, same values)", contrary to "organic solidarity" is based on the differences between individuals and their complementarity. The analysis of the research data will show that the ethical content of solidarity among rappers is the struggle against social and economic inequalities.

In the Haitian context, hip-hop is a field propice to express solidarity and mutual aid. To understand the dimension of solidarity in this culture, I will draw on Becker's perspective of the art world as "a cooperative network in which the same people work together regularly, connecting participants in an established order." An art world consists of the activity of all these cooperating people (1999, p. 99).

For Jolin (2007), solidarity is applied to human life, in the sense that "all men and women on Earth are interconnected and, to strengthen their own humanity, owe each other mutual aid." This is an important aspect of our analysis, as it enables us to understand how rappers from some neighborhoods or different sectors of hip-hop can come together to help each other economically and in the creation of their artistic works. For his part, Raymond Chappuis (1999) saw solidarity as a form of *solidity* of social interactions that can strengthen communities. In this context, "nothing is more solid than the interhuman bond that is part of the genetic equipment of man's being." I conceive solidarity in an ethical perspective that "incites everyone to be responsible for themselves and others" (Chappius, 1999, p. 6). According to Soulet (2004), solidarity is a moral requirement that creates a synergy essential to maintaining social cohesion. The interaction through solidarity and mutual aid could be seen as a lifestyle for most people living in working-class neighborhoods.

Method and Research Design

This chapter follows an inductive approach to refine the object of study based on field data (Creswell, 2014; Lamoureux, 2000). I rely throughout this research on the epistemological position requiring the researcher to take the discourse of actors seriously (Boltanski, 2008; Piron, 2017). François Dubet also suggested that the individual must be considered like an "intellectual" and an "actor capable of consciously mastering, to a certain extent at least, his relationship to the world" (2007, p. 105). For Piron (2017), this kind of research must focus on the local context and the understanding of the people and their practices. This relationship with the world is achieved through the actor's discourse. In my approach, I see a person who practices hip-hop as "someone who possesses ideological and interpretative resources that allow them to understand their world and that cannot be ignored by the sociologist" (Dubet, 2007, p. 225).

I conducted this research from June 2019 to August 2020 in Port-au-Prince, the capital of Haiti, which is also the most populated commune in Haiti. This city has been home to most Haitian hip-hop groups and rappers since 1982. I conducted my doctoral research in several neighborhoods in the capital; the most prominent are Delmas, Pétion-Ville, Centre-ville, Tabarre, Martissant, La Saline, and Carrefour. To recruit interview respondents, I posted an advert on social networks (Facebook and WhatsApp) and in selected media (through hip-hop shows broadcast in the capital), indicating the profile for which I was looking. Potential participants were invited to contact me by phone, instant messaging, or email. The recruitment notice specified that participants had to live in a working-class neighborhood and have posted an online recording of a song in the political hip-hop category with over 10,000 views, i.e., popular songs. Most of the interviewees were recruited by the snowball method, i.e., they were referred to me by third parties, notably by other hip-hoppers.

To examine the influence of solidarity on hip-hop practice in Haiti, I adopted a qualitative research approach. I conducted 36 semi-structured interviews (34 men and 2 women) with participants aged between 19 and 35 years. The duration of the discussions varied between 45 and 90 minutes, I conducted some in the artists' neighborhoods and others in the local recording studios such as *I am music*, *G-One-King's* in downtown Port-au-Prince, *Die Nasty's studio* in Cité Castro, and sometimes in a bar where the atmosphere was calm enough. Initially, I asked the participants about their backgrounds, to find out how they became rappers, and then we discussed how their artistic practices have evolved over time. I also asked them about the difficulties they encountered, and how they imagined their role as a rapper in their community. Solidarity appears as very important in all the aspects of the conversations with Haitian rappers in the context of poverty.

Using both thematic content analysis (TCA) and critical discourse analysis (CDA), my analysis consisted of three different stages. The first stage consisted in transcribing all the interviews completely. Based on the actual content of the interviews, I drew up a list of recurring themes. This phase of the interview analysis is to determine the categories to enable me to make comparisons and bring out singularities among the experiences and issues of the different participants. I assigned a theme to each passage deemed relevant to the kinds of solidarity which characterized Haitian hip-hop, and the analysis brings out the essence of what the rappers said during the interviews.

The second stage involved grouping the themes and subthemes. After reading the corpus, the next step was to codify it into meaningful themes to answer the research question. I assigned a theme to each passage deemed relevant to the research. The themes were then grouped according to recurrence, to distinguish general categories and groups together the elements to be compared. I tried to see how some visions were apprehended by different rappers, depending on their background, ideology, and rap style. This stage enabled me to better organize the corpus so that I could find my way around and better understand how the content and ideas were structured.

The third stage is about interpreting the meaning of the discourse by mobilizing elements of context about the rapper's neighborhood of origin or residence, the situation in the country, the sociocultural context, and the evolution of the hip-hop movement. This step involves interpreting the "subjective meaning" that the hip-hop world holds for the rappers, considering the context in which it is embedded.

Hip-Hop: Between Independent and Commercial Production

Commercial hip-hop is when the artist is funded by organizations, private, or governmental groups for the production, reproduction, and distribution of his work. The artist may also participate in the promotion of products, etc. This trend is called ultraliberalism (Cardet, 2017) and is part of a perspective to improve the image of the rapper to sell his or her records. Thus, "The most important thing in this genre of music is the image of the artist, not the music itself" (Faustin, 2020, p. 39). In the Haitian context, the term "commercial" has often been used pejoratively to describe a certain perversion of hip-hop or a departure from its primary goal, which many believe should be to denounce and criticize the social and political system. In this kind of hip-hop it is very difficult to talk about solidarity and resistance between the rappers.

For itself Independent hip-hop is the type of music in which the artist is not supported by a record company and produces his music with his means and with the help of his relatives or friends. In this way, the artists are free to produce their lyrics as they "really" think about the society, economic system, and politics of the country. The difference between these two visions lies in the treatment of the subjects and the way they perceive solidarity. Very often, underground artists are known for the depth of their discourse. One often gets the feeling that the independent artist has no inhibitions. In this form, hip-hop appears as a free art in which the artist wants to engage as a spokesperson for the community. Hyppia (2016) has shown that art is essentially a miracle, and that a song can awaken consciousness if it is free of constraints. When hip-hop is self-funded through solidarity, the message is often exposed, i.e., rappers name indexical political actors or economic elites involved in corruption or other criminal affairs. This is a common practice among groups like Masters (1999), Règleman Afè Popilè; and artists like 27 Protestataire or 35 Zile embody this trend. There is no way for an underground artist to survive in Haiti without solidarity and mutual aid. There is a spirit of solidarity that has shaped the different generations from Master Dji to the last generation of hip-hop in Haiti. I observe a kind of collective consciousness that leads hip-hop artists to share their knowledge and wealth through the different collaborative networks that have emerged since the 1990s and 2000s.

Sociocultural Understanding of Solidarity in the Haitian Hip-Hop

In the interviews, participants spoke spontaneously of various forms of solidarity they had used during their careers, both at the studio and in their neighborhoods. In some cases, Haitian rappers turned primarily to friends, colleagues, relatives, and family members to raise money to record their songs. Many rappers have developed strategies to cope with the financial challenges and uncertainty of everyday life in Haiti.

Regardless of the generation to which they belong, rappers engage in nonprofit organizations to support specific social causes. Like M18, some participants such as M34, M15, M7, and M6 are very involved in social activities, "I use my status to raise awareness in the community. Sometimes I am called a goodwill ambassador" (M18). Several rappers are volunteers in private or public organizations in the country. Some of the artists I met advocate for children, women victims of violence, or other vulnerable groups in Haitian society, such as small street vendors or farmers: "For several years I have been advocating for people with reduced mobility, and I also support other causes. As a rapper, I have a mission" (M35). That helps them find some contracts to participate in public shows or to do some advertising for these organizations.

Cooperation and solidarity seem to be two important elements for the individual practicing hip-hop in Haiti, so it is important to examine them to understand the rappers' vision and sociopolitical engagement. The rappers interviewed mentioned their practice of solidarity with other actors in the community. One participant explained:

My albums are the result of an important collaboration with other rappers and musicians from the community such as Soldado Razo, Lou Piensa, Aza, Don Roy, ABG, Jawess, Mawon Ann Di, Vanessa Jeudy, Tafa, D-Fi, BlayZ, Samba Zao, Izil and many others. I have also participated in various projects such as A5, Retrouvay, Zansèt, Rockfam, Kilè li ye, Of Ghandi, Le métronome, Fouchard Crew, etc. We know the Haitian proverb: unity is strength. "L'union fait la force" [men anpilchay pa lou]. This is the spirit of hip-hop (M3).

For those who believe in the values of Hip-Hop, helping others is a duty: "It is always a pleasure and at the same time a necessity to participate in the projects of other brothers and sisters in the area" (M15). In turn, the artist has a moral obligation to participate when others are working on his project. If an artist breaks the logic of exchange and refuses to collaborate with others in return, this quickly becomes known in the community. Therefore, a moral sanction is provided for the one who does not respect these inviolable principles: "No one will want to work with you anymore. In Creole, we say that you are a drawn card [*kat make*]" (M34). In this context, it should also be noted that mutual aid, cooperation, and solidarity are values in the Hip-Hop Declaration of Peace:

> "Hip-Hoppas" are encouraged to share their resources. Hip-Hoppas are encouraged to give as much and as often as possible. It is the duty of every Hip-Hop to contribute as much as possible to alleviate human suffering and eliminate injustice. Hip-Hop is respected at the highest level when Hip-Hoppas respect each other. Hip-Hop culture is preserved, maintained, and developed when Hip-Hoppas preserve, maintain, and develop each other.

These discourses give reason to Soulet (2004) who considered solidarity as a moral duty. Sometimes it seems difficult for some rappers to collaborate or cooperate. Collaboration in hip-hop is not without conflict either, but it is "the relationships between actors that count" (Becker, 1999). Those who refuse to help are still in a relationship mode and have their reasons for not cooperating (Conway et al., 2021). But generally, unconditionally making one's talent available to others is a notable fact in hip-hop. One participant believes that collaborating with some of the biggest names in Haitian rap has benefited his career:

> I was influenced by some artists, but they were not necessarily my friends. In short, they are artists I used to listen to, like K-libr, G-bobby, and many others. I have always listened to the best rappers. That's also the case with DRZ, I always listened to him. Blaze One became one of my favorite artists. I especially liked his way of developing the themes, his style, etc. His way of doing things is unusual. For example, I had the opportunity to participate in his

album called "Decolonization." [...] That helped me a lot. [...] It filled me with pride that this artist, whom I love so much, allowed me to participate in his album. One day, I am sure he'll be involved in one of my projects as well. It's good to collaborate. Everything becomes easier. I have collaborated on several projects and several artists also collaborate on my projects (M1).

The analysis of the material shows that the forms of solidarity in hip-hop are very similar to the Haitian *konbit*, a form of solidarity that developed in the countryside, especially in rural communities. This form of solidarity emerged after Haitian Independence in 1804, when slavery was abolished, peasants who owned a piece of land and had no money asked peers and other residents of the community for help in cultivating the land. In return for the help received, a moral debt was created that obligated the person who was helped to help others in return, indefinitely. In *konbit*, resources are also pooled to cook a meal for those working, but there is also singing or dancing to entertain those working in the fields. Even today, a variety of activities take place at a *konbit* site, and each actor must contribute to the success of the day. All contributions, in whatever form, are of equal value. Thus, as a practice of *bossales* (people who identify themselves to African culture and denied the Western culture) in Haiti, the *konbit* is close to the dynamics of Becker's Art Worlds in its cooperative dimension. What rappers call "collabo" in the language of hip-hop, for example, is a model of this kind of collaboration, as it involves the joint efforts of several rappers to make a colleague's musical project a success. Sometimes some rappers cooperate to develop activities that allow them some financial autonomy.

Solidarity and Collaboration Between Haitian Female Rappers

The participation of female rappers in the projects of their male counterparts can also be observed. In this sense, I observed several female artists in other collaborative projects called "Cyphers." In Haiti, several projects of this type have been created by Marina 107 and others, sometimes involving only female artists such as Burning, DS, Tracy Magic, Niska, UX, Tracy, Keemberly, Dona, and others. In other cases, they are mixed cypher projects that involve male and female rappers from the same sector or crew. To make their personal album, the female rappers are also supported by other rappers in the community. A female rapper explained, "In 2015 I collaborated with Piwo Records for my solo project, and this project involved several artists from the community. It was a great experience, and I learned a lot in the process. At the same time, some of them were not even my friends before" (F2). However, it is a challenge to bring together people who did not know each other before and were not used to working together.

Marina 107, whose real name is Ann Raina Cynthia Jean, is a Haitian rap promoter who believes in the importance of solidarity between women to thwart machismo. That is why she created her studio to help people, especially women, in the Haitian hip-hop scene. "I created the studio because I wanted to help women artists," she explained. Many of female rappers are victims when they try to record a sound. "The maestro makes more of an effort to sleep with them than to produce them. And once they've passed through their bed, there's no respect" (Francique, 2021). Solidarity between women appears very important to face the poverty conditions and other challenges in Haiti.

Solidarity: A Way to Face Financial Challenges

I observed solidarity also on a financial level; an artist does not necessarily need a lot of money to realize his musical project. An artist confirms: "When we have a project, a fundraiser is usually organized among friends and family members. And we find money to help each other" (M31). We can observe this is a form of economics in different areas of hip-hop. This is understood as "a set of enterprises organized in the form of cooperatives, mutual societies, associations or foundations, whose internal functioning and activities are based on the principle of solidarity and social benefit." Another participant said: "The money spent on my project is collected among us. This is the way it is for everyone." He admits that in his neighborhoods many of them are producers, arrangers, and instrumentalists. So, it may well be that collaboration is easier to practice in an environment where people know how to identify the human resources available to each other to put them together to satisfy the needs of people. In that way, Chappius (1999) is right when he thinks of solidarity as a *solidity* of relationship between members of a community, because the way rappers process could help them to solidify their relationship together and face social inequalities. Among rappers who identify as activists, solidarity on the financial level is even more notable.

> As an activist and rapper, I must be a role model for others. I must practice what I ask others to practice. Solidarity is a principled position. We share, we help, and we support each other. Hip-hop is a space for experimentation. I've experienced that too when I go to the provinces. Hip-hop is like that. We decide together. Everyone participates. Everyone collaborates as they can. People are united and they share everything. They are stronger when they are united with each other (M33).

These practices are part of the solidarity or social economy because it is an enterprise that combines hybrid resources (market, public, and nonmonetary) and democratic leadership. "Union is strength," which is also the flagship phrase in the Haitian flag, inspires hip-hop. I observed that when an artist prepares a project, he gathers several other artists from his crew and other crews to sing one or more verses. This phenomenon is called "featuring" or "collabo" which is short for collaboration. It seems like this solidarity practice also fits with the vodou culture in Haiti. A participant explained:

Vodou is my life. I was born into vodou; it is the practice of my life. Vodou taught me everything I could learn in the academic world. It was vodou that led me to read certain authors, and it also taught me about forms of solidarity. It was through vodou that I read Marx. Vodou helped me understand the dimensions of history and my spiritual dimensions. Vodou is my way of life, the absence of private property in everything to do with food, or other notions like we're all one... It was vodou that taught me all that. Vodou is my life and solidarity is the way to live it. Vodou is the space that has enabled me to meet people from all walks of life, astral people, material people, and spiritual people. I'm in the practice, in the traditions... I am vodou and vodou is solidarity (M3).

For this rapper, vodou inspired solidarity and other life principles. This artist was raised with his grandmother, and his parents were mostly Marxist progressivist and vodou adepts. His style, known as Vodou rap or rap *rasin*, is not only politically charged but also carries a spiritual message of solidarity between working-class people.

In addition, it is necessary to equip oneself economically: "Saving and making money to meet our needs is important. This allows us to remain authentic" (M34). The rappers' commitment is to denounce inequality and the misery of the poor. Some rappers talk about money as if they must justify or apologize for making, having, or wanting it. Among rappers who call themselves activists, the question of money remains taboo. But they speak about solidarity with pride. Finally, the solidarity experience is a way to legitimize themselves as rappers in the community and to be in concordance with their discourse and values.

The collaboration between rappers is also effective in other aspects of daily life. Depending on the proximity and the needs, some rappers may sleep, eat, and stay for a period of time at another rapper's home. It is important to emphasize that the studios and the working-class neighborhoods are places for experimenting with forms of solidarity that are, in some ways, a reflection of peasants' practices in Haiti, i.e., *konbit* which is linked to the Haitian Vodou.

Several participants believe that the collaborations are intended to help them cope with economic and financial difficulties. For instance, after hours of work in the studio, they collect money to prepare food for dinner together or to buy beers and meats. These modes of practice can be likened to a bossal identity in the logic of Haitian identity duality (Barthélemy, 1989, Célius, 2013). It should be remembered that the *bossal* identity is one close to an ancestral African and Indigenous identity founded on solidarity. The Haitian *konbit* is the result of this "bossal" culture, which advocates the pooling of potential to help each other in the community. This is opposed to the *Creole* identity, which seeks to get closer to the West and to make people more individualistic and selfish.

Solidarity, Sharing, and Mutual Aid: Another Way to Resist and Exist

On several occasions at *I Am Music* studio, I have observed a rising of funds at mealtimes to provide food and drink to be shared among the rappers. Sometimes they send someone to buy and bring them to the studio, other times they prepare their own food. Trying to ask them about this practice, I realized that this has been going on for a long time in some hip-hop communities in Haiti: "Food should not be considered as private property, it is fundamental to us. We must share" (M3). This same spirit of solidarity was observed at *the Die Nasty Records* studio in Cité Castro. M19 also reports that he has experienced this practice in his neighborhood, in Delmas 40 B: "Often the young people collect money on the spot to prepare or buy food. When we want to drink alcohol too. It's the same principle when we want to make a song and publish it. We are brothers and sisters." In many Hip-Hop communities, people with very few economic resources get together to party after long days of work among promoters, rappers, producers, beatmakers, sound engineers, fans, etc. It is linked to two fundamental principles of the Haitian vodou and *konbit*, namely "*Manje kwit pa gen mèt* [cooking-food has no owner]" and "*men anpil chay pa lou* [unity is strength]". This form of solidarity is characteristic of Haitian life during the 19th and 20th centuries. Even today, the *konbit* remains a form of solidarity that still tries to bring hope to peasant areas, for example, in the Ouanaminthe locality during the construction of an irrigation canal in 2023.

Solidarity observed in the recording studios is also practiced in most neighborhoods. It is a tradition of rappers from the 1990s, like Easy One and other rappers from the older generation. A rapper of the new generation explained how solidarity and mutual aid work in his community.

> My neighborhood has influenced my songs and my life a lot. For example, in my first mixtape, I talked about the hunger we experienced in our neighborhood and the solidarity drive we had to put in place to face it. Sometimes, each of us brought something: rice, peas, oil, etc. This food is an example of collaboration. We get together to make something to eat for everyone. We must do it. It's the same way, we help each other. We look for jobs for each other. We all put together the money we earned during our work week, and we made a community meal. That's my reality. All of that has influenced me greatly (M12).

These acts of solidarity demonstrate the cordiality and mutuality that characterize Haitian Hip-Hop. Solidarity is most often observed between members of the same sector or group and between underground artists. However, I observe a kind of solidarity even during tragic events. For example, the death of a rapper. In this context, rappers from different sectors can eventually join to make farewell songs in tribute to the deceased. This was the case during the tragic demise of rappers from the Barikad Crew in 2008, G-Bobby Bon Flo in 2011, or Money

Honey Mike in 2022. For Soulet (2004), this form of cooperation, whatever its nature, can give rise to a synergy that is essential for maintaining social cohesion.

Conclusion

In this chapter, the analysis highlights different kinds of solidarity encountered in hip-hop. Solidarity seems inherent to hip-hop practices in Haiti. For some rappers, rap music is used as a fighting strategy, and for others, it is part of a struggle for recognition. There are various strategies adopted by rappers to keep the movement alive, and we could think of "solidarity" as an inclusive strategy that allows them to survive.

Solidarity is felt at all levels, from preparing an album in the studio, managing daily life, pooling to carry out projects, etc. I was surprised, during the research, by a majority of the participants I met who were invested in "carrier" projects, structuring for their network, which allowed them to improve their professional conditions and those of their colleagues. This is done either through direct involvement within their neighborhood or by starting collective projects, projects to disseminate works (YouTube Channel, television shows, etc.), an ad hoc collective for a signature sale, or a collabo project among others.

I observed that the environments where rappers live, like the ghetto, the studio, and the street, are spaces of resistance against poverty and social inequalities. These spaces are also repositories of a set of discourses evoking lifestyles, claims, expressions of hatred against the capitalist system, etc. The notion of "system" is often evoked to refer to government officials, and economic elites who have no plans to facilitate the inclusion, equity, and emancipation of Haitian youth.

Organizing economically and taking power will allow them to better fight against social exclusion, the poor distribution of wealth, and especially against the exploitation of the underprivileged masses living in working-class neighborhoods. For some young people, especially activist rappers, the practice of political rap reveals a need for social recognition and positioning, because it allows them to better position themselves in the context of exclusion that characterizes their country.

Most Haitian rappers who fight for freedom and prosperity of Haiti sees themselves as activists actors in the sense that "while activist interaction is a material contribution to the movement and solidarity, it is also an exchange in words, communication, and the possibility of speaking, in other words, about whom one is and what one lives" (Cingolani, 2003, p. 128). Speaking as an instrument of denunciation makes hip-hop a place where people meet who have a lot in common, especially the sense of solidarity. This desire to speak about oneself, but also about one's country, one's fellow people, and one's fellow citizens, is above all a desire to be someone in the city is not possible without solidarity.

Based on this research, I conclude that solidarity is part of the life of Haitian rappers. In Hip-hop culture, mutual aid and solidarity are based on the principles of direct action like cooperation, mutual understanding, sharing, and solidarity.

Solidarity is not charity, but it is seen as a way to build a solid community, fortify new social relations, and resist as rappers and activists against unjust systems of power and social inequalities.

References

Askin, N., & Mauskapf, M. (2017). What makes popular culture popular? Product features and optimal differentiation in music. *American Sociological Review, 82*(5), 910–944. https://doi.org/10.1177/0003122417728662

Atsena-Abogo, M.-T. (2016). *La réception du hip-hop chez des rappeurs afro-québécois dans la ville de Québec: appropriation intersectionnelle de problématiquesmultidimensionnelles.* These de doctorat, Université Laval. Corpus UL 32777.pdf (adobe.com).

Averill, G., & Bouyssou, R. (Trad). (2000). Dechoukaj en musique: la chute de la dictature haïtienne. In *Critique internationale* (Vol. 7, pp. 127–142). Culture populaire et politique.

Barthélemy, G. (1989). *Le pays en dehors.* Deschamps.

Becker, H. (1999). *Les Mondes de l'art.* Flammarion.

Béthune, C. (2004). *Pour uneesthétique du rap.* Klincksieck.

Boltanski, L. (2008). Institutions et critique sociale. Une approchepragmatique de la domination. *Tracés. Revue de Sciences humaines,* #08 | 2008, 17–43.

Cardet, M. (2017). *L'effroyable imposture du rap.* Hugoetcie.

Célius, C. (2013). Créolité et bossalité en Haïti selon Gérard Barthélemy, L'Homme *[En ligne],* 207–208. http://journals.openedition.org/lhomme/24697. https://doi.org/10.4000/lhomme.24697

Chappuis, R. (1999). *La solidarité. L'éthique des relations humaines.* Presses universitaires de France.

Cingolani, P. (2003). *La république, les sociologues et la question politique.* Editions La Dispute.

Conway, J. M., Dufour, P., & Masson, D. (2021). *Cross-border solidarities in twenty-first century contexts: Feminist perspectives and activist practices.* Rowman and Littlefield.

Coquery-Vidrovitch, C. (2018). *Les routes de l'esclavage:histoire des traitesafricaines, VIe-XXesiècle.* Albin Michel.

Creswell, J. (2014). *Research design: Qualitative, quantitative, and mixed methods approaches* (4th ed.). Sage.

Dubet, F. (2007). *L'expérience sociologique.* La Découverte.

Faustin, H. (2020). *Influence de la culture hip-hop sur le comportement des adolescents du quartier populaire de Raboteau aux Gonaïves. [Mémoire de licence].* Port-au-Prince: Université d'Étatd'Haïti.

Fernando, J. S.-H. (2004). *The new beats, musique, culture et attitudes du hip-hop.* Kargo &l'Eclat.

Francique, J. (2021). *La femme discrète qui enregistre les chansons de vos trappeurs préférés.* Ayibopost.

Giddens, A. (1990). *Modernity and self-modernity: Self and society in the late modern age.* Polity Press.

Hyppia, D. (2016). Réflexion situationniste sur l'art révolutionnaire et l'art capitaliste, Nouveaux Cahiers du socialisme, Les territoires de l'art, no. 15, Hiver.

Jean-Pierre, J.-S. (2002). *30 ans de musique populaire haïtienne: les moments de turbulence (1960–1990)*.

Jean-Pierre, J.-S. (2019). *Musique populaire haïtienne et pratiques culturelles*. Media tech.

Jolin, L. (2007). Une éthique de la solidarité et de la responsabilité. *Téoros*, *26*(3), 3–5. https://doi.org/10.7202/1071000ar

Lamoureux, A. (2000). *Recherche et méthodologie en sciences humaines*. Etudes vivantes.

Largey, M. (2006). *Vodou Nation: Haitian art music and cultural nationalism*. Press of Chicago.

Larose, S., Rahill, G., & Faustin, H. (2022). Hip-hop Music and Teens from Haiti's Gonaïves Commune. *Actes du colloque étudiant/Art et Politique: les enjeux de la localité dans les pratiques culturelles*. https://www.lastt.inrs.ca/wp-content/uploads/2022/01/ActesColloqueEt.pdf

Lizaire, J. E. (2018). *La pratique du rap enHaïti: un lieu d'autoformation et de subjectivation*. Thèse de doctorat, Université Paris 13.

McAlister, E. (2002). *Rara: Vodou, power and performance in Haiti and its diaspora*. University of California Press.

Piron, F. (2017). Méditation haïtienne: répondre à la violence séparatrice de l'épistémologie positiviste par l'épistémologie du lien. *Sociologie et sociétés*, *49*(1), 33–60. http://hdl.handle.net/20.500.11794/16322

Price, E. (2006). *Hip-hop culture*. ABC Cliot.

Soulet, M.-H. (2004). *La solidarité [Texte imprimé]: exigence morale ou obligation publique?* Academic Press.

Woods, C. (2010). *"The challenges of blues and hip-hop historiography" Kalfou, Inaugural issue* (pp. 38–39). Temple University Press.

Zidani, M. (2019). *Une autobiographie au cœur de l'entrepreneuriatrap: imaginaire, monde et style*. Thèse de doctorat, Université Paris-Saclay.

Section 3

Visual Arts

Chapter 9

Collections and Inclusion: A Portrait of Museum Initiatives in Quebec and Ontario

Mélanie Boucher[1]

Université du Québec en Outaouais, Canada

Abstract

Today's museums seek to be more representative of the social diversity of the communities they serve. Their intention is reflected not only in the exhibitions and public programs they offer, but also in the development of their collections and their uses. The colonial origins of the collections and the gaps in the major art historical narratives that have provided their primary interpretations are more widely recognized. Several recent initiatives are revisiting, for inclusion purposes, the principles of exemplarity, uniqueness, internal organization, and material integrity on which acquisition and its valorization were until recently based. This chapter considers current initiatives undertaken over the past 10 years by the Musée d'art contemporain de Montréal, the Montreal Museum of Fine Arts, the National Gallery of Canada, and the Musée national des beaux-arts du Québec, in the development and use of their collections. It is done by taking as support three strategies established by Maura Reilly (2018) to foster inclusion in exhibitions. These three strategies – areas of study, revisionism, polylogue – are loosely adapted for collections. The four museums were selected for (1) the interest of their initiatives, (2) the complementarity of these institutions, in terms of collecting scope (contemporary, national, or "encyclopedic"), institutional status (major museums, two provincial, one federal, one nonprofit) and location (in major cities, metropolis, or capital city), and their

[1]*Note from the author* This text was written as part of the activities of the "New Uses of Collections in Art Museums" Partnership (SSHRC 2021–2028) of the CIÉCO Research and Inquiry Group. Research assistance was provided by Jessica Minier, a doctoral student at the École des arts et cultures at Université du Québec en Outaouais, assisted by Isabelle Lamothe, a master's student in museology and art practices at UQO. The text was written in French. Translated with www.DeepL.com/Translator (free version)

Accessibility, Diversity, Equity and Inclusion in the Cultural Sector, 135–150
doi:10.1108/978-1-83753-034-220241020

partnership in the "New Uses of Collections in Art Museums" Partnership (SSHRC 2021–2028) of the CIÉCO Research and Inquiry Group. This portrait, through the collections of four institutions, is paradigmatic of a fundamental transformation in Canadian art museums.

Keywords: Art museum; visual arts; equity, diversity and inclusion; collection; collection policies; permanent exhibitions

Introduction

The artist collective Guerrilla Girls presents their 1989 work *Do women have to be naked to get into the Met. Museum* as being the work "that changes it all" (Guerrilla Girls, 2023). This unlimited edition poster reproduces on its left side the reclining nude on a drape of Ingres' painting *La Grande Odalisque* (1814), by affixing this lascivious body – a neoclassical ideal offered to the male gaze – with a gorilla head. The animal's profile sticks out its fangs, seeming to look accusingly at the text that is reproduced in the center-right part. The text consists of a question – Do women have to be naked to get into the Met. Museum? – and statistics. In this New York museum, one of the most important in the world and which has a collection described as encyclopedic, "less than 3% of the artists in the modern art sections are women, but 83% of the nudes are female." This work changed everything by granting an almost instantaneous notoriety to the Guerilla Girls. It also changed everything by revealing, publicly for the first time, the role played by museum collections in maintaining patriarchy. The method adopted by the Guerrilla Girls does not leave room for misinterpretation. On the one hand, only the rooms devoted to the modern and contemporary art collections, which are dedicated to the study, collection, and exhibition of works made from 1890 to the present, are counted. The low representation of women in these rooms cannot, therefore, be the result of a history in which they did not participate. As Linda Nochlin argues in *Why There Have Been no Great Women Artists* (1971), what is missing in the modern and contemporary eras is not women artists but a system suited to the recognition of art that is not white and male. On the other hand, the Guerrilla Girls employed statistics by drawing numerical data whose objectivity cannot be debated.

More than 30 years after that Guerrilla Girls release, is the situation different? Museums and other art exhibition spaces have changed their practices, but equity remains a target, as Anne Dymond demonstrates in *Diversity Counts: Gender, Race, and Representation in Canadian Art Galleries* (2019). Her study seeks to quantify the gender of living artists whose work was exhibited in solo shows between 2000 and 2010 in nearly 100 Canadian contemporary art institutions. Solo exhibition is a reliable indicator of artist success and institutional values (Dymond, 2019, pp. 8–9). Throughout the study, more attention is paid to large-scale institutions and major metropolitan areas. Various findings emerge. Notably, the analysis of internal data is often flawed, and the focus on marginalized groups tends to be at the expense of other equally marginalized groups.

Anne Dymond concludes that it is important for the institution to produce and analyze internal data to counteract unconscious bias and adopt equitable practices.

Re-establishing the numbers to achieved individual exhibitions of living artists that are representative of diversity is a goal that can be reached relatively quickly. The museums and other galleries spaces exhibition programming is generally established over periods of 2–5 years. Changing the composition of collections, on the other hand, takes longer and is more difficult to accomplish. For example, the Metropolitan Museum of Art (2023) Department of Modern and Contemporary Art claims to have committed to this task in 2012: "Modern and Contemporary Art has greatly expanded and diversified its collections, especially through works by women and artists of color." The figures with which the Guerrilla Girls update the same year *Do women have to be naked to get into the Met. Museum?* are however not conclusive. Less than 4% of the artists in the modern art sections are women, while 76% of the nudes are female (Guerrilla Girls, 2023).

Several factors explain the difficulty of changes within collections. The first factor is the composition of a collection, which is inalienable and is made by accumulation. For example, a collection made up of 5,000 works assembled over a period of 50 years would take a long time to change, at an average rate of 100 works added per year. A second reason, intertwined with the first, has to do with collection development methods, which have nothing to do with this mathematical equation. Museum collections are first and foremost collections of collections, which is a little-known museum fact. Museums do not glean what they store piecemeal but remain above all depositories of donations, of private collections, which has two consequences. The first is a dependence on singular tastes, of individuals who do not acquire a priori for societal ends, but to answer very personal motivations – thirst of knowledge, desire of aestheticism, material enrichment, and prestige (Pomian, 1978). The second is the difficulty of rehabilitation in this context. The quantity and impact of donations on a collection will always be greater than the quantity and impact of purchases made by the museum. Changes to historical collections, on the other hand, are also more difficult to make than changes to contemporary art ones – due to the limited availability of works, sometimes only accessible to the wealthy.

In sum, making art museum collections more inclusive and representative is a long-term investment that involves new practices, and statistics are a measure of this. However, statistics are not the only indicator that must be considered to measure change. In systems comparable to Canada's, most museums are state institutions or largely publicly funded. Their social function justifies their raison d'être. The development of a collection that is a better reflection of the community has become a must, helped by a social pressure that is positively received by many professionals. This pressure is sometimes even seized as an opportunity to legitimize positions that were previously difficult to justify. Thus, several recent museum initiatives are revisiting the principles of exemplarity, uniqueness, internal organization, and material integrity on which the justification of acquisition and the development of works in the collections were traditionally based, with a view to inclusion, equity, and diversity. The colonial origins of the collections and the shortcomings of the grand narratives that provided their primary interpretations are more widely recognized.

This chapter provides a portrait of new collection practices in Canada by focusing on four major museums located in large cities in Quebec and Ontario: the Musée d'art contemporain (MAC, Montreal), the National Gallery of Canada (NGC, Ottawa), the Montreal Museum of Fine Arts (MMFA, Montreal), and the Musée national des beaux-arts du Québec (MNBAQ, Quebec City). Three of the museums are federal (NGC) or provincial (MAC, MNBAQ) state institutions, while the fourth is a museum that is also largely publicly funded (MMFA). Their collections are described as encyclopedic (NGC, MMFA), national (MNBAQ – Quebec art collection) or periodic (MAC – contemporary art). The MAC, which is dedicated to contemporary art, is the most recent of the four museums. It was created in 1964 by the Liberal government of the time, which wished to open up to modernity. The two encyclopedic museums, the NGC and the MMFA, were respectively created in 1880 and in 1860, in the humanist and colonialist spirit of the first museums. The MNBAQ opened in 1933, during the economic crisis. Its original mandate was to provide French Canadians (a highly marginalized social group at the time) with a museum that valued their culture and heritage.

The analysis is mainly based on three types of production: strategic plans, acquisition and collection management policies, and permanent exhibitions. These productions offer reliable data, as all museums of the same caliber periodically renew their strategic plans, their "collections" policies, and their collection exhibitions. Only documents in application and exhibitions in progress during the writing of the text (2022–2023) are considered. These products provide a three-part picture of the current relationship to the collection. The strategic plans situate the collections within the museum project. They are used to determine the role of the collections in achieving institutional goals. The acquisition and collection management policies help to determine in greater detail the desired directions and reorientations for each collection, according to collecting areas – periods, disciplines, territories, and others. They also help to put into perspective the initiatives undertaken for the public, with a view to immediate impact. In this regard, permanent exhibitions, which are intended to reflect institutional mandates, remain the best indicator.

These productions will be referred to over the next few pages, according to their relevance to the cases studied. These cases are presented in three sections. Each of these sections reinvests a strategy developed for more inclusive and representative exhibitions, which are increasingly being employed, as several study trips over the last 5 years to the United States, Canada (British Columbia, Ontario, Quebec) as well as France and Italy have made it possible to measure. They are not new to the development of temporary exhibitions; specific research should be undertaken to trace their origins and evolution in relation to these exhibitions. They are, however, resolutely new to permanent exhibitions. These strategies were identified by Maura Reilly, in *Curatorial activism: Towards an Ethics of Curating* (2018). The first considers the area of studies strategy in relation to the MAC's collections. The second strategy, revisionism, serves the study of the MNBAQ's collections and the particular field of modern art. The NGC's Indigenous and Canadian Art exhibition is also examined. The third section reinvests the polylogical strategy, which will be explained in the final section of the chapter. The MBAM is considered in this section, in several fields of collecting as expressed in the gallery and in its collection management policy.

Area of Studies and MAC Collections

Exhibitions that adopt the area of study strategy focus on a marginalized group that they value. For example, they might focus on 19th century women, queer representations, or LGBTQ artists; visible or religious minorities in America; Native art; or cultural reclaiming. These thematic exhibitions highlight specific groups by encouraging the emergence of new issues, names, and realities. New canons and benchmarks are added to the traditional canons and benchmarks of art and its history, which are traditionally on display. The divisions, which are mainly racial, geographical, or gender-based, have the advantage of filling a gap and will continue to do so until the exhibits as a whole become diversified, equitable, and representative. Maura Reilly recognizes disadvantages to this strategy. Colonial and patriarchal referents remain the yardsticks. Additionally, this strategy ghettoizes and flattens the differences of individuals who are labeled in this way (Reilly, 2018, p. 25). They adopt strategic essentialism, as Gayatri Spivak's conceives it. Groups are driven to act as if they have a stable identity, to create belonging and have political clout.

In the realm of collecting, the area of study approach is to establish or develop a field of collecting (e.g., Etruscan art, sculpture, works on paper, or 20th century) so that it forms a more accurate reflection of the corresponding society. A collection of 19th-century Canadian art, for example, would tend to be a mirror of the society living in Canada in the 19th century. This approach, which is difficult to apply to collections of ancient art (where the pool of works is limited), is more easily applied to collections of recent works. In this respect, the Musée d'art contemporain de Montréal is committed to being a "living tableau" of its times. Its strategic plan reflects this commitment, to develop a socially representative collection (2018, p. 4):

> With nearly 8,000 works in its extensive collection, the MAC strives to express plurality, diversity and parity in all its activities, as well as in its acquisitions. As a living picture of the present era, the MAC has the privilege of bearing witness to the essential role of contemporary art in our society and of encouraging the appropriation of this testimony by all audiences.

The collection of approximately 8,000 works is the smallest to be considered in this chapter. It is also the most recent. It was established in 1964, with the opening of the museum, and includes works from 1939 to the present. The MAC is a provincial government corporation that is committed to reflecting ministerial orientations by adhering, in addition, to three specific commitments of the Quebec Government's Cultural Policy (2018):

(1) Enrich the range of activities and services adapted to the needs of people with disabilities, immigrants, or people living in poverty that government cultural corporations offer.
(2) Offer Quebecers free access to museums one Sunday per month.
(3) Implement actions aimed at equality between women and men and equity in the cultural sector.

The third commitment targets gender parity. The institution's Collections Management Policy, published in 2017, also identifies Aboriginal, Inuit, and diverse artists (2017, p. 9). On the institution's website, as consulted 6 years after this publication, the commitment is reinforced (2023a):

> The MAC's collection is representative of Quebec's cultural diversity, including First Nation artists. It is on the lookout for active practices outside the general metropolitan area and respects gender equality.

Marie-Ève Beaupré, former collections curator at MAC, maintains an over-view of donations and purchases through the use of a register (2023). This work tool identifies the disciplines (painting, photography, and other) as well as the origin (artist, gallery, and donor) of acquisitions. It also makes it possible to establish the proportion of artists whose works are entering the collections for the first time – the proportion, which was 67% in 2021, rises to 12% the following year. The register highlights the gender identity according to the male/female binary, the cultural origins, and the geographical distribution of the artists.

In 2022, the MAC launch the MACRepertoire (2023b), which increases the discoverability of the collections. Its content is developed from the collections database and all works are listed. The MACRepertoire work site is also used for open data content sharing. A shared dataset is, according to the research, a first for an art museum in Canada. Several portraits of the collections are thus made available, according to the fields queried, which are grouped into four entries: artists, works, events, and publications. The "artists" and "works" entries group together the fields that provide the portraits. The "artist" entry includes 18 fields. The "nationality" field makes it possible to query and visualize the collections according to several parameters relating to cultural identity. It is, for example, possible to determine the ratio of artists of Canadian origin versus those of other origins, to determine the ratio of artists identifying themselves with one origin versus those identifying themselves with several origins. The "work" entry has 24 fields filled in. The "category," "cultures," and "provenance" fields are the main fields to measure representativeness. Since data on artists and works can be cross-referenced, detailed portraits related to cultural identity are made available. In contrast, gender representation is limited to the male/female binary. And it is not possible, for example, to interview Black, Indigenous, and People of Color (BIPOC), physically disabled or neurodiverse artists. The limitations of the tool are also related to disciplinary categories. Each work is attached to a single discipline, when in fact many acquisitions are more complex. The category "performance" is not referenced. Yet the MAC has works related to this disciple, as evidenced by the collections exhibition *Acts of Presence*. This exhibition, curated by artist Manon de Pauw, focused on "the notions of gesture, manipulation, position taking, and action" (2023b). It included 45 works, originating from or related to performance, grouped in the categories of photography, video/film, mixed media, printmaking, drawing, sculpture, and fiber/paper/material. This limitation for performance highlights the impact of past documentary patterns on current data production – the "performance" category is not referenced because it is not in the in-house data, which has been migrated into the MACRepertoire. The information that could be derived from a "performance" category would otherwise be useful, particularly in capturing the dynamics of forces in gender representation within collections. Performance art was recognized in the 1960s for the role played by women and became associated with feminism in the 1970s.

To promote inclusion and diversity, classification systems need to be enriched, as exemplified by the MACRepertoire and also demonstrated by Hannah Turner in her book *Cataloguing Culture* (2022). However, the addition of categories can also be a hindrance. Patrick Steorn's study of how to include queer in museum collections is eloquent on this subject: "reclassifying objects not only serves to make them available for searching in a database, but adds new historical strata and frames objects so that they fit into established categories" (2017). The author explains that adding – for example, homo-, bi-, or heterosexual – would probably reduce the possibilities of finding queer in collections. In a similar vein, the categories "photo" and "video" come to limit the recognition of "performance."

Revisionism in MNBAQ and NGC

The revisionist approach consists in multiplying the perspectives and increasing the diversity of the groups that are represented in the subject that is exhibited. The revisionist exhibition *Picasso. Figures*, presented in 2021 at the Musée national des beaux-arts du Québec, for example, included a reflection on bodily diversity and a portrait of the women who shared Pablo Picasso's intimacy, many of whom were artists. This exhibition was revisionist, in the sense that Maura Reilly (2018, pp. 24–25) defines it, by inscribing and keeping peripheral the marginalized perspectives (women, non-normative bodies) within the dominant discourse (Picasso):

> While revisionism is an important curatorial strategy, it nevertheless assumes the white, masculinist, Western canon as its center and accepts its hierarchy as a natural given. So, within a revisionist strategy, a fundamental binary opposition is retained,

which means that the Other will always necessarily remain subordinated. And as feminist literary theorist Elaine Showalter cautions, "the feminist obsession with correcting, modifying, supplementing, revising, humanizing, or even attacking male critical theory keeps us dependent upon it and retards our progress in solving our own theoretical problems." We must also be wary of a revisionism that becomes a kind of homage.

The revisionist approach applied to collections is particularly useful for historical bodies of work, which change with difficulty. Since its development can be reoriented, but it remains inalienable, the collection is a lexicon with which the museum must compose and recompose its narratives. The revisionist approach thus favors a contextualization of past choices, while opening up to the perspectives of our times. It serves to multiply the temporalities at work within a single corpus.

The Musée national des beaux-arts du Québec is responsible for more than 36,000 works, from the beginnings of the French colony to the present day. In its collections management policy (2017), the MNBAQ acknowledges its responsibility to review the collections and its difficulty in opening them to a plurality of voices. The policy states in an addendum the lack of in-house expertise:

> The art of the First Nations or of the various cultural communities established in Quebec and especially the contribution of these different groups in the field of contemporary art, particularly around issues of cultural identity, is little or not present in the collections. The MNBAQ must pay particular attention to these different areas of development so that the permanent collection can eventually bear significant witness to them. The development of these segments of the collection requires particular expertise (knowledge of the milieu and the market) and calls for external support.

The policy remains traditional in its approach. It formulates the desire to develop decorative arts and design, graphic arts, installation, digital works, painting, performance, photography, protocols, sculpture, and video/film (2017, p. 4). For greater equity, representativeness, and diversity, it does not target objectives by collecting field. The MNBAQ's permanent collections are structured into seven fields, which are organized according to a chronological, disciplinary, and identity-based logic that obliterates the presence of works by non-Quebec artists, First Nations, and established Quebec diversity (2017, p. 8): ancient art (origins to 1850), ancient art (1850–1900), modern art (1900–1950), contemporary art (1950–2000), current art (2000 to date), decorative arts, and Inuit art. In the policy, only the presentation of modern art (1900–1950) identifies the purchase of works, as a lever to fill gaps – "prioritize major purchase(s) annually that fill significant gaps in this collection" (2017, p. 7).

Between 2014 and 2018, the modern art (1900–1950) curator, Anne-Marie Bouchard, curate the redeployment of the institution's permanent exhibitions, from the origins to the 1950s. The five rooms – *Believing, Becoming, Feeling, Imagining,* and *Challenging* – are grouped under the title *350 years of artistic practice in Québec* (2017–2023). They are varied in style but take a revisionist approach. They offer new perspectives on the collections, stemming from a work in which Anne-Marie Bouchard questions the museum's capacity to present a nonexclusive history of Quebec art (Bouchard, 2023, p. 139):

> The MNBAQ collection has less than 4000 works by women artists out of a total of more than 36 000 pieces. In the absence of systematic classification, it is impossible to generate similar statistics on Aboriginal or diverse artists, but we can safely say that their numbers are certainly lower than those of women artists. Therefore, it is also not possible to cross-reference these data to derive intersectional statistics. Faced with this observation, two questions arise: Are we condemned to rewrite the same history over and over again? Can we be an institution engaged in our community if the history we celebrate is exclusive?

These questions echo the introductory panel of the first room – Believing – which begins with the recognition of this heritage (MNBAQ, 2023):

> Although various cultures were present over the millennia before the arrival of the French, in what is now Quebec, the fate of Native people in Quebec's history is reflected in the history of the Musée national des beaux-arts du Québec's collection. Colonial culture became the benchmark some 500 years ago, and our collection was built on the basis of New France.

This recognition of bias may seem secondary to those unfamiliar with museums' appetite for producing narratives to showcase their assets. For specialists, this recognition of the shortcomings of the permanent exhibition represents a paradigm shift. Until recently, the aim of the permanent exhibition was to enhance the collections, with forms of affirmation linked to their completeness.

To further explore the contribution of the revisionist approach to *350 years of artistic practice in Québec*, the example of *Challenging* is rich in many ways – the French and original title, *Revendiquer*, literally means "claiming." This room covers modern art (1900–1950) yet does not include in its title key figures such as Riopelle, Borduas, or Pellan. It relies on the verb of action, which invites the taking of a stand. As we've seen with the first example provided by the Guerrilla Girls, modernity is a key period for gender equity (male/female) within collections. Under the heading *Revendiquer*, the artists whose works are featured in the exhibition (e.g., their manifestos), as well as any individual who asserts his or her rights, are suggested to speak out. From a thematic yet open approach, the exhibition also amplifies the place given to women. As curator Anne-Marie

Bouchard (2020) explains at a conference, the purchasing priority set out in the General Collection Management Policy is given to women. In the exhibition, this target is achieved by increasing the ratio of women artists whose works are exhibited. It is also achieved through the number of female figures shown, most of whom are neither nudes nor generic representations. These are women, whose names are given and whose singularity is underlined by the treatment of the painting. The portraits occupy a central position, within a spatial layout that opens up to multiple perspectives. The play of holes multiplies visibility. The serial hanging maximizes the volume of space given to the "women" group in the exhibition.

The National Gallery of Canada offers a second example, in the permanent exhibition Aboriginal and Canadian Art (2017). The exhibition covers a period dating back 5,000 years to 1967. As its title suggests, the exhibition focuses on Aboriginal and Canadian art. It aims to give equal visibility to both groups, in rooms that are dedicated to the valorization of the "cultural wealth of the country" (NGC, 2023). The words of the title, as it was at the opening (*Canadian and Indigenous Art*), have been reorganized in this sense. Their inversion is an acknowledgment of self-determination and territorial precedence. It follows the alphabetical order, which is not hierarchical. The exhibition texts also recognize the importance of language for that of the Peoples. All the texts of the exhibition are in the two official languages of the country (English and French), and the texts of the indigenous objects are also translated into the languages of the groups to which they belong – the translations have involved the museum working with several communities. The exhibition is established on a double principle of chronological and circular organization. The productions of European descent are presented in a strict chronology, while the indigenous productions are not limited to this linearity. In the first room of the exhibition, for example, works by contemporary indigenous artists coexist with millennia-old objects. Long-term loans, to fill gaps in the Aboriginal art collections, are also inserted into the exhibition. The strategic location avoids any form of marginalization in the space, which would suggest the marginality of Aboriginal people. In one of the last rooms, this choice even filters the visibility of paintings from the 1950s to 1960s, by Borduas and Riopelle among others. The expected distance, to fully appreciate their large format, is prevented by the height of the display cases in which the Inuit sculptures are placed. The height of the display cases is not determined by the size of the objects inserted. It establishes an equivalence of formats with the paintings.

350 years of artistic practice in Québec, at the MNBAQ, and *Indigenous and Canadian Art*, at the NGC, are both revisionist exhibitions, because they aim for a better balance between groups – female/male at the MNBAQ, aboriginal/non-native at the NGC. As mentioned above, this approach to exhibition can also contribute to the invisibilization of other marginalized groups. At the MNBAQ, the contribution of women is increased, unlike that of First Nations. At the NGC, one of the five pillars of the strategic plan is to "place Indigenous ways of being and knowledge at the heart of our actions." (NGC, 2021, p. 12) The exhibition *Indigenous and Canadian Art* foreshadows the importance of this goal, which is reflected in all areas of collecting – "with an Indigenous lens, to provide a welcoming experience for Indigenous communities." The contribution of women is, by comparison, little recognized. In *Indigenous and Canadian Art*, there is a room dedicated to this group. It's grafted onto the main corridor and can go unnoticed in the tour. This location has the effect of compressing the presence and reducing it in time to a single period in the story.

Polylogue at MMFA

The polylogue exhibition [also call relational], defined by Maura Reilly, reinvests Susan Hardy Aitken's work on the relationship of women to the art historical canon. The term "polylogue," borrowed from Julia Kristeva, invokes a multi-voiced game, a kind of creative bricolage "that would disrupt the monological, colonizing, centristic drives of 'civilization'" (Reilly, 2018, p. 30). Other terms have been adopted to refer to exhibitions that operate through the clash of encounters between objects and fields of knowledge. Werner Hofmann (1989) describes these exhibitions as "worksites of ideas," in that they bring together several perspectives that may conflict with each other. André Gob and Noémie Drouguet (2006 [2003], p. 109) describe as confrontational the exercise of grouping together in an exhibition works and other objects that are not normally associated (an 18th-century African mask with a Renaissance painting, for example). Titles of temporary exhibitions in the collections that are based on the power of unusual encounters – the *Counterpoint* series at the Louvre or *Intrus/ Intruders* (2008) at the MNBAQ (Boucher et al., 2008) – point in the direction of a disruption of balance.

The polylogue exhibition is historically linked to the permanent exhibition. Its first occurrence is record in 1947, with the insertion of a work by Pablo Picasso by the artist at the Louvre Museum (Labonté, 2023). This practice, which gained popularity in the mid-1990s (Francblin, 1995), most often involves the contemporary artist, who is brought to reinvest historical collections under various carte blanche formulas (Boucher & Chevalier, 2018; Boucher et al., 2023). The event effect that was initially sought had little to do with the decolonial approach that motivates many of today's polylogue events. In this respect, the example of *Indigenous and Canadian Art* is atypical because it is not motivated by the shock of the new association but by the relationship to circular time of the First Peoples. The polylogue exhibition has become over the last decade a widespread way of doing things, with which the use of collections has intensified. To the insertion into the permanent exhibition, initially of works that were not part of it and for a short period of time, has been added the contribution of loans for longer periods and then a certain shuffling of existing categories within the collections.

The polylogue exhibition is anchored in the The Montreal Museum of Fine Arts. This art museum is the most committed to the polylogical approach in Eastern Canada, even beyond, since the opening of the Claire and Marc Bourgie Pavilion in 2011. To display some 600 works from the Quebec and Canadian art and fill in the gaps in the collection, curator Jacques des Rochers acquired contemporary Aboriginal works that were inserted into the room devoted to the 1700–1880 period. The introductory panel states that these works offer "a critical and retrospective look." The formula of acquiring recent works to revisit the past is repeated in 2016, with the Michal and Renata and Hornstein Peace Pavilion. This pavilion houses more than 750 works from "Old Masters to contemporary art" (MMFA, 2023) and incorporates, on its six floors, 10 creations by contemporary artists that enter into dialogue with the other works from collections that are on display – including about 100 Horstein couple donations. The opening, in 2019, of the Stéphan Crétier and Stéphany Maillery wing for the arts of the Whole World is also the most ambitious case in this sense. The 10 new galleries include 1,500 works and objects from Africa, Asia, the Mediterranean, the Middle East, Oceania, and the Americas. The All-World Wing focuses on a dialogue between ancient cultures and contemporary artists.

The MBAM's pavilion projects reverse the expected relationship between acquisition and exhibition. Certainly, exhibitions are sometimes programmed to support an acquisition. Permanent exhibitions, however, are normally conceptualized in relation to existing collections. Here, contemporary art is acquired for the exhibition.

The most recent Collection Management Policy (MBAM, 2022), published last year, reflects the approach adopted, which consists of correcting a past through the contribution of the contemporary. This policy makes a particularly significant shift in the polylogical approach, from the exhibition to the collections themselves. The MBAM owns more than 45,000 works. Its permanent collections are divided into 12 collecting areas: (1) Quebec and Canadian Art; (2) Aboriginal Art; (3) Art of the Americas; (4) Art of Oceania; (5) Art of Asia; (6) Art of Africa; (7) Greek, Etruscan, and Roman Art; (8) European Art; (9) Modern International Art; (10) Contemporary Art; (11) Decorative Arts and Design; and (12) Graphic and Photographic Art. The MMFA's policy incorporates a goal of equity, diversity, and representativeness in most fields, which are organized by period, discipline, territory, and cultural group. This widespread integration, in most fields, remains an exception, in the Policies studied. As the MBAM's Policy is more recent than the others studied, it is an indicator of recent change in collection development. With the exception of European art, all the MBAM's collecting fields, organized according to a territorial and cultural logic, actually integrate the recognition of gaps and the updating with contemporary art.

For Asian art, it says, for example:

> Objects will be added to this collection only if they fill a gap in the collection and if their clearly established provenance conforms to current museological, legal and ethical guidelines. In the spirit of the transhistorical, cross-cultural, and thematic reorganization of the collection, the Museum will continue to acquire contemporary Asian works of a polysemic nature that link the past and the present.

For the arts of Africa:

> The focus will remain largely the same, but special attention will
> be given to acquisitions that will promote a challenge to the
> relatively static image of African art conveyed by the historical
> collections. Acquisitions will be made in dialogue with acquisitions
> in contemporary African art. Before any acquisition, thorough
> research will be carried out to verify the provenance of the
> works and to ensure that the wishes of the communities of origin
> are respected.

Collections that are organized by period or by discipline also aim for greater
equity, by targeting gender equity. For contemporary art, it is written, for
example, "inclusion and parity remain a priority for the development of the
collection"; for graphic arts and photography: "the MMFA favors diversity and
wishes to establish gender parity in its future acquisitions."

In relation to the above, a bimodal approach is adopted by the Museum to
equity, diversity, and inclusion in its collections: fields organized by periods and
disciplines adopt a holistic, revisionist approach that targets gender. The fields
organized by territories and cultures, on the other hand, take a polylogical
approach with the contribution of contemporary art. The use of contemporary art
certainly favors the reappropriation by the targeted groups of a collection that
they did not compose. It identifies however the artists of these groups (Asian,
African...) to a unique and same reality.

Conclusion

In *Curatorial Activism*, Maura Reilly demonstrates with numbers the inequity of
gender and cultural groups represented in museums in London (Tate Modern)
and New York (Whitney Museum of American Art, Museum of Modern Art
[MoMA]). About MoMA, the author writes (17):

> In 2004, it re-opened its greatly expanded exhibition spaces and
> unveiled the reinstallation of its prestigious permanent collection,
> featuring art from 1880 to 1970. Of the 410 works in the fourth-
> and fifth-floor galleries, only a paltry 16 were by women. There
> were even fewer works by non-white artists, and those who were
> given exhibition space were segregated in a single room dedicated
> to Diego Rivera and Mexican muralism. A dash through the same
> exhibition galleries in 2015 and 2016 revealed improvements, but
> continuing problems. In 2014, as a testament to the museum's lack
> of inclusiveness, the editors at ArtSlant started a rumor – an April
> Fool's joke, in fact – that MoMA would devote the year 2015
> entirely to women.

Last year, in 2022, MoMA's permanent collection was changed to be more diverse. A Canadian women artist's work was featured, which I observed was a first. The exhibition unfolded without a clear chronology or emphasis on the big names (Pablo Picasso, Andy Warhol, and others). To me, as a scholar who visits MoMA sporadically, this revisionist exhibition in the largest museum of modern art marked a paradigmatic shift from the mid-2010s to the beginning of this decade. As we have seen at the MAC, MNBAQ, NGC, and NGCAM, this shift toward greater inclusion in the collections is also reflected in the decisive contribution made by contemporary art. The contribution of contemporary art to opening up the collections has been recognized. The Guerrilla Girls are contemporary artists who were also the first specialists in the visual arts and museum world to decry the heteronormativity and masculinity of modern and contemporary art museum collections. The artist's contribution to combining works from a priori distinctive universes has also been recognized in the diversification of collections (Boucher & Chevalier, 2018; Boucher et al., 2008, 2023). Exhibitions of artists in collection exhibitions follow in the footsteps of Fred Wilson's *Mining Museum* (1989) at the Maryland Historical Society in Baltimore. They highlight, sometimes disturbingly, the colonial and patriarchal biases of collections. We need to separate the development of collections from this critique by artists and from exhibitions with a temporary focus, in order to take the measure of the change that has recently taken place in the development of collections with a view to greater equity, diversity, and inclusion. In this respect, the four museums considered in this chapter have chosen to make changes to their collections and their development, in line with their mandates and the adjustments that can be made in the short term. These changes are a response to the sociopolitical demands of the moment, as much as they are a response to the new freedom offered to museum professionals, who no longer have to carry out their work according to the doxa-like ways of presenting works. At the same time, they foreshadow new problems: the essentialization of groups newly included in collections and the transposition of present-day values onto a past that is once again shaped by ideals. The integration of contemporary art into historical collections, for example, smooths out and standardizes both periods and disparities of perspective, which begs the question, What will be the impact of today's imperfect fixes, some of them permanent, on the future of collections?

References

Beaupré, M.-E. (2023). *Register. Grey literature.* Musée d'art contemporain de Montréal.

Bouchard, A.-M. (2020). Conférence d'Anne-Marie Bouchard, conservatrice au MNBAQ. In Conférences publiques de la maitrise en muséologie et en pratiques des arts de l'UQO, 25 novembre.

Bouchard, A.-M. (2023). Douter pour se réinventer: la transparence et l'activisme en milieu muséal. In M. Boucher, M. Fraser, & J. Lamoureux (Eds.), *Réinventer la collection. L'art et le musée au temps de l'évènementiel* (pp. 125–140). Presses de l'Université du Québec.

Boucher, M., Béland, M., Bergeron, Y., Drouin, D., Grandbois, M., Martin, M., Montpetit, R., Porter, J. R., & Ouellet, L. (2008). *Intrus/Intruders*. Québec, Musée national des beaux-arts du Québec.

Boucher, M., & Chevalier, G. (2018). Introduction. In M. Boucher & G. Chevalier (Eds.), *Carte blanche. Muséologies, les cahiers d'études supérieures* (Vol. 9, no. 18).

Boucher, M., Fraser, M., & Lamoureux, J. (2023). Penser l'actualité des collections: une introduction. In M. Boucher, M. Fraser, & J. Lamoureux (Eds.), *Réinventer la collection. L'art et le musée au temps de l'évènementiel* (pp. 1–17). Presses de l'Université du Québec.

Dymond, A. (2019). *Diversity counts: Gender, race, and representation in Canadian art galleries*. McGill-Queen's University Press.

Francblin, C. (1995). *Exposer les collections: Le nouveau désordre des musées* (April, no. 201, pp. 31–40). Art Press.

Gob, A., & Drouget, N. (2006 [2003]). *La muséologie: Histoire, développements, enjeux actuels*. Armand Colin.

Gouvernement du Québec. (2018). *Partout, la culture. Politique culturelle du Québec*. https://partoutlaculture.gouv.qc.ca/politique/

Guerrilla Girls. (2023). Guerrilla Girls. https://www.guerrillagirls.com/projects

Hofmann, W. (1989). Exposition. Monument ou chantier d'idées? *Cahiers du Musee National d'Art Moderne, automne*(29), 7–15.

Labonté, M. (2023). Les artistes en art contemporain dans les collections: une recension depuis 1940. In M. Boucher, M. Fraser, & J. Lamoureux (Eds.), *Réinventer la collection. L'art et le musée au temps de l'évènementile* (pp. 231–330). Presses de l'Université du Québec.

Metropolitan Museum of Art. (2023). The Metropolitan Museum of Art. https://www.metmuseum.org/about-the-met/collection-areas/modern-and-contemporary-art

Montreal Museum of Fine Arts. (2022). *Politique générale de gestion des collections du Musée des beaux-arts de Montréal*. Musée des beaux-arts de Montréal. www.mbam.qc.ca/workspace/uploads/files/politique-mbam_2022-05-09_final_publique.pdf

Montreal Museum of Fine Arts. (2023). *Michal and Renata Hornstein Pavilion for Peace*. Montreal Museum of Fine Arts. https://www.mbam.qc.ca/en/the-museum/the-michal-and-renata-hornstein-pavilion-for-peace/

Musée d'art contemporain de Montréal. (2023a). *Musée d'art contemporain de Montréal*. https://macm.org/en/collections/submitting-works-for-acquisition/

Musée d'art contemporain de Montréal. (2017). *La politique de gestion des collections du Musée d'art contemporain de Montréal*. https://macm.org/app/uploads/2017/12/MAC-Politique-de-gestion-des-collections-FINALE.pdf

Musée d'art contemporain de Montréal. (2018). *Plan stratégique. Édition 2018–2022*. https://macm.org/app/uploads/2020/02/Plan-strate%CC%81gique-2018-2022_Approuve%CC%81.pdf

Musée d'art contemporain de Montréal. (2023b). *MACRépertoire*. https://macrepertoire.macm.org/

Musée national des beaux-arts du Québec. (2017). *Politique générale de gestion des collections*. https://d2u082v08vt8dt.cloudfront.net/attachments/000/188/522/original/cbf56b1ea9990e58f1677e6c7ea56830?v=1

Musée national des beaux-arts du Québec. (2023). *Believing. 350 years of artistic practice in Québec*. https://www.mnbaq.org/exposition/croire-1271

150 *Mélanie Boucher*

National Gallery of Canada. (2021). *Transform together. A guide to the National Gallery of Canada's 2021–2026 strategic plan.* https://www.gallery.ca/about/strategic-plan

National Gallery of Canada. (2023). *Indigenous and Canadian art.* https://www.gallery.ca/whats-on/exhibitions-and-galleries/indigenous-and-canadian-art

Nochlins, L. (1971). Why there have been no great women artist. *ARTnews, 22.* https://www.artnews.com/art-news/retrospective/why-have-there-been-no-great-women-artists-4201/

Pomian, K. (1978 [1987]). Entre l'invisible et le visible: la collection. In *Collectionneurs, Amateurs et Curieux. Paris, Venise : XVIᵉ-XVIIIᵉ siècles* (pp. 17–59). Éditions Gallimard.

Reilly, M. (2018). *Curatorial activism: Towards an ethics of curating.* Thames & Hudson.

Chapter 10

Beyond Fakequity: Redefining "Excellence" to Create Space for Equity

Brea M. Heidelberg

Drexel University, USA

Abstract

For many predominantly white arts institutions in the United States, the murders of Breonna Taylor and George Floyd in the summer of 2020 prompted externally initiated calls for equity work. Many of these organizations crafted equity statements, engaged in trainings, and made public displays of their intent to do different and better – however, many did not follow through on those promises (Heidelberg, 2020). While many organizations have indeed engaged in fakequity or "equity talk with no action" (Okuno Consulting, 2017), this may not explain every instance of stalled or incomplete equity action within the arts sector. In the case of fakequity, the remedy is to actually do the work of creating a more inclusive and equitable organization, rather than simply talk about it. However, if there are root causes for stalled equity action aside from fakequity, then organizations are left without guidance on how to identify and address that cause/those causes and move forward. This case examines the primary research question: what organizational practices contribute to stalled equity efforts other than fakequity? Investigating this question led to a secondary research question: what conditions help organizations move beyond stalled equity efforts? In order to address this question, I conducted a single-case study (Yin, 2014) of a midwestern museum to offer a contextualized understanding of identifying and addressing organizational elements that contribute to false starts in equity work within predominantly white arts institutions.

Keywords: DEAI; fakequity; diversity management; organizational culture, organizational excellence

Accessibility, Diversity, Equity and Inclusion in the Cultural Sector, 151–165
Copyright © 2024 Brea M. Heidelberg
Published under exclusive licence by Emerald Publishing Limited
doi:10.1108/978-1-83753-034-220241022

Introduction

This case focuses on an art museum embedded at a large university in the Midwest of the United States. Prior to engagement with a consultant, the museum worked to develop language articulating a commitment to center the experiences of marginalized people. After that initial internal work, the museum received a grant from the Institute of Museum and Library Services. This grant provided funds to hire a consultant to serve as a guide as the organization sought to engage in professional development specifically focused on diversity, equity, access, and inclusion (DEAI), evaluate organizational progress toward centering marginalized voices, and create an institutional plan to continue implementing DEAI strategies. Of special note in the call for proposals was a request that the consultant help the organization shift its institutional culture. The intended results of the engagement were to provide museum staff with the skills to:

- Create an adaptive and inclusive workplace climate.
- Increase the understanding and practice of hiring and retaining staff from marginalized and minoritized backgrounds in order to diversify the Museum's staff, volunteers, and boards.
- Apply what staff learn to their specific museum positions.
- Authentically engage people of diverse races, ethnicities, nationalities, abilities, gender identities, educational backgrounds, and income levels.
- Develop and maintain on-going relationships with a broad range of campus and community partners, especially from those whose voices are underrepresented in the museum.

The museum intended the work to run from March 2020 until November 2021 with multiple in-person elements. However, due to the Covid-19 pandemic, I completed much of the work remotely via zoom – with one in-person engagement near the end of the contract in November 2021. Due to the initial success of the work, the museum extended the contract in the first quarter of 2022 to allow for completion of the DEAI plan.

This chapter uses Yin's (2014) framework for case studies. Yin (2014, p. 16) established the importance of case context, highlighting the significance of understanding the context in addition to the phenomenon under investigation. This is particularly relevant when looking at stalled equity efforts in an organizational context when the inquiry is specifically interested in how that context may influence organizational capacity to engage in sustainable equity work. In addition to overarching research questions, Yin (2014, p. 29) encouraged propositions that help narrow the scope of focus in a case.

My preliminary review of the organization revealed that the museum did not have a readily apparent commitment to equity work. They had taken some initial steps toward creating a more inclusive and welcoming environment – Collections-focused staff spoke at length about efforts to diversify the museum collection with pride for the processes and structures that had been put into place to implement a robust plan to build relationships and community with Black, Indigenous, and

People of Color (BIPOC) artists and collectors. The museum demonstrated this internal work in some external places such as Google Arts and Culture where the museum prominently displayed artwork from BIPOC creators. However, the rest of the organization's externally facing materials did not clearly identify the museum as a space that is for everyone.

During the initial meetings, staff shared instances of stalled attempts at diversifying museum staff. A few staff members shared their efforts to get the museum to think more broadly about the many ways the museum could begin to create a more welcoming and inclusive environment through acquisitions, exhibitions, and associated programming. Staff noted that the museum did not meet attempts to diversify staff and organizational operations with open hostility or antagonistic behavior, but that attempts ultimately stalled because staff lacked direction and felt overwhelmed. On the surface, this looked similar to other organizations who talked about wanting to become more equitable, but ultimately failed to create a meaningful or lasting change (Heidelberg, 2020). However, the fact that the organization kept trying, resulting in a number of stalled attempts, prompted me to consider that there may be more to this particular context than a lack of sincerity. This resulted in the primary research question for this case: what organizational practices contribute to stalled equity efforts other than fakequity, or purposefully engaging in performative action that never becomes substantive (Belfiore et al., 2023; Okuno, 2017). The staff focus on feeling overwhelmed led to a secondary research question: what conditions help organizations move beyond stalled equity efforts?

> To begin answering these research questions, I developed the following proposition: understanding the museum's organizational culture could lead to a more nuanced understanding of the organization's equity efforts and provide insights into how to improve the organization's capacity for equity action. This led to two additional research questions: what organizational culture(s) exist(s) at the museum? And how could the organization's culture(s) potentially impact equity efforts?

Organizational Excellence

The idea of excellence has a longstanding, and problematic, history within the cultural sector in the United States. It is a foundational concept in public arts funding and informs the ways cultural organizations judge themselves and each other. The concept of artistic excellence has been a guiding principle of public arts funding, at the center of the culture wars in the early 1990s, and operated as a political weapon as the arts became further politicized in the mid- to late 1990s (McNeely & Shockley, 2006). Artistic excellence, and the arts spaces that uphold this ideal, has also been a trojan horse for ideals of white supremacy (Domínguez et al., 2020). While organizational excellence is related to the idea of artistic excellence, it receives far less scholarly attention (Voss & Voss, 2020). Organizational excellence – or, more precisely, the drive to be perceived as organizationally excellent – -prompts organizations to continually take on more – more partnerships, bigger projects, and new ventures. This push to take on more often operates independently of stalled or diminishing resources. This case focuses on the ways the concept of organizational excellence can serve as a barrier to equity work. Focusing on a museum located at a midwestern university, this case discusses the importance of including organizational culture as a factor of equity work.

This chapter highlights the issues with organizational excellence as it currently operates within the sector and discusses the way it permeates organizational culture. The chapter goes on to demonstrate why the cultural ecosystem, especially organizational leadership and funders, must thoroughly understand organizational culture – and the toll organizational excellence takes on that culture – before making any attempts to create more accessible, diverse, equitable, and inclusive organizations.

Organizational excellence has a long and fraught history in the world of nonprofit arts. In order to see the nuance of organizational excellence in the field, it is important to first understand how excellence has functioned more broadly in the artistic realm. As a foundational underpinning of gaining support for the creation of the National Endowment for the Arts (NEA) in 1965, excellence as a prerequisite for public funding has served to simultaneously quiet political critics and significantly limit who is eligible for public arts funding (Heidelberg, 2012). Public arts funders at the local, state, and national levels have continued to weaponize the concept of excellence since the inception of the NEA – treating the determinants of excellence as objective, rather than as a social process of constructing and then reifying value (Remender & Lucareli, 1986). As a result, artistic conceptualizations of excellence have focused on artistic expression stemming from white, European, able-bodies, heteronormative, and male perspectives that tend to stem from or aspire to and glorify the middle and upper classes. This creates systemic barriers to symbolic and material support for artists and artistic practices from BIPOC as well as cis women, disabled, nonbinary, and LGBTQ+ creators. While artistic excellence adopts ill-fitted notions of objectivity and attempts to apply them to modes of creativity, organizational excellence adopts ill-fitted notions of efficiency and productivity and attempts to apply them to nonprofit work.

In the for-profit realm, organizational excellence means leadership and management practices used to create a culture committed to sustained periods of high performance (Barnawi, 2022, p. 2918). This is associated with exceeding expectations for outputs, maximizing profits, and minimizing wasted financial resources. As is often the case, the nonprofit interpolation of this idea is warped and made grotesque by the misalignment of business motivations (i.e., profit) and the seemingly forgotten public good aspects of nonprofits' mission-driven purpose. In theory, organizational excellence is something to strive for – organizations should, ideally, minimize waste and work to sustain high quality in their products and services. However, this concept is operating in a capitalistic context. Therefore, in practice, the idea of organizational excellence directly contributes to and exacerbates the worst of the nonprofit industrial complex – a system designed to obscure exploitative practices by encouraging nonprofit organizations to recreate capitalistic and oppressive structures rather than challenge them (INCITE!, 2004). For the nonprofit arts, the result is an interwoven network of artistic and organizational funding practices that center Eurocentric, capitalistic ways of creating and operating. This limits the imagination and opportunity for systemic change toward more accessible, diverse, equitable, and inclusive, expression.

Many in the field have, rightfully, critiqued the white supremacist underpinnings of how the concept of excellence has been used to hoard resources among predominantly white institutions (PWIs) (Borwick, 2022; Conner, 2014; Sidford, 2011). Scholars have also paid considerable attention to defining and warning against the ills of worker burnout (Kanter & Sherman, 2016; Maslach, 2021; Olinske & Hellman, 2017). However, this case study provides value to the field by providing a direct link between the ideas of organizational excellence, burnout, and their collective impact on equity work. While artistic excellence limits what is considered worthy of public funding and other material support, organizational excellence focuses organizational attention on constantly achieving more with fewer material supports. Understanding the impact of organizational excellence on organizational capacity to successfully engage in equity work can be profound for those in organizations trying to create sustainable change as well as the funding institutions that want to support this work.

Organizational change requires energy and time. Equity work requires even more since people must grapple with their own biases and barriers to equity and then do that work on an organizational level. These realities run further afoul of organizational excellence because the time and resources necessary to create real and meaningful change do not have an immediate, tangible payoff in the capitalist terms that often serve as the intellectual underpinnings of grantmaking and final reporting. Therefore, organizational excellence can serve as a significant barrier to actualizing equity plans – even for organizations with a commitment to the work. This case demonstrates how the difficult work undoing the psychological contract of organizational excellence is a necessary step toward actualizing DEIA work.

I argue that the key to combating the negative impact of organizational excellence is to shift organizational culture. Organizational culture is the shared values and beliefs, and the associated manifestations that are established and reinforced by individuals throughout the organization. Organizational culture can be explicit in codified policies and positive or negative reinforcement of behaviors. Organizational culture can also be implicitly communicated via interpersonal interactions and the presence or absence of certain organizational artifacts or practices. While they acknowledge a lack of consensus about a set definition of organizational culture, Abu-Jarad et al. (2010) offered a list of parameters that help articulate what researchers are looking at, for, or measuring in investigations focused on organizational culture: "something that is holistic, historically determined, related to things. . .like rituals and symbols, socially constructed, soft, and difficult to change" (p. 34). Organizational culture has been linked to various organizational phenomena such as overall firm success (Shahzad et al., 2012), employee engagement and productivity, and workplace safety (Wong, 2019).

This chapter discusses the work of one organization as it recognizes, grapples with, and works to overcome the negative impact organizational excellence has had on its organizational culture and its capacity to fully implement plans to become a more accessible, diverse, equitable, and inclusive organization. Written from the vantage point of the author, who acted as an equity consultant for the organization from 2020–2022, this case study demonstrates how, even when there is organizational buy-in to equity work and material support for that work, ideological barriers such as organizational excellence can still stall efforts by having a negative impact on organizational culture. This chapter provides insights on how I worked with the museum to identify this issue and helped them chart a path forward, highlighting negative aspects of organizational excellence and providing institutionally based insights on how to implement equity-focused change.

Methodology

An organizational equity audit was the foundation of all work with the museum. The audit is a mixed-method process looking at how organizational culture is articulated and reinforced across organizational policies, interpersonal interactions, and in the behaviors that are praised, negatively judged, or corrected – all of which aligns with Abu-Jarad et al.'s (2010) overview of elements of organizational culture. The overarching guiding questions are: what organizational culture(s) exist(s) at the museum? And how could the organization's culture(s) potentially impact equity efforts?

I began by conducting a rhetorical analysis of the following organizational documents: community guidelines (developed for and by staff), gallery guides, grant proposals (dated 2018–2020), membership brochures, position descriptions for all staff, staff orientation manual, and public-facing visitor engagement materials. Analyzing the aforementioned internal documents allowed me to see communications norms and patterns, gain insights into organizational policies and procedures that already exist, and begin understanding how institutional values are articulated and reinforced within the organization. From this information, I constructed a survey designed to assess staff knowledge of current organizational commitments, policies, and management norms related to accessibility, diversity, equity, and inclusion. This process also provided organizational context that permitted me to construct a semi-structured interview protocol for staff that further delved into areas indicated as important by the rhetorical analysis: employee recruitment and onboarding, staff understanding of organizational culture, the current organizational climate (from an equity perspective), and institutional memory. Twenty-one of the 26 employees self-selected to participate in the semi-structured interviews.

The rhetorical analysis and semi-structured interviews occurred alongside three professional development workshops facilitated via zoom: facilitating equitable meetings, facilitating difficult conversations, and giving and receiving feedback. During those sessions, questions proposed live and via the chat were recorded to provide additional information about organizational context and operations.

Organizational Audit Findings

Based on survey responses and interview data, the museum had a strong market culture. This type of culture is focused more on externally validated achievement than internal processes and procedures (Cameron & Quinn, 2011, p. 44). The museum is dedicated to always doing more – more partnerships across the university and in the community, more initiatives and collaborations with artists, more and bigger grant-funded projects. There is a dual focus on quantity and quality. This kind of culture is common with staff who are dedicated to their work and desire to have broad-reaching impact. A large percentage of staff interviewed (85%) noted a very heavy workload. Interview respondents that rated their workload as manageable or moderate were predominantly hourly staff who were once overwhelmed, but then cautioned by a supervisor to prioritize their work based on the number of hours they are paid for each week.

According to respondents, when the museum proposed a new grant-funded opportunity, initiative, or partnership, its response was universally "yes." No respondents were able to readily identify a time when the answer was no, and they were unable to determine a clearly articulated decision tree for how it is determined that each opportunity is the right one for the museum. Respondents could easily connect all work to the museum's mission and desire to be a connector and a collaborative partner across the university and in the community. This information was shared with positive reactions, communicative language, and facial expressions that indicate enthusiastic buy-in, even if the impact is that staff are overwhelmed. With a small amount of imagination, it appears that everything presented to the museum is mission critical. Staff struggle to prioritize their work as a result. Universally, there was an acknowledgment that there is not enough time to complete all the work necessary. Additionally, there was organization-wide confusion about how to prioritize work. Staff routinely counted on de facto prioritization based on what was most public-facing and which tasks or projects had a looming or recently lapsed deadline.

The biggest concern with market culture is burnout. When considered in the context of the proposed equity work the organization appeared overall eager to engage in, the museum's emphasis on organizational excellence led, counterintuitively, to a series of stalled efforts and disappointment. Equity work requires time for reflection, diagnosis of root issues, and work to create and maintain change. Essentially, equity work – especially equity work done in spaces where equity was not at the core of the organization's foundation – can be hard and time consuming. Therefore, an organization with workers already overwhelmed with their regular workload are likely to lack the bandwidth to focus on shifting their current organizational culture to prioritize practices to center equity, especially since that work will not be easy and lacks the kind of deadlines that usually prompt museum staff to prioritize particular tasks over others.

In addition to a market culture, the museum also had a strong clan culture present. At its best, this type of organizational culture is like an extended family, with shared values and a sense of cohesion that promotes care for and among employees (Cameron & Quinn, 2011, p. 46). This type of organizational culture exists in organizations where people wish to hire and retain those that are already like them or those that are willing to conform. While this type of replication and mirroring can be about several identity markers, it is often most evident when the clan culture is centered on race/ethnicity, gender identity, and socioeconomic status. The visual presentation of staff on the organization's website indicates the organization is overwhelmingly white. This was confirmed in survey results, where respondents largely identified as white (92%), with only 2% representation of Asian/Asian-American and Hispanic or Latino individuals. There were no Black or Indigenous respondents, and interviews confirmed that there is no one that explicitly identifies that way currently on staff. These findings mirror staffing throughout the museum field in the United States, which tends to be white and female (American Alliance of Museums, 2022).

The homogeneity of museum staff is not limited to race. The clan culture has created a workforce that either subscribes to or is at least amenable to performing "being alike." In practice, this means individuals who identify in ways that align with most of the workforce enter and stay at the organization for extended periods. Over half of survey respondents (55%) have been at the museum for 6 or more years. Additional information gathered during interviews revealed that many start with the museum as an intern or hourly staff member and either remain in the hourly staff position for a prolonged period or work their way up through various roles. As reported by long standing staff in interviews, individuals who recognize or are told they are different appear far less likely to stay and advance within the museum. These elements of similarity and difference may appear to be solely racially or ethnically based – but elements of conflict management style, family structure, and personality fit (regarding small group formation and identity) also play a role. Individuals with caregiver responsibilities (which include children, elderly parents, or domestic partners) tend to struggle in market cultures that do not effectively consider work–life balance (Bear, 2019). At the museum, staff with a variety of caregiver roles work to shift or make alterations to their caregiver duties – often being mindful to avoid mentioning those duties at work – rather than risk not "being like" other staff members who do not have similar responsibilities.

Organizational culture impacts how people show or obscure their identities; it also impacts how power manifests and is wielded throughout the organization. In many instances, organizational culture can be stronger than structural elements introduced to the organization. Despite a relatively flat organizational structure, the museum has a strong hierarchical power structure. This became evident in staff interviews where, universally, individuals mentioned a discrepancy in the stated behavioral norms and the behavior that is permitted by staff with specific roles. Individuals with roles traditionally associated with the creative professions (e.g., curators) appear to have both a perceived and often real ability to circumvent consequences for antisocial behaviors such as yelling at colleagues during meetings, not meeting deadlines, and other behaviors that negatively impact other staff.

In addition to the obvious difference in consequence structure for creative professionals, there is consistent messaging about the importance of their work that was not present for staff working in areas such as community engagement, development, and operations. This implicit messaging about the relative value of work conducted by creative professionals in comparison to work conducted by those in other function areas created hierarchy within the museum, resulting in an "us/them" dichotomy that was present in language patterns across museum staff. This was demonstrated in "we/them" language and language that distanced curators and their work from the work of those ensuring that the museum ran smoothly. In addition to the dichotomized language, non-curatorial staff consistently displayed internalized devaluation of their own work. This was demonstrated by excessive apologies prior to stating an opinion or sharing insights that focused on everyone's position within the organization "I'm sorry, I know I'm not a curator but..."

Hierarchical power structures often replicate themselves throughout an organization and that pattern held true at the museum. In addition to the real and perceived hierarchical divide between traditionally creative roles and roles outside of that narrow definition, there are also positional (salaried and hourly; full-time staff, short-term grant funded, intern) and identity-based (caregiver status, degree status, gender identity) hierarchies that exist within those two structures. While explicit positive messages about the value of each role within the museum were universal, the same internalized devaluing language patterns existed when individuals spoke about their work in relation to the work of others along the aforementioned positional- and identity-based markers. Within the survey and interview responses, there was also confusion regarding individual roles – both the roles individual respondents held as well as their understanding of how others' roles fit into the organization and its mission.

Not Just Another Case of Fakequity

Despite past failures and stalled attempts at sustainable equity work, the museum is not just another example of an organization that claims to want to do better, but is not actually interested in discussing or questioning, let alone changing any problematic practices. Alongside organizational cultural elements that indicated concern for burnout and role confusion there were also indicators of an organization with high levels of empathy present. Museum staff consistently demonstrated community care in two distinct ways: individuals with a more manageable workload expressed concern for their colleagues with higher workloads and individuals who have not personally experienced instances of feeling marginalized expressed concern for colleagues who had. While not universal, a large percentage

(85%) of staff indicated at least two different instances of expressing care, either verbally or through taking on additional work, for colleagues. This was not limited by work function or position within the museum. Additionally, 95% of staff agreed with the following statement in the organizational culture survey: values of equity, fairness, and inclusion are modeled by museum staff. This, coupled with open-ended question responses about staff desire to see sustainable systemic change through the museum indicate ideological buy-in to the values of equity, fairness, and inclusion – despite the lack of operationalization throughout the organization. Despite survey data revealing that some mid-level staff only answered identifying questions, much of the organization felt ready and excited by the prospect of engaging in meaningful equity work. This is a distinct difference from organizations where most, if not all staff are firmly in the resistance end of Wiggins-Romesburg and Githens' (2018) diversity resistance spectrum – a clear indication of the more purposefully deceitful types of fakequity commonly seen in the nonprofit arts (Heidelberg, 2020).

Based on the organizational equity audit findings it was clear to me that the organization was galvanized to not only learn from their past mistakes and false starts – but were also aligning their desire to engage in meaningful equity work with their market culture. While staff and leadership acknowledged that equity work is on-going and that there is no set finish line, this was something they collectively wanted to "get right." While it was clear that staff was sincere in their desire to diversify staff and create an inclusive and equitable environment for internal and external stakeholders, it was also clear that staff lacked knowledge of how to begin the work. When asked whether the museum has specific policies regarding the maintenance of an equitable environment, 24% of respondents answered "yes" and a combined total of 76% of respondents answered "no" or "I'm not sure." The museum had adopted both university-wide policies as well as museum-specific ones throughout the previous 3 years, but most staff were unsure or unaware of them.

Normally when there is confusion about an organization's stance or specific policies, there are trends that indicate that communication about that stance and policies is limited to certain organizational levels or job titles. However, respondents that said "yes" and those that said "no" or "not sure" were evenly distributed throughout the organization. Those that said "yes" to this question focused on the larger university legal language and less on museum-specific information. This same confusion existed regarding museum procedures for reporting equity-related issues and even the organizational equity statement. This indicated a need for a clearly articulated stance and policies, separate from the overall university, that are stated in staff meetings and filtered through the language, policies, and norms that are specific to each department. Finally, given the hierarchical nature of the organization and the power held by positional authority figures, behavior modeling would be key.

It was a more holistic understanding of the organization's culture and norms that allowed me to move beyond surface-level explanations for a lack of progress on equity work and diagnose the interconnected issues in ways that pointed toward clear pathways for change that would stick. Being able to articulate how the organization's culture was incompatible with previous attempts at equity work helped museum staff see how they could make meaningful progress moving forward. Capacity-building in understanding how the clan culture impacted the processes of conflict management and giving and receiving feedback helped staff and leadership understand how to make space for and operate within an organization full of people with different communication and conflict management styles. This is something that had previously been stifled by the organizational culture. Additional capacity-building in facilitating equitable meetings helped staff understand how the hierarchical nature of the organization could often silence those without positional authority, undermining their contributions to the organization. Finally, a deeper understanding of organizational culture and the many ways it can manifest prepared staff for the work of examining and shifting their own organizational culture in service of working toward agreed upon equity goals.

Equity work requires deep work in a few concerted areas at a time. Shifting organizational culture so that general operations allow for deeper engagement across fewer initiatives was presented as a way to combat the negative aspects of a market culture. This was in direct response to staff who stated a desire to infuse their daily work with more equitable practices. A common cycle was that staff would try to consider changes to policies or procedures but would either lack the knowledge or the time to make any real process before having to revert to old procedures and habits to complete the task because they always had so much to do. Based on the results of the equity audit, specifically the market culture of the organization, I recommended a restructuring of the decision-making process that governs how projects are chosen and workflows are created. The cultural inability to say no to new projects and additional work, coupled with the absence of a process for prioritizing work created reactionary processes that devalued and undermined the kind of processes governing routine communication, information, data gathering, and maintenance necessary to ensure that the institution runs smoothly. Staff were excited by the prospect of creating this kind of organizational change, but worried that leadership would not agree. Leadership agreed but struggled with behavior modification – causing confusion. Leaders explicitly stated that they would support staff as they completed current commitments and began taking on less. However, they still worked extra hours and continued taking on additional projects and initiatives.

I engaged in coaching sessions with leadership to address this issue and found that internalized commitment to organizational excellence was to blame. Organizational leaders had reached their respective places of positional authority and power by adhering to the unwritten rules of organizational excellence, behaviors that operate in alignment with burnout culture. They could acknowledge and support staff moving away from those practices but struggled to leave those practices behind themselves. The overarching fear was the presumption that doing fewer projects and initiatives would be perceived by the university, larger community, and funders as simply doing less work, rather than doing better and more equitable work in fewer areas. It was through framing the need to change as modeling behavior that would support the required culture shifts that convinced organizational leaders to alter their practices. I facilitated sessions between staff and leadership where they developed new ways of communicating the work of the museum and its impact, specifically focused on the value of everyday, less visible maintenance tasks of the organization and work to shift those tasks toward more equitable and inclusive practices. A thoughtful and transparent approach to choosing initiatives and prioritizing work modeled processes necessary to select and prioritize work processes, initiatives, and partnerships that would further the organization's equity goals.

Outcomes

Check-ins with staff and leadership at the 6-, 9-, and 12-month marks post engagement saw an organization hitting its stride with internal processes and policies review and change. Staff noted that the hardest shift in organizational culture is holding everyone in the organization accountable for upholding the culture of respect and equity they are trying to cultivate. However, the organization was able to make significant shifts to the more harmful aspects of the market culture as leadership became more comfortable modeling the behavior they wanted staff to embody. This, in turn, allowed staff to create more manageable workloads for themselves. This occurred alongside frank conversations between curatorial and non-curatorial staff about the need for staff throughout the organization to better understand, acknowledge, and respect non-curatorial work.

The result was time and space to build equity into everyday organizational practices while also honoring preexisting commitments. New engagements and initiatives began to be considered through an equity-centered decision tree developed by staff. This decision tree is a living document that the museum continues to tweak as the museum takes on, engages in, and evaluates their work. Staff and leadership report periods where the market culture threatens to take over again – but also note that they hold each other accountable and feel empowered by the knowledge that they, as an organization, have already demonstrated their capacity to create and maintain a culture of care. These outcomes demonstrate the utility of using preexisting positive organizational culture elements to help shift harmful or problematic elements of organizational culture.

Implications for Future Work

Scholars and practitioners frustrated with organizations that have stated equity goals and commitments but have not made progress toward materially changing their organizational structure, processes, or outcomes have outlined a number of culprits for this type of fakequity mostly centered on different forms of insincerity (Hadley et al., 2022). However, this work highlights a different underlying cause to stalled equity efforts within the nonprofit arts sector.

Unchecked, the negative impacts of organizational excellence will continue to thwart organizational equity efforts without coordinated action among organizations, arts service organizations, and funding institutions. Organizations must work to dismantle the institutional practices that align with organizational excellence as discussed here. In addition to material changes to organizational practices, work on changing organizational culture and the associated psychological contracts is necessary. This chapter provided insights into one organization's work to engage in both aspects of this change process.

Arts service organizations must also serve as examples and guides in this work. Additional research into the role arts service organizations can play, beyond their own needs to stop the more common demonstrations of fakequity (Heidelberg, 2020) will help provide a stronger theoretical foundation and hopefully more practical action steps. Finally, funding institutions have the most work to do, since much of organizations' dogmatic adherence to problematic conceptualizations of organizational excellence is done in service of attaining and maintaining eligibility for grant funding. Funding institutions should continue and expand upon work called for from Sidford (2011) and the Helicon Collaborative (2017) to not only diversify public arts funding, but also to consider how public arts funding systemically undermines and excludes organizations run by and serving those that operate outside of white, cis, heteronormative, upper class, and able-bodied norms.

Conclusion

This chapter contributes to a more holistic understanding of why organizations with sincere aspirations may have struggled to operationalize equity work. While there are certainly organizations who have and are actively practicing fakequity by claiming to engage in equity work while still perpetrating harm, they do not represent the full scope of organizations struggling to create meaningful and sustainable change toward a more equitable organization and cultural ecosystem. This chapter argues that further investigations into the negative impact of organizational excellence, specifically as it pertains to organizational equity work, the following research questions should be explored: How does organizational excellence manifest in organizational practices and procedures in nonprofit arts organizations? What are the pros and cons of organizational adherence to the ideal of organizational excellence? How can funding institutions help create standards for organizations that exist outside of the problematic aspects of organizational excellence as it currently stands?

This suggested research can and should occur alongside other investigations into the more pernicious examples of fakequity so that the field can determine more robust responses to this issue. This case suggests that there needs to be a purposeful delineation between malicious fakequity and fakequity that results from institutional issues other than deliberate and continuous inequitable practices. Otherwise, the field runs the risk of addressing only the symptoms of inequity rather than root causes of continued inequities in the field. This outcome would further exacerbate social justice fatigue and burnout for those working for organizational justice (Faeq & Ismael, 2022; Nazir et al., 2019) and risk attrition of the people working hardest to create necessary change toward cultural ecosystems that accurately reflect the population and are more equitable and inclusive.

References

Abu-Jarad, I. Y., Yusof, N. A., & Nikbin, D. (2010). A review paper on organizational culture and organizational performance. *International Journal of Business and Social Science, 1*(3), 26–46.

Barnawi, M. (2022). Organizational excellence models failure and success factors of organizational excellence and challenges mitigation. *Open Journal of Business and Management, 10*(6), 2915–2938. https://doi.org/10.4236/ojbm.2022.106144

Bear, J. B. (2019). The caregiving ambition framework. *Academy of Management Review, 44*(1), 99–125.

Belfiore, E., Hadley, S., Heidelberg, B. M., & Rosenstein, C. (2023). Cultural democracy, cultural equity, and cultural policy: Perspectives from the UK and USA. *The Journal of Arts Management, Law, and Society, 53*(3), 157–168.

Borwick, D. (2022). *Excellence in community engagement.* Arts Engaged. https://www.artsengaged.com/excellence

Cameron, K. S., & Quinn, R. E. (2011). *Diagnosing and changing organizational culture based on the competing values framework* (3rd ed.). Jossey-Bass.

Conner, L. (2014). Divining "artistic excellence". *We the Audience.* https://www.artsjournal.com/wetheaudience/2014/05/devining-artistic-excellence.html

Domínguez, S., Weffer, S. E., & Embrick, D. G. (2020). White sanctuaries: White supremacy, racism, space, and fine arts in two metropolitan museums. *American Behavioral Scientist, 64*(14), 2028–2043. https://doi.org/10.1177/0002764220975077

Faeq, D. K., & Ismael, Z. N. (2022). Analyzing the relationships between organizational justice and job performance. *International Journal of Engineering Business Management, 6*(5), 14–25.

Hadley, S., Heidelberg, B., & Belfiore, E. (2022). Reflexivity and the perpetuation of inequality in the cultural sector: Half awake in a fake empire? *Journal for Cultural Research, 1*(22), 244–265. https://doi.org/10.1080/14797585.2022.2111220

Heidelberg, B. M. (2012). *The language of cultural policy advocacy: Leadership, message, and rhetorical style.* Doctoral dissertation, The Ohio State University.

Heidelberg, B. M. (2020). Artful avoidance: Initial considerations for measuring diversity resistance in cultural organizations. In K. Thomas (Ed.), *Diversity resistance in organizations* (pp. 149–164). Routledge.

Helicon Collaborative. (2017). *Not just money: Equity issues in cultural philanthropy.* Sundara Foundation.

INCITE! (2004). *Beyond the non-profit industrial complex.* INCITE! https://incite-national.org/beyond-the-non-profit-industrial-complex/

Ithaka S+R & American Alliance of Museums. (2022). *Art museum staff demographic survey 2022.* American Alliance of Museums.

Kanter, B., & Sherman, A. (2016). *The happy, healthy nonprofit: Strategies for impact without burnout.* John Wiley & Sons.

Maslach, C. (2021). *Burnout.* Malor.

McNeely, C. L., & Shockley, G. E. (2006). Deconstructing U.S. arts policy: A dialectical exposition of the excellence-access debate. *Social Justice, 33*(2), 45–62.

Nazir, S., Shafi, A., Atif, M. M., Qun, W., & Abdullah, S. M. (2019). How organizational justice and perceived organizational support facilitate employees' innovative behavior at work. *Employee Relations, 41*(6), 1288–1311.

Okuno Consulting. (2017). *Fakequity [Infographic].* https://fakequity.files.wordpress.com/2015/08/fakiequit5.jpg

Olinske, J. L., & Hellman, C. M. (2017). Leadership in the human service nonprofit organization: The influence of the board of directors on executive director well-being and burnout. *Human Service Organizations: Management, Leadership & Governance, 41*(2), 95–105.

Remender, P. A., & Lucareli, R. (1986). In search of artistic excellence: The social construction of artistic values. *Studies in Art Education, 27*(4), 209–212. https://doi.org/10.2307/1320916

Shahzad, F., Luqman, R. A., Khan, A. R., & Shabbir, L. (2012). Impact of organizational culture on organizational performance: An overview. *Interdisciplinary Journal of Contemporary Research in Business, 3*(9), 975–985.

Sidford, H. (2011). *Fusing arts, culture and social change.* Philanthropy at Its Best, National Committee for Responsive Philanthropy. https://www.ncrp.org/publication/fusing-arts-culture-social-change

Voss, Z., & Voss, G. (2020). *The alchemy of high-performing arts organizations.* SMU DataArts. https://www.wallacefoundation.org/knowledge-center/pages/the-alchemy-of-high-performing-arts-organizations.aspx

Wiggins-Romesburg, C. A., & Githens, R. P. (2018). The psychology of diversity resistance and integration. *Human Resource Development Review, 17*(2), 179–198.

Wong, C. (2019). Changing organizational culture: From embedded bias to equity & inclusion. *Professional Safety, 64*(08), 26–30.

Yin, R. K. (2014). *Case study research: Design and methods* (Applied social research methods). Sage publications.

Chapter 11

Toward an Inclusive Cultural Participation: The Case of Chilean Museums

Jesús Heredia-Carroza[a], Javier Reyes-Martínez[b] and Fátima Gigirey[a]

[a]Universidad de Sevilla, Spain
[b]Centro de Investigación y Docencia Económicas (CIDE), Mexico

Abstract

The purpose of this chapter is to explore the attendance at museums of disabled people in Chile. To address this issue, we propose a logistic regression analysis by type of disability (i.e., physical or mobility difficulty, muteness or difficulty in speech, mental or intellectual difficulty, deafness or difficulty hearing, blindness or difficulty seeing) and severity of disability (i.e., two or more conditions in one individual). We use the National Survey of Cultural Participation in Chile 2017 ($N = 12{,}151$), a study whose main aim is to explore cultural participation and the factors that influence disabled people. Preliminary results indicate that only some disabilities negatively influence attendance at museums (e.g., physical disabilities); furthermore, the severity of the disability is also a relevant factor, considering it shows a negative influence on attendance at museums. These results suggest several implications for the infrastructure in museums, as well as repercussions in policies, procedures, funding, and financial management in museums that, if addressed, would foster inclusive environments for all individuals in Chile.

Keywords: Disability; cultural participation; diversity and inclusion; museum attendance; Chile

Introduction

The right of access to culture is included in the Universal Declaration of Human Rights (1948) and the Convention on the Rights of Persons with Disabilities (2006). However, the effective participation of individuals with disabilities is still a

Accessibility, Diversity, Equity and Inclusion in the Cultural Sector, 167–181

Copyright © 2024 Jesús Heredia-Carroza, Javier Reyes-Martínez and Fátima Gigirey

Published under exclusive licence by Emerald Publishing Limited

doi:10.1108/978-1-83753-034-220241025

challenge in our societies. Most researchers who study the cultural attendance of people with disabilities focus on the physical barriers to cultural services or in the disability in itself but assume that like the rest of nondisabled people, individuals with disabilities are influenced by factors such as the family environment, educational attainment, or the result of personal empowerment.

The purpose of this chapter is to determine how disabilities are associated with the attendance of museums in Chile and what factors have an impact in this cultural participation.[1] To fulfill this aim, we propose a logistic regression analysis with data from the 2017 National Survey of Cultural Participation in Chile (*Encuesta Nacional de Participación Cultural 2017* or ENPC in Spanish).

Results show differences in participation that depend on the kind of disability. For instance, individuals with intellectual disability are more likely to have a diminished attendance than those without intellectual disability. This is mainly explained by the difficulty they have in understanding the artistic work and even in understanding the signs of the route through the museum. In addition, these people struggle with their financial situation which also determines museum attendance. On the contrary, family environment or social capital encourages cultural participation to a good extent. It may suggest that museum attendance becomes more relevant when individuals with a disability attend with others. These conclusions may help policymakers design and implement effective cultural policies that promote access to museums for people with disabilities and thus ensure their cultural rights.

Literature Review

The Concept of Functional Diversity

Medical and social conditions explain the disability (Yoon et al., 2021). The medical conception defined disability as an exclusively personal or individual characteristic that abstracts from the social context in which the person operates. On the contrary, the social perspective is aware of the oppressive structures of a social context that is not sensitive to the real needs of people with disabilities (Ferreira, 2008). The Convention on the Rights of Persons with Disabilities (CRPD) defined disability as the result of "long-term physical, mental, intellectual

---

[1]Chile is the country in Latin America with the highest Human Development Index (HDI), despite having a smaller population (19.67 million people), in comparison to other countries in the region (OECD, 2023). In regard to population, average age of the Chilean is 35.5 years old, and 17.6% of population experience at least one disability (ENDISC, 2022).

Chile has 320 museums that are distributed unevenly throughout the territory, most of them concentrated in the central regions and urban areas of the country (SNPC, 2021). According to the *Servicio Nacional del Patrimonio Cultural* (SNPC, 2021), museums are medium and small in scale. In addition, in 2022, visits at museums have reported a substantial increment of 80%, in comparison to the two pandemic previous years, although they have not recovered levels of visitants before the COVID-19 episode (SNPC, 2023).

or sensory impairments that in interaction with various barriers may hinder their full and effective participation on an equal basis with others."[2] The CRPD rejects the medical model of disability, which focuses on individual disability, and is closer to a social model (Ferri et al., 2022; Kanter, 2017; Yoon et al., 2021). Thus, disability must be conceived not as an objective characteristic applicable to the person but as an interpretative construction inscribed in the culture in which the individual develops (Ferreira, 2008).

Besides, disabilities can operate in different ways. For instance, an invisible disability is a condition where there are no noticeable physical signs or other signals to indicate limitations (e.g., intellectual disabilities), whereas a visible disability shows outward manifestations to the casual observer – e.g., physical disabilities (Ysasi et al., 2018). The level of stigma and discrimination in distinctive aspects of life are conditioned by these characteristics and can constitute an important barrier to social and cultural participation.

Infrastructure as a Barrier to Cultural Participation

Depending on the characteristics that define the disability, the barriers to cultural participation will be different. Social participation barriers are defined as "the conditions or factors in a person's environment that have the effect of limiting or impeding their functioning and that create disability, which in turn leads to a lower level of social participation and exclusion" (WHO, 2011).

Some of the most mentioned barriers to people with a disability are related to cultural infrastructure. For instance, evidence shows that factors such as physical accessibility to the location, inaccessible content, insufficient seating in museums, or the absence of sign language interpreters significantly impact cultural participation (Argyropoulos & Kanari, 2015; Leahy & Ferri, 2022). For instance, in museums, Renel (2019) emphasized navigation signals as a central barrier. When signals are difficult to understand, they minimize the cultural experience of people with intellectual disabilities – i.e., signals could make the navigation or orientation in the place difficult or may obscure the meaning of the piece. Regarding historical heritage sites, the most prominent physical barriers are the lack of adapted transport to make the trip, the cost of transport, and the fact that some people with disability depend on a caregiver to get around (Charlton, 1998; Gratton, 2020; Mesquita & Carneiro, 2016). Good building design and accessibility can be good facilitators: avoid glass doors, steps, and so on (Leahy & Ferri, 2022).

Besides physical barriers, sometimes policymakers overlook other types of disabilities such as cognitive or intellectual disabilities (Cho & Jolley, 2016). Understanding the text is particularly important in the case of people with these disabilities. Mastrogiuseppe et al. (2021) identified as the main barrier for these individuals the codification of the explanatory texts that are found in the historical heritage sites. In this case, a complex vocabulary and syntax may operate as obstacles that make the understanding difficult. Another type of barrier refers

---

[2]CRPD, Article 1.

to accessibility to communication. People with disabilities sometimes feel that they have minimal attention when it comes to guided tours in sign language or for the visually impaired (Ferri et al., 2022). Some also complain that people working in the cultural sector sometimes lack the skills to provide access information to a variety of people with disabilities (Constantinou et al., 2018; Ferri et al., 2022; Weisen, 2012).

Infrastructure as a Facilitator to Cultural Participation

Besides barriers to cultural participation, it is relevant to enumerate those aspects that can play a role as facilitators. For instance, the use of technologies is a good facilitator to cultural participation, mainly in places of historical heritage and museums (Agostiano, 2016; Heredia-Carroza, Palma, Chavarría-Ortiz, et al., 2023; Renel, 2019; Seale et al., 2021). Studies linking technologies and the cultural participation of people with intellectual disabilities are optimistic about the potential capacity of technologies to encourage the participation of these individuals (Adkins et al., 2012). Positive effects of using technologies for people with deafness have also been reported (Constantinou et al., 2016).

Accessibility for those with visual impairment is limited even in museums where visibility strategies have been implemented (Mesquita & Carneiro, 2016). Some museums explore new forms of touch-based exploration (Argyropoulos & Kanari, 2015; Cho & Jolley, 2016). For instance, in the United States, organizations such as the Metropolitan Museum of Art, the Solomon R. Guggenheim Museum, the Touch Museum, and the Children's Museum of Central Wisconsin have implemented specific programs for people who are blind or have some degree of vision loss (Cho & Jolley, 2016). Many museums are implementing various programs and facilitators such as tactile exhibitions, audio guides, relief sculptures, or information in Braille (Argyropoulos & Kanari, 2015; Reich et al., 2011). However, there are still many barriers to attendance. For example, in Greece, the duration and number of these specialized programs are very limited, and in many historical heritage sites, people with any type of disability are not considered equal citizens (Argyropoulos & Kanari, 2015; Lid, 2016).

Educational Attainment and Socioeconomic Level

Other sociodemographic and social factors have been acknowledged to be related with attendance at museums of individuals with disabilities. The financial barrier is another issue to overcome. According to Akyurek and Bumin (2017), people with disabilities have a higher cost of living in relation to the income they receive. In general, these individuals also have a lower educational level with a lower probability of being in a situation of occupation (Oliveira et al., 2015; Queirós et al., 2015). These lower incomes directly affect cultural participation (Ahmed et al., 2022). On some occasions, there is an amount of limited individual income, but we must also highlight the lack of public support to bring organizations closer to cultural policy (Ferri et al., 2022).

These inequalities do not affect all types of disabilities in the same way. Intellectual disability is the most exposed to exclusion. In comparison, individuals with physical disabilities have better socioeconomic prospects than those with cognitive disabilities (Queirós et al., 2015). Other studies also show how family socioeconomic perspectives are a strong predictor in later life development in people with disabilities (Queirós et al., 2015). Finally, although technologies facilitate the approach of people with disabilities to culture, it also discriminates according to income (Leahy & Ferri, 2022).

Social and Cultural Capital

Social capital is defined as the set of resources that are linked to membership in a specific group. The group provides resources that serve as a basis for the establishment of a status or personal value (Bourdieu, 1986; Heredia-Carroza, Palma, & Aguado, 2023). Social capital determines cultural participation (Bourdieu, 1986; Neveu, 2018; Putnam, 2001; Upright, 2004). Membership in a club or association enhances social capital by facilitating the establishment of a network of contacts among individuals with diverse skills and backgrounds. Individuals with disabilities and their families relate more to other members of the community (Chenoweth & Stehlik, 2004; Clear, 1999) that eventually can promote cultural attendance. In addition, there is a strong relationship between socioeconomic status and social capital (Courty & Zhang, 2018; Di Maggio & Mohr, 1985; Heredia-Carroza, Aguado, et al., 2023; van Eijck, 1997).

Cultural capital refers to certificates, academic certificates, and other forms of institutionalized education, along with cultural participation and consumption of several cultural practices (Hyyppä, 2010). Early stages of socialization in cultural settings are factors that lead to greater participation throughout life (Upright, 2004). These suggest that people take cues from both their environment and their social networks in the formation of preferences and that these preferences tend to accumulate (Nagel, 2010; Relish, 1997; Yaish & Katz-Gerro, 2012). Empirical evidence shows that a significant part of parental influence is transmitted through parental cultural involvement (Nagel, 2010; Nagel et al., 1997; Yaish & Katz-Gerro, 2012). Children who come from well-off and highly educated families – i.e., with more cultural capital – are more active in cultural participation than those who come from families with a lower level of education (Nagel, 2010). The same happens with children with disabilities who are born to these types of families.

According to previous exposition, it follows that disabilities can play a key role to individuals in regard to cultural participation, particularly at museum attendance. Therefore, an important research question emerges: what is the relationship between people with disabilities and their visits to museums in Chile? But also, how might additional social inequalities effect this relationship?

Methods

The Survey and the Sampling

To determine the relationship between disabilities and the attendance of museums in Chile, we employed data from the 2017 National Survey of Cultural Participation in Chile (Encuesta Nacional de Participación Cultural 2017 or ENPC in Spanish). Its main purpose is to characterize cultural participation practices of the Chilean population over 15 years of age (Ministerio de las Culturas, las Artes y el Patrimonio, 2018).

Data from this survey are representative at the regional and national levels for urban areas and were collected using a stratified and three-stage probabilistic and complex sampling. In this three-stage sampling process, blocks, homes, and individuals were selected, in that order. 12,151 households were surveyed during August 2017 to December 2017. The interview was conducted face-to-face, employing an electronic device, in Spanish (Ministerio de las Culturas, las Artes y el Patrimonio, 2018).

Measurements

The main indicator in this study is the attendance at museums variable, which indicates whether an individual attended museums during the last year or not. Another important indicator is the presence of disability conditions. In this case, interviewees are categorized according to not reporting a disability, those who indicate physical disability, hearing or speech impairment, intellectual disability, or visual disability.

Other variables in the analysis, employed as control variables, are related to several socioeconomic conditions and individual traits. These indicators have been associated in the field as relevant to attending museums. For instance, the Indigenous variable indicates whether an individual identifies themselves as Indigenous or not. The socioeconomic indicator classifies participants according to their socioeconomic level. The sex variable also categorizes individuals into men or women. The age variable indicates the interviewee's age. In the education indicator, interviewees are grouped into those who have attained professional education and those who have not. In regard to participation in social groups or organizations, we also included the social capital variable. Finally, two variables are related to cultural capital: art education and stimuli by parents during infancy. Both measures indicate whether an interviewee had these incentives or not.

Data Analysis Technique

To answer the research question, we employed a logistic regression. Logistic regression is a type of analysis that is used to predict the outcome of a dichotomous variable based on a set of predictor variables. It also allows us to calculate the odds that one event occurred or not. We integrated the statistical model by the attendance at museums (as dependent or outcome variable) and the different types of disabilities (as the main independent variable). We also added other variables as independent variables that have been evidenced to influence the attendance: the Indigenous self-ascription, socioeconomic level, gender, age, education, social capital, art education, and stimuli during infancy indicators (i.e., as control variables).

Results

Concerning attendance at museums, 16.2% of interviewees participated in this activity, whereas 83.8% did not. In the case of the presence of disabilities, data show that 88.4% of interviewees do not report experiencing a disability, while 7.3% indicate a physical disability, 1.8% a hearing or speech impairment, 0.4% an intellectual disability, and 2.1% a visual disability.

Results from the statistical analysis (i.e., the logit regression) show that those individuals who report physical and intellectual disability are less prone to attend museums, in comparison to those who do not report any disability. In terms of odds ratio, those who indicated physical and intellectual disabilities had 0.45 and 0.29 times odds (respectively) of reporting attendance at a museum in the last year, in comparison to those without any disability; in other words, a lesser probability.[3] As observed from these three conditions, intellectual disabilities have a greater impact on attendance – i.e., it diminishes participation in a greater probability than physical disabilities. Contrary, individuals who mention a hearing or speech impairment have more probabilities to attend museums (2.06 times odds), in comparison to those individuals who do not report a condition of disability.

Concerning other relevant sociodemographic and social categories (i.e., as control variables), self-ascribing as Indigenous and being a woman do not have any significant result on the chance to attend museums. In the case of age, the analysis indicates that the probability of attending museums reduces with age (0.98 times odds). It means that older people participate less in this type of cultural activity. Also, socioeconomic level matters. Those interviewees from the higher socioeconomic strata (level 4 and 5) have a greater chance to attend museums (1.69 and 2.29 times odds, respectively) in comparison to those from the lower socioeconomic level (level 1).

Furthermore, to those individuals from the lower socioeconomic strata (level 2 and 3), attendance was not statistically significant, which indicates a null relationship between individuals and participation (i.e., it is not relevant to them). Education attainment is another indicator related to attendance at museums. In this analysis, those who have attained professional education had 1.72 times the odds to attend museums, in contrast to individuals with nonprofessional

---

[3]Odds ratio expresses a change in one variable in relation with another. It is a value where a score above 1 indicates a positive association (more probability), whereas a score below 1 suggests a negative relationship. In addition, the further a value is from 1.0, the greater the association it suggests.

education. Similarly, people who received artistic education during childhood, as well as those who received stimuli from parents, have a greater chance to attend museums (2.10 and 1.54 times odds, respectively), in contrast to those who did not report this education or stimuli. In addition, interviewees who report participating in social or civic organizations have higher probabilities to attend museums (1.99 times odds), in comparison to those who do not participate. From all these indicators, the highest probability is for the upper socioeconomic levels. However, this probability is even lesser than the likelihood of intellectual disability, which may suggest that disabilities may have a (more) important role in attendance at museums than other socioeconomic traits (see Table A1 in Appendix 1).

Discussion

We believe that the factors that favor or limit cultural participation are the same for the study of any population group, whether they present a degree of disability or not. However, this work not only makes it possible to study cultural participation by type of disability but also highlights that the results obtained for this population group are the same as for those who are not disabled. Some of the results obtained in the literature review are representative for all people who participate in culture, whether or not they have some degree of disability.

Most countries have laws that protect the cultural rights of people with disabilities with the objective of removing barriers to access. However, many of these norms focus on physical mobility but neglect other types of disabilities such as cognitive (Cho & Jolley, 2016). This explains why intellectual disability reports are the most likely to diminish the attendance followed by the physical ones. On the contrary, those with hearing or speech impairment have more probability to attend museums that highlight the importance of the sign language interpreters in cultural centers (Argyropoulos & Kanari, 2015). In this sense, this study shows how communication has an impact on cultural participation: the possibility of seeing or understanding the artistic work is a good mechanism to encourage attendance.

Our results about socioeconomic level and education attainment are consistent with the literature review. Higher socioeconomic status reports higher participation in comparison to lower (Courty & Zhang, 2018; Di Maggio & Mohr, 1985; Di Maggio & Useem, 1980; Reyes-Martínez & Andrade-Guzmán, 2023; van Eijck, 1997). In addition, according to the review, the cost of living for people with disabilities is higher than their incomes (Akyurek & Bumin, 2017). Therefore, cultural attendance seems like a privilege for those who can afford it. Our study also shows how parental influence has an impact on cultural participation. Empirical evidence shows that a significant part of parental influence is transmitted through parental cultural involvement (Nagel, 2010; Yaish & Katz-Gerro, 2012). This result is also consistent with other studies such as Di Maggio and Useem (1980) and Queirós et al. (2015), which indicated that family socioeconomic perspectives are a strong predictor in later life development of people with disabilities. In addition, well-educated parents invest heavily in their children's education, which makes them more exposed to cultural events.

Relative to education, the analysis reports the significance of artistic education, as Di Maggio and Useem (1980) predicted. In this sense, these authors highlight that a person's educational level is the main predictor of their attendance at museums and performing arts events: individuals with a secondary or university education are much more likely to value the arts than those with less educational level. The second element that these authors highlight as a determinant of cultural participation is the curricular presence of one or more artistic disciplines in the school.

Finally, social capital is a good predictor of cultural participation. The OECD's statistics has identified the social capital in four ways: (1) personal relationships, (2) social media support, (3) civic engagements, and (4) cooperative standards (Sakalauskas et al., 2021). In addition, other factors such as gender, age, race, or socioeconomic status can encourage or restrict access to social capital (Webber, 2005). Individuals with disabilities participate in cultural activities within groups or associations. Association encourages empowerment and at the same time enables cultural participation (Evans et al., 2017; Fawcett et al., 1994; Niesz et al., 2008; Yoon et al., 2021).

Conclusions

Functional diversity also implies diverse ways of relating to culture. Inequity in access to culture does not affect all people with disabilities equally. In this sense, people with intellectual disabilities are the ones at greater risk of exclusion, followed by physical disabilities. In both cases, there is a possibility for improvement: for the first group, facilitating the interpretation of works of art or improving navigation signals would be measures that would encourage participation, and for the second, improving access facilities emerges as one of the points to consider.

Although visual disability was not significant in our model, this deserves some attention. Traditionally, museum attendance was closely related to visual appreciation. However, different kinds of museums based on touch are emerging now in the main artistic center as MET or Guggenheim Museum. Probably, this type of experience will improve the participation in museums of individuals with these conditions.

The effective cultural participation of people with disabilities is still a challenge in our societies. The study shows that social participation by these people is strongly favored by a process of personal empowerment. This is expressed through the education received by parents and at school. The existence of cultural organizations also encourages participation. This idea highlights the importance of associations of people as a vehicle for empowerment and social participation.

In addition, it is necessary to reinforce artistic education at school. It is well known that knowledge in art is related to cultural participation. In the case of people with disabilities, this is not only beneficial from a clinical point of view but also provides incentives to attend museums.

However, there are some financial barriers to overcome. Although people with disabilities are more prone to be at risk of social exclusion, it is reported that a high level of income improves the possibilities to access a social life and culture. In this sense, public funding support for organizations would be a good mechanism that would allow cultural participation of low-level income people with disabilities.

Implications for Management

Findings emphasize how attendance at museums depends on several conditions related to inequalities: being able, being at the highest socioeconomic levels, being young, attaining professional education, and possessing social and cultural capital. This situation accentuates the way cultural institutions and politics exclude distinctive vulnerable groups. It follows, to policymakers and politicians, the need to design, build, promote, and maintain cultural policies against ableism, classism, and ageism that seem very ingrained in the management and operation of museums and other cultural spaces, despite the advances in the field during the last decades. A change in this perspective not only requires a transformation in the narrative of cultural bureaus or offices but also demands the necessary budget to integrate discourses and practices. Indeed, cultural policies concerning museums need a renovation that focuses on the people and debunks myths about disabilities: public and private institutions should guarantee access to the cultural rights of everyone.

In addition, the inclusion of individuals in situations of disability would demand specific programs and interventions in museums, most of them at the level of objectives, conceptualization, infrastructure, training, and promotion. These imply the determined action of practitioners in the field, among them, cultural promoters and managers, directors of cultural institutions, public workers in the cultural sector, and artists. The reduced cultural participation, particularly acute in people with intellectual disabilities, indicates the lack of arrangements for this group. What measures are required to facilitate individuals with disabilities access to museums? How can museums approach these individuals? How may practitioners help to transform the experiences at museums?

Funding

The first author (J.H.C.) disclosed receipt of financial support for the research, authorship, and/or publication of this article. The author acknowledges financial support from Ayudas para la Recualificación del Sistema Universitario Español en su Modalidad Margarita Salas granted by the Resolución de 29 de noviembre de 2021 of Universidad de Sevilla, financed by the European Union-NextGenerationEU.

Declarations of Conflicting Interests

No potential conflict of interest was reported by the authors.

References

Adkins, K. W., Molloy, C., Weiss, S. K., Reynolds, A., Goldman, S. E., Burnette, C., Clemons, T., Fawkes, D., & Malow, B. A. (2012). Effects of a standardized pamphlet on insomnia in children with autism spectrum disorders. *Pediatrics, 130,* 139–144. https://doi.org/10.1542/peds.2012-0900K

Agostiano, M. (2016). The 'compensatory solutions' for an alternative accessibility of cultural heritage sites. In A. Arenghi, I. Garofolo, & O. Sørmoen (Eds.), *Accessibility as a key enabling knowledge for enhancement of cultural heritage* (pp. 131–147). Franco Angeli.

Ahmed, S. K., Jeffries, D., Chakraborty, A., Carslake, T., Lietz, P., Rahayu, B., Armstrong, D., Kaushik, A., & Sundarsagar, K. (2022). Teacher professional development for disability inclusion in low- and middle-income Asia-Pacific countries: An evidence and gap map. *Campbell Systematic Reviews, 18*(4), 1287. https://doi.org/10.1002/cl2.1287

Akyurek, G., & Bumin, G. (2017). Community participation in people with disabilities. In M. Huri (Ed.), *Occupational therapy—Occupation focused holistic practice in rehabilitation.* InTech. https://doi.org/10.5772/intechopen.68470

Argyropoulos, V., & Kanari, C. (2015). Re-imagining the museum through "touch": Reflections of individuals with visual disability on their experience of museum-visiting in Greece. *ALTER – European Journal of Disability Research/Revue Européenne de Recherche sur le Handicap, 9.* https://doi.org/10.1016/j.alter.2014. 12.005

Bourdieu, P. (1986). The forms of capital. In J. Richardson (Ed.), *Handbook of theory and research for the sociology of education.* Greenwood.

Charlton, J. I. (1998). The dimensions of disability oppression: An overview. In J. Charlton (Ed.), *Nothing about us without us: Disability oppression and empowerment.* University of California Press. https://doi.org/10.1525/california/ 9780520207950.003.0002

Chenoweth, L., & Stehlik, D. (2004). Implications of social capital for the inclusion of people with disabilities and families in community life. *International Journal of Inclusive Education, 8*(1), 59–72. https://doi.org/10.1080/1360311032000139467

Cho, H., & Jolley, A. (2016). Museum education for children with disabilities: Development of the nature senses traveling trunk. *Journal of Museum Education, 41*(3), 220–229. https://doi.org/10.1080/10598650.2016.1193313

Clear, M. (1999). Caring culture and the politics of parent/Professional relations. *Australian Journal of Social Issues, 34*(2), 119–136. https://doi.org/10.1002/j.1839-4655.1999.tb01073.x

Constantinou, V., Kosmas, P., Parmaxi, A., Ioannou, A., Klironomos, I., Antona, M., Stephanidis, C., & Zaphiris, P. (2018). Towards the use of social computing for social inclusion: An overview of the literature. In P. Zaphiris & A. Ioannou (Eds.), *Learning and collaboration technologies. Design, development and technological innovation.* Springer International Publishing. https://doi.org/10.1007/978-3-319-91743-6_28

Constantinou, V., Loizides, F., & Ioannou, A. (2016). A personal tour of cultural heritage for deaf museum visitors. In Paper presented at the Euro-Mediterranean Conference. https://ktisis.cut.ac.cy/handle/10488/9285

Courty, P., & Zhang, F. (2018). Cultural participation in major Chinese cities. *Journal of Cultural Economics, 42*(4), 543–592.

Di Maggio, P., & Mohr, J. (1985). Cultural capital, educational attainment, and marital selection. *American Journal of Sociology, 90*(6), 1231–1261.

Di Maggio, P. D., & Useem, M. (1980). The arts in education and cultural participation: The social role of aesthetic education and the arts. *Journal of Aesthetic Education, 14*(4), 55. https://doi.org/10.2307/3332369

ENDISC. (2022). *Estudio Nacional de la Discapacidad 2022*. Servicio Nacional del Patrimonio Culural.

Evans, T., Bellon, M., & Matthews, B. (2017). Leisure as a human right: An exploration of people with disabilities' perceptions of leisure, arts and recreation participation through Australian community access services. *Annals of Leisure Research, 20*(3), 331–348. https://doi.org/10.1080/11745398.2017.1307120

Fawcett, S. B., White, G. W., Balcazar, F. E., Suarez-Balcazar, Y., Mathews, R. M., Paine-Andrews, A., Seekins, T., & Smith, J. F. (1994). A contextual-behavioral model of empowerment: Case studies involving people with physical disabilities. *American Journal of Community Psychology, 22*(4), 471–496. https://doi.org/10.1007/BF02506890

Ferreira, M. A. V. (2008). Una aproximación sociológica a la discapacidad desde el modelo social: Apuntes caracteriológicos [A sociological approach to disability based on the social model: Some characteriological sketches]. *Reis, 124*, 141. https://doi.org/10.2307/40184909

Ferri, D., Leahy, A., Šubic, N., & Urzel, L. (2022). Implementing the right of people with disabilities to participate in cultural life across five European countries: Narratives and counternarratives. *Journal of Human Rights Practice*. https://doi.org/10.1093/jhuman/huac035

Gratton, N. (2020). People with learning disabilities and access to mainstream arts and culture: A participatory action research approach. *British Journal of Learning Disabilites, 48*(2), 106–114. https://doi.org/10.1111/bld.12303

Heredia-Carroza, J., Palma, L., Chavarría-Ortiz, C., & de Sancha-Navarro, J. (2023). Consumption habits of recorded music: Determinants of flamenco albums acquisition. *Sage Open, 13*(3). https://doi.org/10.1177/2158440231195202

Heredia-Carroza, J., Aguado, L. F., & Tejedor-Estupiñán, J. M. (2023). La economía y gestión de la cultura popular como motor de desarrollo territorial. *Revista Finanzas y Política Económica, 15*(2). https://doi.org/10.14718/revfinanzpolitecon.v15.n2.2023.1

Heredia-Carroza, J., Palma, L., & Aguado, L. F. (2023). Does copyright understand intangible heritage? The case of Flamenco in Spain. *International Journal of Heritage Studies, 29*(6). https://doi.org/10.1080/13527258.2023.2208102

Hyyppä, M. T. (2010). How does cultural participation contribute to social capital and well-being? In *Healthy ties*. Springer. https://doi.org/10.1007/978-90-481-9606-7_5

Kanter, A. (2017). *The development of disability rights under international law: From charity*. https://www.routledge.com/The-Development-of-Disability-Rights-Under-International-Law-From-Charity/Kanter/p/book/9781138094338

Leahy, A., & Ferri, D. (2022). Barriers and facilitators to cultural participation by people with disabilities: A narrative literature review. *Scandinavian Journal of Disability Research, 24*(1), 68–81. https://doi.org/10.16993/sjdr.86

Lid, I. M. (2016). Access to cultural heritage: A multiscaled approach. In A. Arenghi, I. Garofolo, & O. Sørmoen (Eds.), *Accessibility as a key enabling knowledge for enhancement of cultural heritage* (pp. 77–89). Franco Angeli.

Mastrogiuseppe, M., Span, S., & Bortolotti, E. (2021). Improving accessibility to cultural heritage for people with intellectual disabilities: A tool for observing the obstacles and facilitators for the access to knowledge. *Alter, 15*(2), 113–123. https://doi.org/10.1016/j.alter.2020.06.016

Mesquita, S., & Carneiro, M. J. (2016). Accessibility of European museums to visitors with visual impairments. *Disability & Society, 31*(3), 373–388. https://doi.org/10.1080/09687599.2016.1167671

Ministerio de las Culturas, las Artes y el Patrimonio. (2018). *Encuesta Nacional de Participación Cultural 2017*. Ministerio de las Culturas, las Artes y el Patrimonio.

Nagel, I. (2010). Cultural participation between the ages of 14 and 24: Intergenerational transmission or cultural mobility? *European Sociological Review, 26*(5), 541–556. https://doi.org/10.1093/esr/jcp037

Nagel, I., Ganzeboom, H., Haanstra, F., & Oud, W. (1997). Effects of art education in secondary schools on cultural participation in later life. *Journal of Art & Design Education, 16*(3), 325–331. https://doi.org/10.1111/1468-5949.00093

Neveu, E. (2018). Bourdieu's capitals: Sociologizing an economic concept. In T. Medvetz & J. J. Sallaz (Eds.), *The Oxford handbook of Pierre Bourdeau* (Part IV, Chapter 15). Oxford University Press.

Niesz, T., Koch, L., & Rumrill, P. (2008). The empowerment of people with disabilities through qualitative research. *Work (Reading, Mass.), 31*, 113–125.

OECD. (2023). *Panorama económico de Chile*. OECD.

Oliveira, P. M. P. de, Mariano, M. R., Pagliuca, L. M. F., Silva, J. M. da, Almeida, P. C. de, & Oliveira, G. O. B. (2015). Socio-economic profile of people with disabilities: A health impact. *Health, 7*(5). https://doi.org/10.4236/health.2015.75075

Putnam, R. (2001). Social capital: Measurement and consequences. *Isuma-Canadian Journal of Policy Research, 2*(5), 41–51.

Queirós, F. C., Wehby, G. L., & Halpern, C. T. (2015). Developmental disabilities and socioeconomic outcomes in young adulthood. *Public Health Reports, 130*(3), 213–221. https://doi.org/10.1177/003335491513000308

Reich, C., Lindgren-Streicher, A., Beyer, M., Levent, N., & Pursley, J. (2011). *Speaking out on art and museums: A study on the needs and preferences of adults who are blind or have low vision*. https://www.semanticscholar.org/paper/!-Speaking-Out-on-Art-and-Museums%3A-A-Study-on-the-Reich-Lindgren-Streicher/6dd0bfd50d09cf05816d2181121903aa5ce561b3

Relish, M. (1997). It's not all education: Network measures as sources of cultural competency. *Poetics, 25*(2), 121–139. https://doi.org/10.1016/S0304-422X(97)00011-9

Renel, W. (2019). Sonic accessibility: Increasing social equity through the inclusive design of sound in museums and heritage sites. *Curator: The Museum Journal, 62*, 377–402. https://onlinelibrary.wiley.com/doi/10.1111/cura.12311

Reyes-Martínez, J., & Andrade-Guzmán, C. A. (2023). Derechos sociales y culturales en el trabajo artístico: un análisis exploratorio de artistas chilenos y mexicanos durantes tiempos pandémicos. *Revista Finanzas y Pol'tiica Económica, 15*(2), 441–464. https://doi.org/10.14718/revfinanzpolitecon.v15.n2.2023.6

Sakalauskas, L., Dulskis, V., Lauzikas, R., Miliauskas, A., & Plikynas, D. (2021). A probabilistic model of the impact of cultural participation on social capital. *Journal of Mathematical Sociology, 45*(2), 65–78. https://doi.org/10.1080/0022250X.2020.1725002

Seale, J., Garcia Carrizosa, H., Rix, J., Sheehy, K., & Hayhoe, S. (2021). A participatory approach to the evaluation of participatory museum research projects. *International Journal of Research and Method in Education, 44*(1), 20–40. https://doi.org/10.1080/1743727X.2019.1706468

SNPC. (2021). *Estadísticas usuarios museos regionales y especializados.* Servicio Nacional del Patrimonio Cultural.

SNPC. (2023). *Panorama de los museos.* Reporte 2023. Servicio Nacional del Patrimonio Cultural.

Upright, C. B. (2004). Social capital and cultural participation. *Poetics, 32*(2), 129–143. https://doi.org/10.1016/j.poetic.2004.02.002

van Eijck, K. (1997). The impact of family background and educational attainment on cultural consumption: A sibling analysis. *Poetics, 25*(4), 195–224. https://doi.org/10.1016/S0304-422X(97)00017-X

Webber, M. (2005). Social capital and mental health. In J. Tew (Ed.), *Social perspectives in mental health. Developing social models to understand and work with mental distress* (pp. 90–111). Jessica Kingsley Publishers.

Weisen, M. (2012). Digital access to culture. *Journal of Assistive Technologies, 6*(2), 163–166. https://doi.org/10.1108/17549451211235028

WHO. (2011). *World report on disability.* World Health Organization. http://www.who.int/disabilities/worldreport/2011/report.pdf

Yaish, M., & Katz-Gerro, T. (2012). Disentangling 'cultural capital': The consequences of cultural and economic resources for taste and participation. *European Sociological Review, 28*(2), 169–185. https://doi.org/10.1093/esr/jcq056

Yoon, J. H., Ellison, C., & Essl, P. (2021). Shifting the perspective from 'incapable' to 'capable' for artists with cognitive disability; case studies in Australia and South Korea. *Disability & Society, 36*(3), 443–467. https://doi.org/10.1080/09687599.2020.1751079

Ysasi, N., Becton, A., & Chen, R. (2018). Stigmatizing effects of visible versus invisible disabilities. *Journal of Disability Studies, 4*(1), 22–29.

Appendix 1

Table A1. Logit Results of the Attendance at Museums, Coefficients, and Odds Ratios.

Variables	Coeff	Odds Ratio	Linearized Std. Err.	t	P > t	[95% Conf. Interval]	
Disability							
Physical disability[a]	−0.79	0.46	0.21	−3.73	0.000	−1.20	−0.37
Hearing or speech impairment[a]	0.73	2.07	0.31	2.37	0.018	0.12	1.33
Intellectual disability[a]	−1.23	0.29	0.62	−1.98	0.048	−2.44	−0.01
Visual disability[a]	0.22	1.25	0.24	0.93	0.353	−0.25	0.68
Indigenous							
Yes[b]	0.05	1.05	0.14	0.38	0.701	−0.22	0.33
Age	−0.02	0.98	0.00	−8.66	0.000	−0.02	−0.02
Socioeconomic Level (Quintile)							
Q2[c]	0.11	1.11	0.11	0.96	0.340	−0.11	0.33
Q3[c]	0.19	1.20	0.11	1.64	0.102	−0.04	0.41
Q4[c]	0.53	1.70	0.11	4.71	0.000	0.31	0.75
Q5[c]	0.83	2.30	0.15	5.37	0.000	0.53	1.14
Sex							
Women[d]	−0.01	0.99	0.07	−0.13	0.895	−0.15	0.13
Education Attainment							
Professional[e]	0.55	1.73	0.12	4.73	0.000	0.32	0.77
Art Education During Infancy							
Yes[f]	0.74	2.10	0.10	7.11	0.000	0.54	0.95
Stimuli by Parents During Infancy							
Yes[f]	0.44	1.55	0.10	4.25	0.000	0.23	0.64
Social Capital							
Yes[f]	0.69	2.00	0.09	7.50	0.000	0.51	0.87
Cons	−1.53	0.22	0.15	−9.98	0.000	−1.83	−1.23
N	11,806						
P	0.0000						

Note: In comparison to a) No disability, b) No, c) Q1, d) Men, e) Non-professional, f) No.

Section 4

Events

Chapter 12

The Super Bowl: An Opportunity for Equity, Diversity, and Inclusion Initiatives for Arts Organizations

Tiffany Bourgeois

Ohio State University, USA

Abstract

This chapter offers a case study (Yin, 2018) of Super Bowl LIII as a special opportunity for diversity, equity, and inclusion (DEI) initiatives for arts organizations. It uses mega-event legacy theory (Preuss, 2015) to frame the outcomes as legacies. The Atlanta Super Bowl Host Committee created a specific initiative entitled Legacy 53. The Legacy 53 initiative consists of five pillars: Business Connection, Capital Improvement Project, Civil Rights and Social Justice, Sustainability, and Youth Engagement (Reed, 2018). This study offers a particular perspective on DEI structures because it examines the Civil Rights and Social Justice pillar's public art project that involved community-driven installations across Atlanta with partners including WonderRoot, an arts organization. The project highlights how administrators can prepare for and take advantage of this unique funding opportunity during future Super Bowls. By reviewing literature on mega-events, urban development, the Olympics, and Super Bowls, I examine the funding structure of the Atlanta Super Bowl Host Committee and investigate how arts organizations relate to DEI initiatives. This work addresses a gap in the literature by highlighting funding with a focus related to systemic justice because it is a unique approach that does not reflect historical Super Bowl funding trends.

Keywords: Equity; mega events; arts organizations; Super Bowl; legacy

Accessibility, Diversity, Equity and Inclusion in the Cultural Sector, 185–197
Copyright © 2024 Tiffany Bourgeois
Published under exclusive licence by Emerald Publishing Limited
doi:10.1108/978-1-83753-034-220241027

Introduction

The Atlanta Super Bowl Host Committee created a specific initiative entitled Legacy 53. The Legacy 53 initiative consisted of five pillars: Business Connection, Capital Improvement Project, Civil Rights and Social Justice, Sustainability, and Youth Engagement (Reed, 2018). This chapter offers a case study (Yin, 2018) of Super Bowl LIII as a special opportunity for diversity, equity, and inclusion (DEI) initiatives for arts organizations. Specifically, it uses mega-event legacy theory (Preuss, 2015) to frame the outcomes of the sports mega-event as legacies to examine the Civil Rights and Social Justice pillar's public art project that involved community-driven mural installations across Atlanta. This chapter highlights Super Bowl LIII partnership with WonderRoot, an arts organization, to facilitate the Off the Wall Project. The project aimed to share "elements of Atlanta's civil rights and social justice journey, elevating key stories and ideas present in [the] city's pursuit of civil rights, human rights, and a more equitable future for all Atlantans" through murals, media, and community conversations (Off the Wall, n.d., para. 1).

This work uses a cultural outcomes lens to understand diversity and equity associated with the cultural programming of the Super Bowl. It also highlights how administrators can prepare for and take advantage of this unique funding opportunity during future Super Bowls. By reviewing literature on mega-events, urban development, the Olympics, and the Super Bowl, I examine the funding structure of the Atlanta Super Bowl Host Committee and investigate how arts organizations relate to DEI initiatives. Mega-event legacy theory provides a theoretical framework to understand the relationship between the mega-event and the region that hosts it by examining the lasting effects. The funds arts organizations receive from host committees are examples of the lasting effects of the Super Bowl. This work addresses a gap in the literature by highlighting funding opportunities related to systemic justice for arts organizations. It adds to the fields of arts management, mega-events, and sports because this unique funding approach does not reflect historical Super Bowl funding trends. In the future, arts organizations in cities that will host upcoming Super Bowls can prepare to take advantage of unique funding opportunities from host committees by reviewing the host committee goals and determine if they align with the mission of the organization. Specifically, highlighting opportunities for collaboration and funding could provide unique instances to support organizations with DEI initiatives. The Super Bowl, although a temporary event, could address systemic issues when coupled with arts organizations whose mission and programming are focused on DEI.

This investigation addresses the following research questions:

- In what ways did the funding structure of the Atlanta Super Bowl Host Committee for Super Bowl LIII enable DEI initiatives?
- In what ways did Super Bowl LIII engage with local arts organizations to create lasting legacies?

Background and Rationale

The National Football League (NFL) is a powerful organization in sports in the United States. It is one of the most popular and profitable sporting leagues and dominates US viewership and ratings (Oates & Furness, 2014). For example, one individual team, the Dallas Cowboys, has a worth of more than $8 billion dollars. Since the NFL is one of the most significant engines of contemporary culture (Oates & Furness, 2014), examining the cultural outcomes of the Super Bowl, its culminating and championship event, fits within this context of this research aim.

Although this chapter highlights NFL-specific initiatives that engage with accessibility, diversity, equity, and inclusion (ADEI), it is important to acknowledge the historical and continued struggles with these issues. For instance, scholars have emphasized the racist nature of mascots (Bruyneel, 2016; Davis, 1993; Davis-Delano et al., 2020; Fryberg et al., 2008). The league also lacks racial diversity in leadership and employment given the racial makeup of the players (Conlin & Emerson, 2006; DeMartini & Butler, 2022). The NFL has a history of racial norming (Gasquoine, 2022; Hobson, 2021) and negative responses to players' social justice efforts (Montez de Oca, 2021; Niven, 2020). For example, in 2016, Colin Kaepernick, a San Francisco 49ers quarterback, kneeled during the US national anthem to protest police brutality. Some considered his protest polarizing, and he received widespread criticism. In 2017, Kaepernick became a free agent but was not signed to any team, which many consider punishment for his exercising his First Amendment rights.

In order to address a variety of issues related to systemic racism associated with the organization and the United States, the NFL created programming and initiatives related to ADEI. Specifically, it began the Inspire Change initiative during the 2018 season with the hope of creating a world that is equitable and just (NFL, n.d.a; Rugg, 2020). As of 2023, "the NFL and its teams have surpassed their $250 million commitment to combat systemic racism – four years ahead of schedule" (NFL, n.d.b, para. 3). In addition to league-wide efforts, some Super Bowl–specific initiatives relate to ADEI. One initiative that has occurred during multiple Super Bowl games that exemplifies the NFL's engagement with ADEI action is the Business Connect program. The program identifies and connects qualified, local minority-, woman-, veteran-, or LGBT-owned businesses with the NFL and its vendors for contracting purposes during the Super Bowl. It also provides networking, educational, and other business development resources to prepare local participating companies for future contract opportunities (Umontuen, 2018). In Atlanta, the mission was to bring event production dollars to the city while elevating diverse locally owned businesses. More than 200 local businesses participated in the program (Umontuen, 2018).

The Atlanta Super Bowl Host Committee managed the logistics of the championship game, which was held on February 3, 2019, between the New England Patriots and the Los Angeles Rams. Specifically, the nonprofit organization acted as "the liaison between the NFL, the City of Atlanta and the local community. Formed in 2017 under the Championship Hosting Division of the Atlanta Sports Council, the Host Committee planned, organized, and supported activities and events that will enhance the Super Bowl LIII experience for the city, state, and region" (Atlanta Super Bowl Host Committee Announces Partnership with On Location Experiences, 2018). The Atlanta Super Bowl Host Committee used Legacy 53 as a means for lasting outcomes. Legacy 53 created a lasting legacy for the city, reflecting the committee's mission for the Super Bowl to leave a positive impact on Atlanta (Tucker, 2018). It boasts the lasting legacy of Super Bowl LIII across the five pillars of Business Connect (supplier diversity, civil rights and social justice, capital investment, sustainability, and youth engagement). It also included a $2.4 million renovation of John F. Kennedy Park in Atlanta's historic Westside neighborhood; 30 murals installed around the city through the Off the Wall program; and participation by more than *200* local, diverse, and certified businesses in Business Connect. In addition, the program collected 42,446 of e-waste pounds for recycling and planted more than 20,000 trees in Atlanta and the surrounding communities (Atlanta Super Bowl LIII Host Committee, 2019). This chapter focuses specifically on the Off the Wall program.

Literature Review

This literature review focuses on Super Bowl–specific outcomes related to arts and culture and extends beyond them to be more comprehensive and reflective of the field. Scholars like Inoue and Havard (2014) and David et al. (2008) have emphasized Super Bowl–specific outcomes, continuing the discussion on economic and tourism impacts, which are common in literature when discussing mega-events. Inoue and Havard (2014) investigated the determinants and consequences of the perceived social impact of a sports event. For instance, the relationship between arts organizations and funding is highlighted by the discussion of attendees' psychological benefits from the sports event's support for a charitable cause. Similarly, scholars like Groothuis and Rotthoff (2016) have examined the economic impacts and build-on additional effects of the Super Bowl through the lens of civic pride, which is like Kim and Walker's (2012) discussion of the psychological impacts of the Super Bowl on a community. These include community pride, as a result of changes in the community's image and community excitement. These intangible benefits can be examined through the lens of public goods. Benefits in form of public goods do exist but stem mainly from public funds rather than from the team and the event. This article highlights how receiving public funds can facilitate potential engagement for arts and cultural organizations with the Super Bowl (Groothuis & Rotthoff, 2016). Lastly, Lee and Krohn (2013) deepened the perspective of resident support of the event, as noted by Kim and Walker (2012). Their perspective is relevant to this study because responses by the community could impact how arts organizations engage with different opportunities associated with the Super Bowl. Specifically, the Legacy 53 initiative's Civil Rights and Social Justice pillar offers a particular opportunity focused on DEI through the community-driven public art project, Off the Wall. These scholars have provided frameworks for understanding outcomes associated with the Super Bowl outside of the general economic impact, which is relevant to this examination of arts organization engagement with Super Bowl LIII.

Theoretical Framework

This chapter emphasizes how Super Bowl LIII was a unique opportunity for DEI initiatives for arts organizations and fits within the greater framework of mega-event legacies using case study methodology (Creswell, 2007; Yin, 2018). Preuss's (2015) theory highlighted a framework that is useful for understanding how social justice initiatives can provide lasting impacts due to changes after the event, an examination of the space and the intention associated with the initiative. Although this chapter focuses on Super Bowl LIII, there are other examples, such as the Olympics and the World Cup, that support similar cultural outcomes through arts and culture programming. Preuss's (2015) framework includes components to determine a mega-event legacy. Specifically, he noted what constitutes an event-related change, who is affected by the change, how the legacy affects a particular stakeholder, and when the legacy begins and how long it lasts (Preuss, 2015, p. 649). Although the Super Bowl is a sports mega-event, the outcomes of the host committee's initiatives relate to cultural experiences and activities. This chapter uses the mega-event legacy theory framework to better understand the goals and long-term impacts of Super Bowl LIII.

In order to have a clear foundational understanding of the Super Bowl, scholars like Hiller (1995) and Müller (2015) have highlighted the general structure of a mega-event. Garcia (2008), Bourgeois (2019), and Bourgeois and Socolof (2022) focused on the cultural outcomes of sports mega-events, which is relevant for this study in understanding the relationship between host committees and arts organizations. Other scholars have focused on Super Bowl–specific outcomes (David et al., 2008). This work on Super Bowl LIII is grounded in an understanding of the economic and financial components of sports mega-events (Candid, n.d.). Lastly, Baumann and Matheson (2018), Matheson (2005), Matheson and Baade (2006), and Kim and Walker (2012) added to the perspective on the Super Bowl's economic impact, its effects on tourism, and its social impacts.

Mega-Event Legacy Theory

Preuss's discussion of mega-event legacy theory focused on an event-related change. This chapter examines legacy that is grounded in diversity and equity. Specifically, through the Legacy 53 initiative, the host committee affected change by supporting its Civil Rights and Social Justice pillar. The creation of murals through the Off the Wall project fits within this framework. This is an event-related change because the murals were created by the host committee in conjunction with WonderRoot. The mission of the arts organization was "to unite artists and community to inspire positive social change" (Candid, n.d.). The goal of the project was to share "elements of Atlanta's civil rights and social justice journey, elevating key stories and ideas present in [the] city's pursuit of civil rights, human rights and a more equitable future for all Atlantans" through murals, media, and community conversations (Off the Wall, n.d., para. 1). This work uses a cultural outcomes lens to understand diversity and equity associated with the cultural programming of the Super Bowl.

The framework to understand the relationship between the Super Bowl and the region that hosts it by examining the lasting effects related to diversity and equity is grounded in Preuss's legacy framework. Preuss (2015) included six characteristics within his definition of legacy: time, new initiatives, value, tangibility, space, and intention. In general, each Super Bowl Host Committee's initiatives can fit within this context. Funds associated with awards to support programming from local nonprofit organizations to continue after the event fit the criteria that requires a legacy last longer than the event. There is also the creation of new programmatic opportunities due to the awards. The idea that impacts can be positive or negative reflects Preuss's discussion of value. This concept relates explicitly to organizations that received funds as positive impacts and those that did not receive funds as negative impacts (Bourgeois & Socolof, 2022). The construction or development of physical spaces emphasizes the tangible nature of Preuss's fourth characteristic. The dispersion of funds within a specific city or region highlights space-specific requirements of legacy. There can be intentional and unintentional consequences due a variety of factors, like perspectives of stakeholders. This chapter adds to the discussion by explicitly applying Preuss's framework to the Off the Wall project associated with Super Bowl LIII and its relationship with ADEI.

Methodology

This article uses case study methodology to examine Super Bowl LIII as a special opportunity for DEI initiatives for arts organizations. Specifically, this investigation examines the Off the Wall Project that was supported by the Atlanta host committee and facilitated by WonderRoot. Using works by Yin (2018), Creswell (2007), and Stake (1995), I examine different sources to a support a comprehensive perspective. Data from the NFL and national and local sources serve as the foundation for this investigation.

The analytical strategy that directs this work is a reliance on theoretical propositions (Yin, 2018) for understanding DEI initiatives for Super Bowl LIII. Mega-event legacy theory (Preuss, 2007, 2015) guides the case study by framing the analysis and pointing to relevant contextual conditions. Preuss's framework that includes time, new initiatives, value, space, tangibility, and intentionality as a means for analysis supports the understanding of outcomes of mega-events. It serves as the foundation for this work. National and local sources were used to create a Super Bowl database that lists Super Bowl activities related to arts and culture organizations and funding. The data were coded by identifying themes, creating linkages, and establishing patterns (Saldana, 2009). In addition to coding, I reviewed archival data as secondary sources from entities like Beam

Imagination that highlighted the desired purposes of the murals using a material culture approach.

Findings

Super Bowl LIII highlighted opportunities for DEI through its Off the Wall initiative with WonderRoot. This organization was established in 2004 with a mission to unite artists and the community to encourage social change (Abbott, 2023). It was cofounded by Chris Appleton, Alex West, and Witt Wisebraum. Appleton took on the role of the executive director and became the prominent figurehead of the organization (Abbott, 2023). At the height of its operations, WonderRoot had eight staff members and an annual budget of close to $1 million (Emerson, 2019). The prominent arts organization provided space for artists, hosted events, and supported programming that reflected its dedication to Atlanta youth, community, and organizers before it closed in 2019. The closure of the organization was preceded by controversy. Former employees and members of the Atlanta art community penned an open letter that accused Appleton of abusive behavior, including charges of racism, financial misconduct, and discrimination against vulnerable groups (Abbott, 2023). Appleton was placed on leave, and Brian Tolleson was placed as interim executive director. A third-party law firm was hired to investigate the claims. The report from the law firm confirmed that Appleton repeatedly behaved in an "unprofessional manner" with his staff and had challenges with financial management. The investigation did not find any evidence of sexual impropriety or racism (ArtsATL, 2019). Appleton later resigned, and the organization was unable to survive due to lack of financial support (Emerson, 2019).

The Off the Wall initiative was one of the last programs that WonderRoot supported before the organization closed. It provided opportunities for artists and community members to work together and collaborate to create murals as a legacy. The creation and implementation of lasting legacy initiatives falls under the purview of the Super Bowl Host Committee. By reviewing the roles and outcomes associated with the Atlanta Super Bowl Host Committee, this investigation notes the intention of having a positive impact on the Atlanta community with initiatives that focus on civil rights and social justice. Through murals, media, and community conversations the Off the Wall project was created to show the civil rights and social justice history and present the city's pursuit of a more equitable future for Atlantans (Off the Wall, n.d., para. 1).

The Off the Wall project was part of the Civil Rights and Social Justice pillar that was initiated by WonderRoot and the Atlanta Super Bowl Host Committee. It took place from June 2018 to February 2019 with 11 different artists, the majority of the whom were people of color and associated with Atlanta. Interestingly, one of the artists was selected by the Atlanta community (Off the Wall, n.d.). A description of creating the murals highlights an inclusive process. Specifically, there were 43 conversations with community partners that engaged over 1,000 participants. The community conversations were able to collectively inform the creation of the murals. The artist created the mural designs based on these community conversations. WonderRoot facilitated multiple feedback sessions to invite residents to comment on the design concepts (Off the Wall, n.d.).

Using Preuss's framework to understand legacy includes six characteristics: time, new initiatives, value tangibility, space, and intention. The Off the Wall project fulfills the first criterion, time. Specifically, it requires the outcome to last "longer than the event and its directly initiated impacts. Legacies can derive from structures already completed before the event, but most legacies stem from changed location factors after the event takes place" (Preuss, 2015, p. 647). Although the project was focused on the celebration of the Super Bowl, there are still some murals available for viewing since the completion of the championship game. For instance, *Helping Hands* by Muhammad Yungai is viewable at the Woodruff Library at the Atlanta University Center and fulfills the criteria of change that occurs after the event. Also, legacy requires "new opportunities out of an initial impact and may even develo[p] its own dynamics over time as the environment changes" (Preuss, 2015, p. 647). The Off the Wall project was a new opportunity that was created due to the Super Bowl. The collaboration and community involvement created new opportunities for artists and work founded in DEI. The spaces have developed over time. For instance, the initial act of creating the murals physically changed the appearance of the locations. Also, the changing state of the murals as time progresses reflects these criteria. Next, the outcome should consist "of changes that bring positive outcomes for some stakeholders and negative outcomes for others" (Preuss, 2015, p. 647). Value associated with the Off the Wall mural project is complicated by the temporary nature of the host committee and the closing of WonderRoot. For instance, it had appropriate elements for positive value because local artists had an opportunity to create works with the support of formal institutions and community members. Yet, the lack of ownership of the murals makes it difficult to note who is responsible for their upkeep and maintenance. This has resulted in deterioration of the murals and the spaces that house them. The deteriorated structures con-structed during and for sports mega-events are referred to as white elephants. The tangibility of the formal structures of the murals fulfills the Preuss' perspective. The Off the Wall project's focus on Atlanta ensured that it embodied the spatial element of the framework. It was "limited to a defined space, that is, a city" (Preuss, 2015, p. 647). The civil rights and social justice theme of Legacy 53 effectively related to Atlanta. The murals fit the needs of the Super Bowl and embodied the culture and history of the city grounded in the civil rights move-ment, housing historically Black colleges and universities and institutions related to human rights. Lastly, legacies can "be developed indirectly by the event" (Preuss, 2015, p. 647). In general, host committees note the positive impacts they intend for the mega-event to have. Yet, there can be some unintended negative consequences. The intention for Super Bowl LIII was to have a positive impact on the Atlanta community and highlight the city's journey with civil rights and social justice. Yet, the lack of clear ownership over the murals after the Super Bowl resulted in unintended negative outcomes.

Discussion

The Off the Wall Project does fit the general framework for mega-event legacies, but Preuss's elements of time, tangibility, and intention emphasize a richer connection to the pursuits of this study because of how they support the creation and implementation of similar initiatives in the future. For instance, there will be a Super Bowl each year that will provide opportunities for long-term impacts. New host committees will continually determine the lasting impacts their programming and initiatives will have on the communities they serve. Also, the tangibility of the outcomes associated with the initiatives affects how stakeholders will engage with them. The intention is relevant to this study when examining the long-term upkeep of the structures, which affects the communities that house the murals.

The Off the Wall project relates to Preuss's discussion of time within the context of structures being in place post the Super Bowl and how other host committees can engage with it for future championships. Specifically, the Atlanta Super Bowl Host Committee used Legacy 53 as a means for creating lasting outcomes that exemplified the intention of their mission for the Super Bowl to leave a positive impact on Atlanta (Tucker, 2018). Preuss described time as lasting longer than the event and its directly initiated impacts. Legacies can derive from structures completed before the event, but most legacies stem from changes to location factors after the event takes places (Preuss, p. 647). The longevity of the murals associated with the Off the Wall project is explicitly connected to Super Bowl LIII. The project is an example as how sports mega-events engage with arts organizations and DEIA initiatives. The annual nature of the championship game provides a framework for review of past initiatives. In addition, the temporary time frame of the Super Bowl allows for visitors to examine or view the art after the championship game.

Preuss's discussion of tangibility is relevant to the Off the Wall project. Specifically, he stated, "it may be tangible or intangible, or material or non-material" (Preuss, 2015, p. 647). Artists created tangible works that allowed for citizens of Atlanta or visitors to experience using necessary materials to support the creation of the murals. The content of the work that highlighted the elements related to civil rights and a more equitable future is pertinent to the discussion of DEI initiatives. For instance, the project is a tangible example of the initiative. Also the materials used to create the mural and the content are examples of tangibility. There is also an intangible element that comes from experiencing the artwork. It can happen collectively, when viewing with others, or singly, when viewing by oneself. Reflection on the content, its history, and its present relevance is a nonmaterial element that is relevant to the understanding and long-term impact of the murals. The host committee for Super Bowl LIII supported DEI through Off the Wall as their Civil Rights and Social Justice pillar's public art project. Specifically, the content of the murals that is grounded in civil and human rights is an example of a DEI initiative facilitated by the arts organization, WonderRoot.

The explicit intention of the project is also grounded in DEI because of the focus on civil and human rights and the pursuit of a more equitable future (Off the Wall, n.d., para. 1). The creation of the murals was thoughtfully designed and emphasized community involvement. Yet, the closure of WonderRoot and the temporary nature of the Super Bowl Host Committee reflect no formal oversight of the future of the murals. This can result in deterioration, which impacts how Atlanta residents and visitors experience the murals and hinders their ability to explore the themes presented in the art related to DEI.

Conclusion

This chapter used mega-event legacy theory as a lens to examine how the funding structure of the Atlanta Super Bowl Host Committee for Super Bowl LIII participated in DEI initiatives and engagement with local arts organizations. Super Bowl LIII did engage with ADEI through explicit Legacy 53 initiatives. The host committee and the collaborating arts organization, WonderRoot, grounded the Off the Wall project in Atlanta's civil rights and social justice history and engaged with local artists and community members. The creation of tangible pieces of art and intangible experiences between viewers of the murals that occurred after the Super Bowl fit Preuss's framework. Also, it reveals intention when engaging with artists that focused on themes relevant to civil and human rights and potential deterioration of the murals due to lack of ownership as outcomes. Specifically, the history of civil rights and social justice in Atlanta is represented in the content of the murals and their location. Due to changes surrounding leadership, WonderRoot is no longer an organization, and the host committee was a temporary organization. Since the organizational leadership that began the project is no longer functioning, it is unclear what will happen to the murals. This chapter identifies how the Super Bowl engages with accessibility, DEI, and arts organizations. It provides arts and cultural organizations a framework for identifying how to engage with a sports mega-event and potential outcomes. Next steps for this work include a long-term review of the condition of the murals and how community members and visitors engage with the pieces to investigate if the murals are fulfilling their original goal.

References

Abbott, D. (2023, September 10). *What happened to WonderRoot? An Atlanta arts center.* CultureFrontier. https://www.culturefrontier.com/wonderroot/

ArtsATL. (2019, August 3). *WonderRoot, founded to pursue social justice through art, closes after 15 years.* https://www.artsatl.org/popular-arts-nonprofit-wonderroot-closes-down-for-good-after-15-years/

Atlanta Super Bowl Host Committee announces partnership with on location experiences. (2018, March 22). *Business Wire.* https://www.businesswire.com/news/home/20180322005752/en/Atlanta-Super-Bowl-Host-Committee-Announces-Partnership-with-On-Location-Experiences. Accessed on November 22, 2023.

Atlanta Super Bowl LIII Host Committee. (2019, February 11). Atlanta wins big as host to Super Bowl LIII. *Wayback Machine.* https://web.archive.org/web/20190514183231/http://atlsuperbowl53.com/atlanta-wins-big-as-host-to-super-bowl-liii/

Baumann, R., & Matheson, V. (2018). Mega-events and tourism: The case of Brazil: World Cup tourism. *Contemporary Economic Policy, 36*(2), 292–301. https://doi.org/10.1111/coep.12270

Bourgeois, T. (2019). London 2012 Olympics: Exercises in cultural diplomacy. *Place Branding and Public Diplomacy, 15*(3), 198–205. https://doi.org/10.1057/s41254-017-0084-4

Bourgeois, T., & Socolof, J. (2022). Super Bowl LII: Rural arts and cultural institution engagement. *American Journal of Arts Management, 10*(22).

Bruyneel, K. (2016). Race, colonialism, and the politics of Indian sports names and mascots: The Washington Football Team case. *Native American and Indigenous Studies, 3*(2), 1–24. https://doi.org/10.5749/natiindistudj.3.2.0001

Candid. (n.d.). *WonderRoot Inc—GuideStar profile.* https://www.guidestar.org/profile/56-2482941#financials. Accessed on March 12, 2023.

Conlin, M., & Emerson, P. M. (2006). Discrimination in hiring versus retention and promotion: An empirical analysis of within-firm treatment of players in the NFL. *Journal of Law, Economics, and Organization, 22*(1), 115–136. https://doi.org/10.1093/jleo/ewj005

Creswell, J. W. (2007). *Qualitative inquiry and research design: Choosing among five approaches* (2nd ed., pp. xvii, 395). Sage Publications.

David, P., Horton, B., & German, T. (2008). Dynamics of entertainment and affect in a Super Bowl audience: A multilevel approach. *Communication Research, 35*(3), 398–420. https://doi.org/10.1177/0093650208315965

Davis, L. R. (1993). Protest against the use of native American mascots: A challenge to traditional American identity. *Journal of Sport & Social Issues, 17*(1), 9–22. https://doi.org/10.1177/019372359301700103

Davis-Delano, L. R., Gone, J. P., & Fryberg, S. A. (2020). The psychosocial effects of native American mascots: A comprehensive review of empirical research findings. *Race, Ethnicity and Education, 23*(5), 613–633. https://doi.org/10.1080/13613324.2020.1772221

DeMartini, A. L., & Butler, B. N. (2022). Perspective: National Football League teams need chief diversity officers. *Frontiers in Sports and Active Living, 4.* https://www.frontiersin.org/articles/10.3389/fspor.2022.891516

Emerson, B. (2019, August 2). WonderRoot, troubled arts organization, is disbanded. *Atlanta Journal-Constitution.* https://www.ajc.com/entertainment/arts–theater/wonderroot-troubled-arts-organization-disbanded/fLEeKknuyIv6oV6TjtyhaM/

Fryberg, S. A., Markus, H. R., Oyserman, D., & Stone, J. M. (2008). Of warrior chiefs and Indian princesses: The psychological consequences of American Indian mascots. *Basic and Applied Social Psychology, 30*(3), 208–218. https://doi.org/10.1080/01973530802375003

Garcia, B. (2008). One hundred years of cultural programming within the Olympic Games (1912–2012): Origins, evolution and projections. *International Journal of Cultural Policy, 14*(4), 361–376. https://doi.org/10.1080/10286630802445849

Gasquoine, P. G. (2022). Performance-based alternatives to race-norms in neuropsychological assessment. *Cortex, 148,* 231–238. https://doi.org/10.1016/j.cortex.2021.12.003

Groothuis, P. A., & Rotthoff, K. W. (2016). The economic impact and civic pride effects of sports teams and mega-events: Do the public and the professionals agree?

Economic Affairs, 36(1), 21–32. https://doi-org.proxy.lib.ohio-state.edu/10.1111/ecaf.12156

Hiller, H. (1995). Conventions as mega-events—A new model for convention host city relationships. *Tourism Management, 16*(5), 375–379. https://doi.org/10.1016/02615177(95)00041-L

Hobson, W. (2021, August 3). How "race-norming" was built into the NFL concussion settlement. *Washington Post.* https://www.washingtonpost.com/sports/2021/08/02/race-norming-nfl-concussion-settlement/

Inoue, Y., & Havard, C. T. (2014). Determinants and consequences of the perceived social impact of a sport event. *Journal of Sport Management, 28*(3), 295–310.

Kim, W., & Walker, M. (2012). Measuring the social impacts associated with Super Bowl XLIII: Preliminary development of a psychic income scale. *Sport Management Review, 15*(1), 91–108. https://doi-org.proxy.lib.ohio-state.edu/10.1016/j.smr.2011.05.007

Lee, S., & Krohn, B. D. (2013). A study of psychological support from local residents for hosting mega-sporting events: A case of the 2012 Indianapolis super bowl XLVI. *Event Management, 17*(4), 361–376. https://doi.org/10.3727/152599513X13769392444585

Matheson, V. A. (2005). Contrary evidence on the economic effect of the Super Bowl on the victorious city. *Journal of Sports Economics, 6*(4), 420–428. https://doi.org.proxy.lib.ohio-state.edu/10.1177/1527002504267489

Matheson, V. A., & Baade, R. A. (2006, January 1). Padding required: Assessing the economic impact of the Super Bowl. *European Sport Management Quarterly, 6*(4), 353–374.

Montez de Oca, J. (2021). Marketing politics and resistance: Mobilizing black pain in national football league publicity. *Sociology of Sport Journal, 38*(2), 101–110. https://doi.org/10.1123/ssj.2021-0005

Müller, M. (2015). What makes an event a mega-event? Definitions and sizes. *Leisure Studies, 34*(6), 627–642. https://doi.org/10.1080/02614367.2014.993333

National Football League. (n.d.a). *History of NFL's inspire change initiative.* https://www.nfl.com/videos/history-of-nfl-s-inspire-change-initiative. Accessed on March 12, 2023.

National Football League. (n.d.b). *NFL expands commitment to social justice with new 5-year players coalition partnership.* https://www.nfl.com/news/nfl-expands-commitment-to-social-justice-with-new-5-year-players-coalition-partn. Accessed on March 12, 2023.

Niven, D. (2020). Stifling workplace activism: The consequences of anthem protests for NFL players. *Social Science Quarterly, 101*(2), 641–655. https://doi.org/10.1111/ssqu.12756

Oates, T. P., & Furness, Z. (Eds.). (2014). *The NFL: Critical and cultural perspectives.* Temple University Press. https://www.jstor.org/stable/j.ctt14bsvzs

Off the Wall. (n.d.). *Off the Wall.* https://www.offthewallatl.org/. Accessed on March 12, 2023.

Preuss, H. (2007). The conceptualisation and measurement of mega sport event legacies. *Journal of Sport & Tourism, 12*(3–4), 207–228.

Preuss, H. (2015). A framework for identifying the legacies of a mega sport event. *Leisure Studies, 34*(6), 643–664.

Reed, K. (2018, June 26). Atlanta Super Bowl Committee announces legacy 53, a community *11Alive*. https://www.11alive.com/article/sports/nfl/superbowl/atlanta-super-bowl-committee-announces-legacy-53-a-community-engagement-initiative/85-567595922

Rugg, A. (2020). Incorporating the protests: The NFL, social justice, and the constrained activism of the "Inspire Change" campaign. *Communication & Sport*, *8*(4–5), 611–628. https://doi.org/10.1177/2167479519896325

Saldana, J. (2009). *The coding manual for qualitative researchers*. Sage Publications.

Stake, R. (1995). *The arts of case study research*. Sage Publications.

Tucker, T. (2018, June 26). *Atlanta's Super Bowl launches "Legacy 53" program*. The Atlanta Journal-Constitution. https://www.ajc.com/sports/atlanta-super-bowl-launches-legacyprogram/9z5qMccVgfTZZWFMUFWTkN/

Umontuen, I. (2018, June 29). *The Atlanta Super Bowl Host Committee to announce the launch of "Legacy 53" service initiative*. The Atlanta Voice. https://theatlantavoice.com/atlantassuperbowlcommittee-will-launch-legacy-53/

Yin, R. (2018). *Case study research and applications: Design methods* (6th ed.). Sage.

Chapter 13

Local and Popular Cultural Festivals as Venues for the Promotion of Equity, Diversity, and Inclusion: The Case of the Petronio Álvarez Pacific Music Festival in Colombia

Luis F. Aguado[a]*, Alexei Arbona*[a] *and Jesús Heredia-Carroza*[b]

[a]Pontificia Universidad Javeriana Cali, Colombia
[b]Universidad de Sevilla, Spain

Abstract

This chapter offers empirical evidence of the contribution of a local and popular festival to diversity and inclusion in the hosting territory. With this in mind, three impacts (economic, social, and cultural) are determined and measured from the triple perspective of the creation of value of cultural assets. We show the case of the XXII edition of the *Petronio Álvarez Pacific Music Festival* held in the city of Cali (Colombia) from August 15th to 20th, 2018. The estimates were taken from three sources: (i) an input–output model adapted for the economy of the city of Cali, (ii) A face-to-face survey of 1,030 festival attendees over 18 years old, and (iii) A face-to-face survey of a representatives of each of the 173 business positions that took part in the Festival (e.g., handicrafts, musical instruments, traditional beverages, cuisine, hairstyles, and cosmetics). The results show that the festival: (i) generates inclusive material wealth, which is measured through income and employment for Afro-colombian communities, traditionally marginalized and economically disadvantaged; (ii) is shown as an opportunity to promote intercultural dialogue and diversity for the local community and tourists; and (iii) the community attending the festival (both locals and tourists) contribute to the cultural enrichment of the territory. The applied method might be replicated for other festivals case of studies in other countries in

Accessibility, Diversity, Equity and Inclusion in the Cultural Sector, 199–213
Copyright © 2024 Luis F. Aguado, Alexei Arbona and Jesús Heredia-Carroza
Published under exclusive licence by Emerald Publishing Limited
doi:10.1108/978-1-83753-034-220241029

order to generate evidence that can be used for designing cultural policies which encourage diversity and equity in a specific territory.

Keywords: Diversity and inclusion; cultural festival; economic value; social value; cultural value; Petronio Álvarez Pacific music festival

Introduction

Culture and Economy present a nexus associated with the generation of cultural value (Frey, 2000; Throsby, 2001). Many of the elements of this value are not easily measured and estimated from an economic perspective; shared beliefs, customs, and rituals of a festival contribute to the achievement of cultural, social, and economic development, reflected on the competitiveness of the territories (Boyd, 2020; Garcia & Judd, 2012; Heredia-Carroza, Aguado, et al., 2023; World Bank Group, 2015). According to UNESCO (2022) cultural and creative sectors constitute the main assets that generate income and jobs focused on innovation, social inclusion, and environmental care. Cultural festivals have an impact on the territories that host them from multiple perspectives: economically, through job creation; socially, through promoting values such as diversity, inclusion, and equity; and, culturally through preserving and innovating with cultural and artistic expression that reflect the intangible heritage of a community.

A music festival is defined as "a musical event of large attendance and certain duration consisting of performances by various bands and artists in a limited period of time and space" (Brandão & De Oliveira, 2019). As Frey (2020) has pointed out, music festivals are "an art form in constant flux," which allows recreating and expressing memories and experiences of a specific community, socializing and gathering family and friends, and also allows an intergenerational transfer of culture, which interacts positively with communities of different ethnic backgrounds, attracting tourism and wealth (Zhuang et al., 2023).

In this context, local and popular cultural festivals are events that play an important role in the social and economic development of a community and express its intangible cultural heritage (Getz, 2010; Palma et al., 2013; UNESCO, 2015). These festivals show a positive relationship between culture, territory, and local development (OECD, 2005; UNESCO & World Bank, 2021). Specifically, cultural festivals play a multidimensional social role, contributing to: (i) improving people's quality of life (Dwyer & Jago, 2018; Getz et al., 2018; Pavluković et al., 2019); (ii) Promoting diversity, inclusion, and equity (Belfiore, 2020; Laing & Mair, 2015); and, finally, (iii) Generating wealth represented by income and employment (Snowball, 2008) focused on the local population who are traditionally in vulnerability conditions (Aguado et al., 2021; Saayman & Rossouw, 2011).

In equity terms, any type of action or measure that limit people's participation in economic life (e.g., in the labor market) constitutes a barrier to the society development and prosperity (Buckman et al., 2021). According to the Council of Europe (2017) more diverse and inclusive societies reflect higher levels of equity and social justice that translate into better competitiveness and development outcomes (OECD, 2022). This chapter shows the contribution of Petronio Álvarez Pacific Music Festival (hereinafter, El Petronio) to diversity, inclusion, and equity in the host city within the context of value generation in the cultural sector. Diversity recognizes, understands, and agrees differences among people reflected in their own features and backgrounds (e.g., age, gender, ethnic, self-recognition, disability, religion, sexual orientation, and class). Inclusion and equity encourage a fair ecosystem which makes fell the people heard, supported, and integrated, without barriers that imply discrimination and intolerance toward differences.

Finally, the results obtained contribute to the empirical literature on the economic, social, and cultural effects generated by cultural festivals in the territory. Firstly, few studies have empirically measured these effects. Secondly, the results invite cultural policymakers to improve the information they provide to different agents (artists, cultural managers, and the community in general) about the impact of this type of event on the territory, and its contribution to diversity, inclusion, and equity.

Local and Popular Cultural Festivals: An Intervention Strategy Focused on Diversity and Inclusion

This section introduces the concept that embodies the complexity and multidimensional nature of the value associated with cultural activities and events. To this end, we present a systematic interaction of the cultural, social, and economic values associated with festivals, which contribute to a strategy of sustainability, and a more complete understanding of the impacts of these events (see Table 13.1), consisting of economic, social, and cultural value. The latter is reflected in key empirical elements for the promotion and stimulation of the economic and institutional relationships linked to the sustainable use of cultural resources as a strategy for local economic development, assuming cultural diversity as a public good that improves the way in which societies function.

El Petronio is the most prestigious cultural event of marimba music, and Afro-Colombian Pacific traditional songs and dances. This music and dances were included in the Representative List of the Intangible Cultural Heritage of Humanity by UNESCO in 2015. The case of El Petronio illustrates how intangible heritage can encourage the socioeconomic development of the territory which hosts it (Cali, Colombia). It was measured through the triple perspective of the value generation of cultural goods (Heredia-Carroza et al., 2019; Rivera et al., 2008; SACO, 2016; Throsby, 2003; Wallstam, 2022). This offers an approximation of the wide variety of ways in which quantitative data express and measure the value generated by a cultural festival.

As illustrated in Table 13.1, a cultural festival (e.g., popular music, local dances, and gastronomy) is a way of expressing the intangible cultural heritage associated with the idiosyncrasy and past of a territory (Heredia-Carroza, Palma, & Aguado, 2023). Its cultural value, reflecting the heritage of the past, is embodied in the sentiments invoked by the attendees/participants, which are

Table 13.1. Cultural, Social, and Economic Value Generated by a Cultural Festival in Cali (Colombia).

Type of Value	Description	Implementation in the Territory	Contribution to Diversity and Inclusion
Cultural	Generates an ecosystem to conserve and develop the cultural heritage of the territory and enrich the stock of cultural capital of the people.	Protection and preservation of own cultural expressions and traditions.	The festival represents, preserves, and innovates in cultural and artistic expressions that reflect the customs, traditions, and diversity of the population of the Colombian Pacific. This population is mostly characterized (Urrea et al., 2021): (1) being of African descent, (2) with high levels of poverty.
Social	Source of positive cultural exchanges for locals and tourists that improve the quality of life in the territory. Encourages diversity and inclusion.	Participation/Attendance: Meeting and integration with family and friends. Bridge for intercultural dialogue among people with different ethnic and social backgrounds through music, dance, gastronomy, and traditional crafts.	
Economic	Source of new income and employment. Contributes to generate brand and image to the territory as a tourist destination.	Employment for artists, creative artists and the value chain that supports the event (e.g., local transportation, hotels, equipment rental, and stage logistics). Unique and authentic experience that attracts attendees to the region.	

positively tied in with their personal well-being, the evolution of skills for cultural participation and the preservation, transfer and protection of cultural heritage gathered over time (Heredia-Carroza, Palma et al., 2023). Its social value is manifested in the present through multiple channels such as social cohesion, positive cultural interaction among culturally distinct population groups, and the promotion of values such as diversity and tolerance. Its economic value can be seen in the ability of the festival to generate income and employment resulting from the celebration, which boosts the local economy. Likewise, the celebration of the festival can offer a territory a competitive advantage against competing tourist destinations, by offering an option to attract tourists (national and international) looking for new and varied cultural experiences.

In short, a local and popular cultural festival represents an ideal vehicle for the advancement of diversity and inclusion. These events contribute to the elimination of barriers that divide and prevent large segments of the population from their active involvement in the cultural, social, and economic life of the environment in which they live. Specifically, a local and popular cultural festival facilitates, in the context of supply, from its conception and production, the involvement of artists and creative individuals from vulnerable communities (ethnic minorities in conditions of poverty) focused on traditional skills associated with music, dance, gastronomy and ancestral crafts. In the context of demand, it enables the participation and attendance of local communities that are identified by their customs and traditions, while conserving, preserving, and valuing these customs and traditions to national and international audiences for their cultural enrichment, and the enjoyment of unique and authentic experiences.

The Petronio Álvarez Pacific Music Festival (Cali, Colombia): Contribution to the Diversity and Inclusion of the Hosting Territory

The Petronio Álvarez Pacific Music Festival is an institution that facilitates the setting in motion of commitments and specific activities designed to create opportunities for economic inclusion for the Afro-Colombian population. The *Petronio Álvarez Pacific Music Festival*, as a cultural event, enables the people of the Colombian Pacific, throughout its 6 days' duration, to recreate and express the memories and experiences of their place of birth, socialize and reconnect with family and friends. The city of Cali, as organizer and host of the festival, recognizes the abundance of its cultural diversity which, in turn, is a source of multiple cultural, social, and economic benefits.

Profile: *The Petronio Álvarez Pacific Music Festival*

From the standpoint of cultural economics (Towse, 2019), one can define Petronio as a cultural good. For more than two uninterrupted decades of celebration, it has preserved the customs and traditions associated with the cultural heritage of the inhabitants of the Colombian Pacific. Its distinctive elements allow it to express creativity and add a stamp of content and meaning to the music, dance, crafts, food and drinks, costumes, and hairstyles, from this region. Table 13.2 offers a more complete picture of the nature of the festival, the different areas in which it occurs, and pinpoints the channels through which the values described above are created.

Table 13.2. Nature and Main Characteristics: *The Petronio Álvarez Pacific Music Festival.*

Official Name	Petronio Álvarez Pacific Music Festival
City that hosts it and season of the celebration	Santiago de Cali, Colombia, August of each year
Starting year, duration, and number of editions	August 1997; 6 days; 26 editions.
Description	The festival is the most significant meeting place for the people of the Pacific region in Colombia. It focuses on their traditional music, and recreates the traditional arts and crafts that express their identity.
Program	The program is made up of five events, (i) The main focus is the competition of groups in Afro-Colombian Pacific airs and music – marimba and traditional songs, chirimia, Cauca violin, free group; (ii) The Petronito with child musicians between 6 and 14 years of age; (iii) academic encounters; (iv) pedagogical quilombo, a space that promotes integration, coexistence, and respect for the culture of the Pacific; (v) commercial exhibition of traditional cultural expression: crafts and designs, cuisine and local drinks, sweets and soft drinks, hairstyles and cosmetics.
Credentials	Cultural Heritage of the Nation (Law 1472 of 2011, Congress of the Republic of Colombia). In 2015, the marimba music and traditional songs and dances of the Colombian Pacific region were included in the Representative List of the Intangible Cultural Heritage of Humanity by UNESCO. "Festival de Música del Pacífico Petronio Álvarez" is a joint trademark owned by the Municipality of Cali

Table 13.2. *(Continued)*

Official Name	Petronio Álvarez Pacific Music Festival
	(resolution No. 29152 of the Superintendence of Industry and Commerce of the Republic of Colombia).
Festival Management	The person in charge, organizer, and financier of the festival is the Mayor's Office of Cali. The festival has its own regulations set by a group of advisory bodies: Conceptual Committee (to advise on the planning and development of the festival); Jury Regulation of the Music Contest; Regulation of the commercial sample of traditional expressions of the Pacific.
Scenarios	The festival takes place in a single venue, called the Petronio Citadel (Village), temporarily built to host the three main events: the music contest, the pedagogical quilombo, and the commercial exhibition of traditional cultural expression. The events are contiguous and take place simultaneously within the Citadel.
Creative talent	1,108 creative artists: 431 musicians (musical contest) + 173 musicians (Guests) + 504 artisans in 173 commercial stalls.
Attendees	368,650 attendees during the 6 days of the festival. An average attendee spends 2.69 days; thus, we estimate that the festival was visited by 137,045 individuals. Using the filter question of the survey that asked about the main reason to visit the city of Cali on the dates of the festival, enabled us to estimate that 74,349 individual attendees whose main reason for visiting the city of Cali was to attend the festival.
Festival organization costs	COP $ 5,168 million (USD 1.75 million), 86% is set by the Mayor's Office of Cali.
Access to events	Admission for attendees to the citadel (village) is free.

Source: Aguado et al. (2021, Table 13.1, p. 311).

Methodological Aspects

To provide an empirical measure of the cultural, social, and economic value generated by the festival and to estimate indicators of diversity and inclusion, we used three sources of information:

(1) *Survey of attendees.*[1] We obtained the spending of the attendees and the assessment of the nonmonetary (social, cultural) values from a questionnaire applied through a face-to-face survey to people over 18 years of age during the festival. August 15th–20th, 2018. We selected respondents using systematic sampling techniques by geographic place of residence (Bethlehem, 2009). In total, we attained 1,030 attendee surveys (636 local residents and 394 tourists). The attendee surveys provide a 95% confidence level and a 3.0% margin of error for all attendees. To reach this sample, we made a total of 1,376 survey attempts, 346 of which did not pass the filter question: "Is attending the Petronio Álvarez Festival the main reason why you are in Cali today?" This question is essential to estimate the economic value, in the sense that it implies the reason without which the trip would not have been made, in the case of nonlocal attendees (from the rest of Colombia and abroad). In the case of local residents, it is understood as the reason that keeps them, in the specific season, in the city (see United Nations, 2000).

(2) *Survey to commercial stalls:* Application of a face-to-face survey instrument to the representatives of each of the 173 commercial stalls that participated in the sample of traditional expressions of the Afro-Colombian Pacific (49 of handicrafts, instruments, and design; 48 of traditional and native beverages; 59 of traditional cuisines; 7 of sweets, snacks, and soft drinks and 10 of hairstyles and cosmetics). The survey made it possible to describe the types of services/products sold at the stall, as well as if the business currently operates in a municipality other than Cali, if it buys inputs in a municipality in the Pacific region, how many people work by type of employment (creative, support), among other relevant information.

(3) *Input–output model adapted to the economy of the city of Cali.*[2] This model transforms the sources of demand (spending/investment in the organization of the festival + spending by attendees) into effects on production and employment in the impact area, defined as the city of Cali (SACO, 2019). The structure of the model is as follows: $X = [I - A]^{(-1)} D$, where X is a vector showing the gross value of firms' production, I represents the identity matrix, A represents the input–output coefficients. The latter represents the inter-sectoral purchase flows per unit of production reflecting the direct and indirect relationships of the productive structure of an economy; D is the vector of demand for production by agents (consumers, firms, and government).

---

[1]The questionnaire and the database from the surveys are available on request.
[2]The structure and results of the input–output model are available on request.

Contribution of the Petronio to Diversity and Inclusion in Figures

The results provide a clear relationship: festival → territory → local development, which is evidenced by the creation of value (economic, social, and cultural), which is manifested in the improvements and expansion in the different dimensions that have impacted the well-being of the population in a positive way, and the geographical location that hosts the festival. From improvements in social cohesion and the reinforcement of the identity of local residents with their places of origin, increases in the personal well-being of those who enjoy the festival as attendees (e.g., an escape from routine, have a moment to escape from the stress of everyday life, the transmission of cultural values), the improvement of skills for new artists and creative artists (e.g., innovation in styles, a platform to exhibit new works), the preservation, transfer, and protection of cultural heritage, employment opportunities for artists and creative artists of ethnic populations in conditions of poverty, attraction of tourists to the territory. The figures and indicators presented below have been estimated based on microdata from the three sources of information listed in the previous section.

Cultural Impact: 97.7% and 96.4%, respectively, of the festival's attendees agreed that the festival contributes to their cultural enrichment and preserves the cultural expressions and traditions of the Afro-Colombian Pacific. *Social impact:* 95.8% and 98.2%, respectively, of the attendees agreed that the celebration of the festival contributes to the integration and cohesion of the Afro-descendant communities of the Pacific with the other communities that live in the city, and contributes to the image of Cali as a city that houses and encourages cultural diversity. *Economic Impact*: 94.3% of attendees agreed that the celebration of the festival contributes to the generation of new income and employment in the city of Cali and the Colombian Pacific. Thirty-nine percent of the tourists (national + international) attending the festival visited the city of Cali for the first time. *Ethnic self-identification of attendees*: 43% Afro-descendant, 4.6% indigenous, and 52% the rest (mestizo, white).

Inclusion by gender and age: The festival is visited mostly by women. In fact, 61.2% of the attendees are women, especially in the case of attendees from Cali and the Pacific. In the case of tourists (from other cities in Colombia and abroad), this percentage is 57.4%. By age range, the profile of the attendees indicates that they are mostly young. For all the origins of residence of the attendees, the age is concentrated between 18 and 35 years old.

Diversity and integration of the Afro-Colombian Pacific culture as part of the cultural identity of the city of Cali. In the city of Cali, 14.62% of the population recognizes itself as Black, Mulatto, Afro-descendant, and Afro-Colombian (DANE, 2023). However, for 89.6% of local attendees who recognize themselves as white/Mestizo, the festival represents their culture and identity.

Economic inclusion, between the economy of the city of Cali and the rest of the municipalities of the Colombian Pacific region, through the economic impact generated by the festival. These municipalities have high levels of monetary poverty among their population: The exhibition of traditional handicrafts from the Pacific region, which takes place in the Petronio citadel, is made up of 173 commercial stalls: 123 are permanent (they operate during the rest of the year in Cali and/or in their places of origin) and 50 are temporarily built for the festival. Ninety-three are family-owned, 23 are collectively owned, and 57 are individually owned. The festival generates income and employment in the Pacific municipalities through a double channel: (i) the income received by exhibitors coming from the Pacific and (ii) the purchase of inputs (e.g., local products, seeds, fibers) for the preparation of food, beverages and handicrafts from these municipalities. The economic impact on the economy of Colombia's Pacific municipalities, other than Cali, amounts to $12,031 million (US$4.1 million), generating 319 jobs equivalent to 172 full-time jobs.

Employment in the Petronio: The 173 stalls sampled of traditional activities of the Pacific generated a total of 929 direct full-time employment. Of these, 503 were creative (e.g., cooks, hairdressers, costume designers, craftsmen) and 426 support staff (e.g., waiters, salespeople).

The economy of the Petronio Álvarez Pacific Music Festival: The festival has a cost of $5,168 million (US$1.75 million) and mobilizes resources of $42,644 million (US$14.4 million), comprising organizational expenses and those of the attendees. The economic impact on the economy of the city of Cali and its metropolitan area is $116,724 million (US$39.4 million), generating 3,551 jobs, equivalent to 1,849 full-time jobs. Expectations: 95.6% of attendees believed that the experience of attending the festival met or exceeded their expectations.

Programming: 93.5% of the attendees had a favorable opinion about the programming of the festival.

Fig. 13.1 presents a synthesis of the generation of value to the city of Cali and the Colombian Pacific by the festival.

Conclusions

In this case study, we presented a practical approach that gathered empirical evidence on the generation of value of cultural assets associated with intangible cultural heritage. This includes the value associated with preserving and protecting traditions, festivals, and memories, which implies keeping in the present time dialogues and knowledge among different cultures, which are key to the promotion of a creative and innovative environment and to encourage diversity and socioeconomic inclusion of ethnic populations in territories with high levels of poverty.

The evidence provided shows that the experience of attending the *Petronio Álvarez Pacific Music Festival* as a spectator contributes to one's own cultural enrichment (97%), to the image of Cali as a city that hosts and encourages cultural diversity (98.2%) and to the generation of income and employment for the city (94.3%). In the same way, the celebration of the festival attracts tourists to the city who will later repeat the visit. In terms of creative talent, the festival gives work to 1,108 creatives within the Petronio Citadel: 503 artisans on the exhibition of traditional cultural activities of the Pacific and 431 musicians (musical contest) + 173 musicians (Guests).

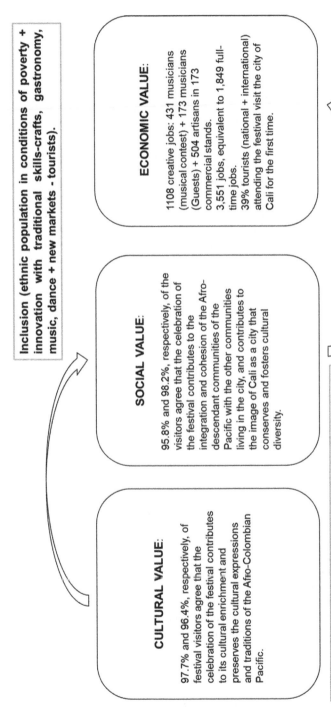

Fig. 13.1. Value Creation. The Petronio Álvarez Pacific Music Festival (Cali, Colombia).

The economic benefits of the festival are not limited to Cali as its host city. They spread to the entire Colombian Pacific region through two channels. The first of these distributes income and employment for the rest of the municipalities of the Colombian Pacific, through the income received by exhibitors from sales in the traditional cuisine and arts and crafts, which, in turn, involves the purchase of local input in their places of origin. The second channel operates through the income received by musicians and artists from the Pacific within the framework of the festival, which also constitutes a platform for the recognition of new musical talent.

In this sense, likewise the economic data of the festival and its impact on Cali, we can observe El Petronio festival's contribution to EDI in the appraisal of the cultural heritage of a part of the population traditionally marginalized (Afro-Colombian population). During the festival people can enjoy different manifestations of this cultural heritage (music, gastronomy, handicraft, among others). It is very important to highlight the bold decision about this celebration, where equity, diversity, and inclusion have an important role. For, first time in Colombia, Afro-Colombian people have the opportunity to show their knowledge, traditions, and cultural heritage in order to demonstrate their cultural wealth and strengthen their sense of belonging to a huge community in this country.

Opportunities are opened for local cultural policy, to increase participation/attendance: (i) a more territorially decentralized festival in the city, which without losing the central focus of the festival unit, creates opportunities for the participation of more local people in the festival, (ii) an educational strategy during the festival that offers a deeper knowledge of the culture of the Pacific for locals and attendees. This in turn improves the experience of the attendee, from contact with the music, traditional cuisine, and arts and crafts, and (iii) a more efficient communication strategy at local, national, and international levels on the relevance of the festival, with the aim of attracting new audiences.

Funding

The first (LFA) and second (AA) authors thank the Inclusion for Peace Program (IPA) of the International Organization for Migration (mission in Colombia), and the Office of Research and Development of the *Pontificia Universidad Javeriana* Cali, Colombia. The third author (J.H.C.) discloses receipt of financial support for the research, authorship, and/or publication of this article. The authors acknowledge financial support from *Ayudas para la Recualificación del Sistema Universitario Español en su Modalidad Margarita Salas* granted by the Spanish Ministry of Universities through the *Resolución de 29 de noviembre de 2021 de Universidad de Sevilla*, financed by the European Union – NextGenerationEU.

Declaration of Conflicting Interests

No potential conflict of interest was reported by the authors.

References

Aguado, L., Arbona, A., Palma, L., & Heredia–Carroza, J. (2021). How to value a cultural festival? The case of Petronio Álvarez Pacific Music Festival in Colombia. *Development Studies Research*, ·8(1), 309–316. https://doi.org/10.1080/21665095. 2021.1979417

Belfiore, E. (2020). Whose cultural value? Representation, power and creative industries. *International Journal of Cultural Policy*, 26(3). https://doi.org/10.1080/ 10286632.2018.1495713

Bethlehem, J. (2009). *Applied survey methods: A statistical perspective, Chapter 4.* Wiley.

Boyd, S. (2020). Cultural and heritage tourism in contemporary cities. In A. M. Morrison & J. A. Coca-Stefaniak (Eds.), *Routledge handbook of tourism cities.* Routledge.

Brandão, A., & De Oliveira, R. (2019). Internationalization strategies in music festivals. *Scientific Annals of Economics and Business*, 66, 91–112.

Buckman, S., Choi, L., Daly, M., & Seitelman, L. (2021). The economic gains from equity. *Brookings Papers on Economic Activity*, 71–111. https://www.brookings.edu/ wp-content/uploads/2021/09/15985-BPEA-BPEA-FA21_WEB_Buckman-et-al.pdf

Council of Europe. (2017). *Cultural participation and inclusive societies – A thematic report based on the indicator framework on culture and democracy.* Council of Europe Publishing.

DANE. (2023). *Geovisor de Autorreconocimiento Étnico.* Departamento Nacional de Estadística, Gobierno de Colombia.

Dwyer, L., & Jago, L. (2018). Valuing the impacts of festivals. In J. Mair (Ed.), *The Routledge handbook of festivals* (pp. 43–52). Routledge.

Frey, B. (2000). *Art and economics.* Springer-Verlag.

Frey, B. (2020). Festivals. In R. Towse & T. Navarrete Hernández (Eds.), *A handbook of cultural economics, Chapter 29* (pp. 262–265). Edward Elgar Publishing.

Garcia, M., & Judd, D. (2012). Competitive cities. In P. John, K. Mossberger, & S. E. Clarke (Eds.), *The Oxford handbook of urban politics.* Oxford Handbooks. https:// doi.org/10.1093/oxfordhb/9780195367867.013.0024

Getz, D. (2010). The nature and scope of festival studies. *International Journal of Events Management Research*, 5(1), 1–47. https://doi.org/10.1108/17852951011029298

Getz, D., Andersson, T., Armbrecht, J., & Lundberg, E. (2018). The value of festivals. In J. Mair (Ed.), *The Routledge handbook of festivals* (pp. 22–30). Routledge.

Heredia-Carroza, J., Palma Martos, L., & Aguado, L. F. (2019). Why does copyright ignore performers? The case of Flamenco in Spain. *The Journal of Arts Management, Law, and Society*, 49(5), 347–364. https://doi.org/10.1080/10632921.2019. 1646682

Heredia-Carroza, J., Aguado, L. F., & Tejedor-Estupiñán, J. M. (2023). La Economía y gestión de la cultura popular como motor de desarrollo territorial. *Revista Finanzas y Política Económica*, 15(2). https://doi.org/10.14718/revfinanzpolitceon. v15.n2.2023.1

Heredia-Carroza, J., Palma, L., & Aguado, L. F. (2023). Does copyright understand intangible heritage? The case of flamenco in Spain. *International Journal of Heritage Studies.* https://doi.org/10.1080/13527258.2023.2208102

Heredia-Carroza, J., Palma, L., de Sancha-Navarro, J., & Chavarría-Ortiz, C. (2023). Consumption habits of recorded music: Determinants of flamenco albums acquisition. *Sage Open, 13*(3). https://doi.org/10.1177/21582440231195202

Laing, J., & Mair, J. (2015). Music festivals and social inclusion – The festival organizers' perspective. *Leisure Sciences, 37*(3), 252–268. https://doi.org/10.1080/01490400.2014.991009

OECD. (2005). *Culture and local development.* Organisation for Economic Co-operation and Development, OECD Publishing.

OECD. (2022). *The culture fix: Creative people, places and industries, local economic and employment development (LEED).* OECD Publishing. https://doi.org/10.1787/991bb520-en

Palma, M., Palma, L., & Aguado, L. (2013). Determinants of cultural and popular celebration attendance: The case study of Seville Spring Fiestas. *Journal of Cultural Economics, 37*(1), 87–107. https://doi.org/10.1007/s10824-012-9167-5

Pavluković, V., Armenski, T., & Alcántara–Pilar, J. (2019). The impact of music festivals on local communities and their quality of life: Comparation of Serbia and Hungary. In A. Campón–Cerro, J. Hernández–Mogollón, & J. Folgado–Fernández (Eds.), *Best practices in hospitality and tourism marketing and management. Applying quality of life research (Best Practices)* (pp. 217–237). Springer.

Rivera, M., Hara, T., & Kock, G. (2008). Economic impact of cultural events: The case of the Zora! festival. *Journal of Heritage Tourism, 3*(2), 121–137. https://doi.org/10.1080/17438730802138139

Saayman, M., & Rossouw, R. (2011). The significance of festivals to regional economies: Measuring the economic value of the Grahamstown National Arts Festival in South Africa. *Tourism Economics, 17*(3), 603–624. https://doi.org/10.5367/te.2011.0

SACO. (2016). *National Arts Festival. Monitoring and evaluation: Key development indicator report on a DAC intervention.* South African Cultural Observatory, SACO. Department of Arts and Culture, Republic of South Africa.

SACO. (2019). *An input–output model for the cultural and creative industries in South Africa and possible extension.* South African Cultural Observatory, SACO. Department of Arts and Culture, Republic of South Africa.

Snowball, J. (2008). *Measuring the value of culture. Methods and examples in cultural economics.* Springer Verlag.

Throsby, D. (2001). *Economics and culture.* Cambridge University Press.

Throsby, D. (2003). Determining the value of cultural goods: How much (or how little) does contingent valuation tell us? *Journal of Cultural Economics, 27*, 275–285. https://doi.org/10.1023/A:1026353905772

Towse, R. (2019). *A textbook of cultural economics* (2nd ed.). Cambridge University Press.

UNESCO & World Bank. (2021). *Cities, culture, creativity: Leveraging culture and creativity for sustainable urban development and inclusive growth.* UNESCO, World Bank.

UNESCO. (2015). *Festival statistics: Key concepts and current practices.* UNESCO.

UNESCO. (2022). *Re|shaping policies for creativity: Addressing culture as a global public good.* United Nations Educational, Scientific and Cultural Organization (UNESCO).

United Nations. (2000). Recommendations on tourism statistics. Statistical Papers, Series M, 83 United Nations Publication Series M N° 83 (Rev–1.0).

Urrea, F., Ramírez, H., & Carabalí, B. (2021). *Brechas étnico–raciales en Colombia.* USAID/Colombia, ACDI/VOCA Colombia, Universidad del Valle, Facultad de Ciencias Sociales y Económicas.

Wallstam, M. (2022). Maintaining the status quo: The nature and role of policy stakeholders' perceptions of event value. *International Journal of Event and Festival Management, 13*(2), 219–234. https://doi.org/10.1108/IJEFM–06–2021–0053

World Bank Group. (2015). *Competitive cities for jobs and growth: Appendices to six case studies of economically successful cities.* World Bank.

Zhuang, M., Zhang, H., Li, p., Shen, C., Xiao, X., & Zhang, J. (2023). Connecting tourists to musical destinations: The role of musical geographical imagination and aesthetic responses in music tourism. *Tourism Management, 98*, 104768. https://doi.org/10.1016/j.tourman.2023.104768

Chapter 14

Digital Transformation of Events and Live Performances

Stephen Boyle, Carmen Reaiche and Mohammadreza Akbari

James Cook University, Australia

Abstract

In our current context, constant adaptation to emerging trends is crucial. There has been much discussion about digital transformation affecting all sectors. The art and event sector is no different and has been directly affected by digitalization, but what influence does this movement have on the management of these events? At the event management level, digital transformation entails organizational adjustments to roles, personal competencies, management techniques and technologies, and, more importantly, leadership philosophies to develop digital inclusion initiatives to attain broader participation in the arts.

Digital transformation's integration into events takes various forms, especially in response to challenges like the pandemic. While it creates opportunities for engagement, it also poses challenges, potentially isolating community members without digital access. The digitalization of an event must be considered at all levels to connect to the participants. Evidence in this chapter is displayed through a hybrid curated and Fringe arts festival: North Australian Festival of Arts, a leading industry example exhibiting new digital transformation models in the Australian arts. We will explore key factors underlying how digital transformation must enhance the experience and access by creating an environment that is familiar to attendees but has enough originality to make the event special and digitally inclusive. This chapter concludes by suggesting key constructs of digital transformation models for event and live performances to embrace digital inclusiveness in the arts.

Keywords: Digital transformation; arts festivals; regional communities; access and inclusion; emerging technologies

Accessibility, Diversity, Equity and Inclusion in the Cultural Sector, 215–226
Copyright © 2024 Stephen Boyle, Carmen Reaiche and Mohammadreza Akbari
Published under exclusive licence by Emerald Publishing Limited
doi:10.1108/978-1-83753-034-220241032

Introduction: Digital Inclusion and the Australian Arts Sector

Technology and art have long been intertwined. Technology innovation encourages artistic expression by enabling artists to either invent new technology or adapt existing ones to foster the creative process. In the past 20 years, digital technology has developed and spread quickly, and information and communication technologies are being used more frequently for a variety of purposes, including artistic expression, and extending the reach to audiences (Alacovska et al., 2020). Even one of the most recent breakthroughs, artificial intelligence (AI), has already made its way into the studios of artists and the creative process (PwC, 2022) However, the arts are putting institutions under growing pressure to adopt digital transformation due to shifting consumer interactions and expectations for novel experiences (Australian Competition and Consumer Commission, n.d.). In this section, the focus is on digital inclusion, the capability of an audience to reach and engage with their favorite art genre, and the ability of the artist to adjust and deliver a unique online experience.

In a very short time, a much wider range of other key activities – from purchasing tickets to attending museum tours and participating in live events – have moved online. We are seeing firsthand digital transformation models across the various sectors within the arts industry and consequently the growing need for a digital inclusive ecosystem, if these digital technology models are to become effective.

However, this quick digitization is happening at a time when some community members still face significant obstacles to participating online. Bridging this digital divide is the goal of digital inclusion. The National Agreement on Closing the Gap (2020) report, put forward the idea that all Australians ought to have access to and be able to fully utilise digital technology for managing their wellbeing, accessing recreational services, being part of the community, and maintaining some degree of social interactions with friends, family, and people around the world.

The way we live and work has been fast changing thanks to connected digital technologies, even before COVID-19 disrupted the world (Akbari & Hopkins, 2022). The forced social exclusion and isolation experienced under COVID-19 hastened the migration to online services, and these enablers will continue to play a significant role in the new normal. Nearly all Australians have access to internet infrastructure, yet more than 2.5 million people are still without it (Thomas et al., 2020). According to The Australian Digital Inclusion Index (2020), access, affordability, and digital ability are key elements impacting individuals living in some regional areas who fall outside of the digital reach. The issue is that the numerous advantages of the digital economy are not being widely distributed and too many Australians continue to experience significant hurdles to fully access and/or experience online involvement and, therefore, are less able to engage with the arts.

Recently, a number of projects have surfaced in an urgent effort to make the digital art society more accountable, equitable, and accessible (Li, 2020). These programs cross the boundaries between the public, private, and government sectors. They form the basis of an emerging new business model for the arts ecosystem which presents the notion of "stakeholder integration." This ecosystem business model is based on the concept of value created in collaboration with artists and how that value is then shared with other key stakeholders and the community (Drejer et al., 2019). Therefore, for value creation to effectuate, it is important that stakeholders recognize that changes in the digital arena are only effective if we identify inclusive digital ecosystems. Let's now discuss how digital technologies impact arts business models in particular.

How Digital Technologies Change Business Models for the Arts: Automate, Transform, and Engage (ATE)

By enabling new methods of creating and extracting value, new exchange mechanisms and transaction architectures, and new boundary-spanning organizational forms, digital technologies have been a primary driver of new innovative business models (Akbari et al., 2022). Key changes to innovative business model construction in the arts can be classified into three broad categories: automation, transformation, and audience engagement.

For the arts, automation refers to situations where a business uses digital technologies to streamline or improve ongoing events and live performances and service provision. The use of technology to automate activities related to the conception, development, and dissemination of artistic works is referred to as automation in the arts. This automation can include automated ticket sales, automated virtual program creation, and other functional aspects of the business delivery of services.

However, it can also include things like digital music composition tools, visual effects animation programs, and algorithms for producing art or supporting the design process. Automation in the arts frequently aims to streamline and accelerate the creative process so that artists can concentrate on the artistic rather than the technical components of their work. In this process, an inclusive digital ecosystem plays a key part in enabling the success of automation. Automation should be considered a two-way process – it impacts the business but also reaches the audience. For that, we must consider the audience's capability as well as capacity to access new technology.

The term "transformation" describes situations in which these new business models can replace established ones by utilizing digital technologies (Schroeder et al., 2019). The incorporation of digital technology into the conventional arts field is referred to as "digital transformation" in the arts. Through this approach, artists, arts groups, and cultural institutions can explore new avenues of expression and creativity, expand their audiences, and enhance the sector's overall sustainability. Audience engagement refers to events significantly increasing audience connectivity while delivering a unique experience (Li, 2020). The emergence of these new digital ecosystem business models constitutes a network of interconnected artists, events, and technologies that simultaneously is challenged by the degree of an audience's digital engagement and social interaction.

Everything is digital today! There is no doubt that digitalization is here to stay, if not in full, in different ways and to different levels, often developing a blended mode or style of programming. However, there is still a lot of baiting and switching that utterly falls short of what attendees are hoping for. Many events have "digital" advertising or promotional imagery that depicts futuristic digital engagement platforms. However, these events still require a lot of traditional or manual methods of completing tasks, for example, when people attend the event or log into the recommended apps or programs. This seems to be a common response from event managers to their fear of losing a complete audience cluster: attendees that represent a blend of traditional and digital adoption. But at the same time, the digital transition is a permanent trend. Technology has become an inextricable element of our daily lives, and as a result, we are seeing increasing societal integration of technology and the exponential growth of the digital world. The digital revolution is already having a big impact on how the arts audience engages with and appreciates industry trends. As technology develops further, it is expected to become an even bigger factor in the future of the arts and culture sector, presenting both new opportunities and challenges.

To some extent, the audience will need to get familiar with these new platforms and technologies in order to access and participate in art and cultural events as a result of the growing reliance on digital technology. This could include social media and other online resources for finding and following musicians and organizations, online ticketing services, virtual or augmented reality activities, and more. The degree to which an audience must adapt, however, may vary depending on their access to technology. How and to what level this adoption occurs relies on a number of factors, including but not limited to demographic differences. The main demographic factors that can impact both access to and understanding of how to use technology (referred to as digital literacy) often include the age of the user, socioeconomic factors, and geographic location. In Australia in particular, the geographic location of a community or individual can bring challenges to accessing digital infrastructure, including those who live in rural or remote locations.

All locations outside of Australia's major cities are referred to as "rural and remote." These regions fall into one of four categories according to the Australian Standard Geographical Classification System: inner regional, outer regional, remote, or very remote. Over two-thirds (69%) of the population of Australia live in major cities, making it one of the most urbanized nations in the world. However, one in five (20%) live in inner regional areas and one in 10 (9%) in outer remote areas. One of the defining features of remote communities is that technology, in particular, is one of the main services that is less accessible (Infrastructure Partnerships Australia, 2022).

The unequal distribution of access to digital platforms and online cultural events among various demographic groups is also referred to as the "digital gap" among the performing arts audience. As a result, not everyone will have the same opportunity to appreciate and engage with performing arts, which may result in a loss in the diversity of both the audience and the works being produced.

It can be challenging for remote communities to properly interact with and participate in the arts due to their limited access to technology. These communities frequently struggle with a variety of difficulties relating to social inclusion and internet access. The arts, particularly event managers, could consider that an effective ecosystem business model to stimulate "engagement" is one that provides a unique experience combining both art exposure and social inclusion. Diversity and digital access are intertwined concepts which are evident in remote communities. Ensuring equal access to digital resources and platforms promotes diversity by enabling underrepresented individuals and communities to participate, contribute, and obtain the many advantages of the digital realm. It can be said that it enhances cultural educational opportunities, promotes economic empowerment, and contributes to more inclusive and equitable digital spaces.

Regrettably, digital participation does not always translate into social inclusion. The degree to which internet users can effectively use their access varies according to their socioeconomic status, offline resources, the kinds of devices they can afford and maintain, the location from which they can access the internet, such as whether they rely on mobile data plans or access through an internet service provider (Reisdorf & Rhinesmith, 2020), and other factors, such as digital skills (Dutton & Reisdorf, 2019).

It is important to consider all the above factors to develop digital inclusion initiatives to attain broader participation in the digitalization of the arts. This can help increase access to arts and culture for communities that might not otherwise have the chance to experience the arts and can help foster a more inclusive and diverse cultural landscape. Therefore, it becomes imperative to ensure that the tools and platforms used for the digitalization of the arts are accessible and user-friendly for individuals in remote communities, taking into account factors such as limited internet connectivity and varying levels of digital literacy.

What are other issues for the arts in relation to ATE? In the process of automation, a diverse range of technology, including AI, has been adopted (Stark, 2020). Art made by artists and event performances are not just about production and digitalization but also about keeping the human touch and emotions, which AI cannot do. AI may not have the same ability that artists have to create and design in a way that is sensitive to human emotions and experiences.

Therefore, automation capabilities should focus on helping artists eliminate monotonous chores so that artists can focus on their creative work. AI, for example, can facilitate platforms to simulate reality event attendance. AI can also be used to create virtual reality platforms that duplicate real-world events, including art exhibitions. Through the use of computer graphics and other technologies, these platforms give users the ability to interact with virtual places and things and create an immersive experience. They might also include social networking tools that enable users to communicate with others in the virtual world. This could be a useful tool for people who are unable to attend events in person due to travel distances, physical restrictions, or other circumstances.

The use of technology in the arts does, however, raise a number of problems in addition to digital participation, such as the risk that automation could supplant human creativity, how technology will affect art's ability to transform, and how technology will be used to engage audiences in novel and creative ways. Authenticity loss, uniformity of artistic expression, and the potential for technology to further marginalize particular populations are a few issues to be concerned about. The use of technology in the arts raises other ethical questions, such as those related to copyright and intellectual property. Furthermore, there are concerns that the application of technology in the arts may result in a decline in cultural diversity.

The adoption of digital technologies in all sectors is rapidly expanding but not without difficulties. The music industry, for example, struggled for many years to develop and adopt a successful business model, moving from sales of physical products (CDs) to licensing access (streaming). As more and more digital technology becomes available and is adopted, developing innovative business models for arts event managers and organizers will be critical for their continued success and attainment of financial, social, and artistic goals. Let's examine some of the key constructs and characteristics of the Arts' sector.

The Key Constructs of Digital Transformation Models in the Arts

Defining Business Models

Due to the variety of definitions, there is potential for a wide range of interpretations of what constitutes a business model. General terms used to describe the business model include, for example, a framework (Afuah, 2004), a conceptual tool (Osterwalder et al., 2005), and many others. We can pinpoint three similar constructs despite major conceptual divergences when defining business models. The first is that the business model is the opportunity for exploration and stakeholder integration. Second, value capture and proposition are intertwined. Third, new business models are significantly enabled by digital technologies.

A business model reflecting digital transformation in the arts can emerge from the value proposition that the artist and/or performance offers to its audience, the inclusiveness of the audience to whom it offers that value, and, of course, its sources of sustainable revenue.

It can also happen in the way value is recognized, produced, distributed, and captured; in the digital tasks required to produce and provide value to audiences; and in the organizational skills on which these tasks rely. These structures are dynamically connected to one another and are tightly interconnected to key stakeholders of the ecosystem in which the nature of arts and/or performance is recognized. Financial returns are nonetheless crucial for performing artists who, while they don't prioritize making a profit, still need to pay their bills while maintaining their social and cultural goals.

Digital transformation business models are only effective if they generate more revenue than expenditure. Taking into account that technology can be costly; the digital transformation business model needs to generate new value, performances, or audiences by identifying new value-generating opportunities, developing new digital experiences, or creating new ways of producing, delivering, and capturing digital performances. It is the role of key stakeholders, particularly those with the power for decision-making, to enable this digital transformation business model and value creation. It is important to note that it is an integrative effort and not one assigned to a single stakeholder, as the proposed models are "integrative ecosystems" *per se*. Fig. 14.1 provides a brief overview of these models, keeping in mind that as technology changes, the new business models must adapt and undertake performance monitoring and improvement. It is also important to remember that digital inclusiveness is required to bridge the digital gap.

The continual shift of economies and societies toward various organizational paradigms that are heavily influenced by digital technology is at the center of current discussions affecting the arts. The following case study demonstrates an emerging digital inclusive ecosystem – a promising new business model for the arts.

The North Australian Festival of Arts

The North Australian Festival of Arts was established in 2019 in Townsville, Queensland. The event was borne from an initiative of the Commonwealth Games held in 2018 in Brisbane. Townsville was named one of the four event cities alongside the Gold Coast, Brisbane, and Cairns. According to the NAFA website "During the Commonwealth Games, the Queensland Government provided funding for each event city to create and run an arts and cultural festival" (NAFA, 2023). The aim of the festival was to create additional cultural experiences and opportunities for the local communities and to the people visiting the region to attend the supporting events. Townsville's Festival 2018 attracted

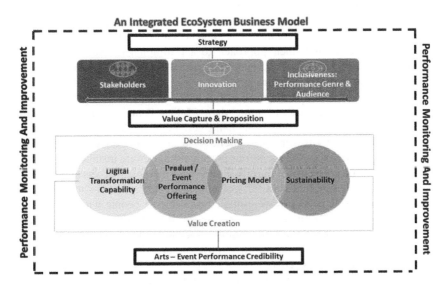

Fig. 14.1.   An Integrated EcoSystem Business Model for the Arts.

100,000 people who attended events and performances across 12 days (NAFA, 2023).

Townsville is a regional city in the state of Queensland in Australia, with an approximate population of 196,800 (Australian Bureau of Statistics Estimated Resident Population, June 30, 2020). It lies approximately half-way between the tip of Cape York and Brisbane (the state's capital).

NAFA in its current form is a hybrid curated and fringe arts and cultural festival. In the spirit of Fringe Festivals across the globe, NAFA has an inclusive, organic, and open access side that features all forms of art and performance. To NAFA organizers, "open access" means that there are no curators, no program directors, no themes, or content criteria that artists have to fulfill when registering their show.

The festival is formed around the mantra: anyone with a story to tell and a venue to host it. No matter who you are, where you come from, or what art form you represent, everyone is welcome at NAFA. As the festival grows, the open access definition also extends to the audiences to ensure the removal of any barriers that prevent people from attending, be that physical, societal, financial, or otherwise (NAFA, 2023).

After successfully debuting in 2019, the festivals held in 2020 and 2021 had to adapt and evolve with the ever-changing COVID-19 pandemic. Although many challenges have been faced, the festival has continued to bring the North Australian community alive throughout the difficult times faced by the arts and culture community.

NAFA offers hundreds of different performances, experiences, and venues and has become a signature event held in Townsville for the community to enjoy throughout a month-long celebration of the arts (NAFA, 2023).

In 2020 and 2021, there were severe restrictions placed due to the COVID-19 pandemic. As such, many artists scheduled to perform were unable to travel, and there were restrictions on the number of audiences allowed at performances. This led organizers to rethink their approach to a traditional festival and begin to adopt new hybrid models of delivery. This strategy resulted in rebuilding arts attendance and the local economy.

The year 2022 saw NAFA return in full with 105 shows, 427 individual performances, and attendances of more than 52,000. Being a regional city, the festival organizers faced a number of challenges, including distance (Townsville is approximately 1,350 km from Brisbane) and insufficient venues to hold all the events and performances. As such, four portable venues were installed, essentially doubling the venue capacity of the city. In line with their open access and focus on inclusivity, it was reported that 92% of audiences surveyed felt "welcome and included," and 98% of shows were made accessible to people with a disability (Culture Counts, 2022). In addition, 89% agreed that attending the festival made them feel positive about their community, and 86% agreed the content of the festival "reflected a broad and inclusive range of voices" (Culture Counts, 2022).

From the artists' perspective, 30% of the projects undertaken included artists from an Aboriginal and Torres Strait Islander background and 68% from culturally diverse backgrounds. The artists also highly praised the festival for its inclusion and diversity agenda (Culture Counts, 2022).

While the festival has thus far achieved this agenda, there are still a number of future challenges and opportunities identified by the festival management. These include providing access to a more diverse audience, especially those who face social, economic, and geographic barriers in accessing arts and culture. The event organizers are exploring how to include digital technologies to overcome these in future festivals. In future festivals, it is planned to record a number of local artists' projects from an audience perspective and then have the ability to stream these into locations where people can't access the physical venue. These may include aged care facilities and remote communities. In this way, audiences can be thought of in three layers – locals, "out of towners," and digital attendees.

To take advantage of the third layer of digital audiences, a new business model is needed where these virtual performances can be revenue-generating. The concept is to utilize a virtual venue where these performances are viewed and sell these to other festivals around the world. Local artists can then maximize the number of people seeing their work without having to travel and deal with the costs and logistics of moving their performances to other locations.

Other digital technologies can also be employed to provide greater access for patrons. These include augmented reality, such as interactive site maps indicating accessibility pathways for those with disabilities, and digital interactive programs. The intent is to provide greater accessibility to all members of the community and provide a multilayered open access platform.

However, there are still challenges to be faced as festivals pivot to online and virtual operations. These may include a lack of IT infrastructure in different communities (particularly those in remote locations), individual access to technology, and digital literacy. It has to be accepted that there is a potential digital divide in our communities, and if we are to be truly inclusive and embrace an increasingly diverse community of stakeholders (both artists and audiences), then investment in technology at the community level and education and training in the use of this technology at the individual level will become increasingly important.

Conclusion

The NAFA has an inclusive, natural, and open access side that showcases all forms of art and performance, in the spirit of Fringe Festivals throughout the world. Unlike most art festivals, open access means that no one makes the selection of which events to include. When registering their event, artists are not required to meet any themes, content, or program director requirements. Anyone with a story to share and a place to host it is the festival's credo. To ensure the removal of all barriers – physical, sociological, financial, digital, or otherwise – that hinder individuals from accessing the art, the open access term needs to expand to include the audiences as the festival grows. The festivals held in 2020 and 2021 had to adapt, undertake digital transformation, and change to keep up with the COVID-19 pandemic after making their successful debut in 2019 and 2020, respectively. Despite numerous obstacles, the festival has persisted in energizing the North Australian region, reaching remote communities in the area, despite the challenging times the arts and cultural community has experienced. Therefore, let's examine some of the lessons learned in this period of adaptation that led to the proposal of new business models for digital transformation.

Lessons Learned/Key Construct Proposed Model

The next major technological paradigm shift is creating a new line of demarcation between the current digital/virtual world and the following one, in the same way that the previous shift divided the analogue/physical world from the digital/virtual world.

Depending on the particular environment and objectives of the model, the key construct for the proposed model for arts digital transformation may change. However, a digital transformation model for the arts might take into account a few important concepts, such as:

• Engaging audiences with digital technologies, such as social media and online platforms, to reach and interact with both new and existing audiences.
• Monetization: Creating new digital revenue streams through platforms, including online ticket sales, streaming services, and digital goods.
• Accessibility: Using digital tools like closed captioning, audio description, and translation services, making the arts more available to diverse audiences.
• Preservation and archiving: Making use of digital technologies to safeguard and store artistic creations, for instance, by scanning physical collections and building digital repositories.
• Cooperation and cocreation: Promoting artistic and audience collaboration and cocreation via digital channels, such as by facilitating online forums and virtual workshops.

The following actions can be taken to prevent the digital gap among audiences for performing arts:

• Offer free or inexpensive technology and internet connectivity, including lending or donating equipment and giving residents in remote areas access to free or inexpensive Wi-Fi.
• Teach audience members how to use technology and the internet to attend virtual events and other online resources. Provide digital literacy education.
• Create accessible virtual experiences by ensuring that online activities can be accessed by people with disabilities and by providing alternate participation channels, such audio-only options.
• Partner with neighborhood organizations to reach underserved communities and offer technology, internet access, and instruction in digital literacy.

- Prioritize diversity and inclusion in programming by considering the varied demands of the audience and making adaptations to account for varying degrees of technology access and expertise.

Automate, Transform, and Engage (Minimum Standard)

When adopting digital technology with the aim of increasing accessibility and diversity in the arts and cultural sector, the business model needs to be inclusive of all stakeholders. All stakeholders from management, government, local communities, artists, and audiences need to be considered in the development of a strategy that will result in an inclusive digital ecosystem. In this way, we can build sustainable business practices and minimize further marginalizing those who face barriers to engaging with the technology and establish a more inclusive and diverse approach to engaging audiences with the arts.

References

Afuah, A. (2004). *Business models: A strategic management approach.* McGraw-Hill/ Irwin.

Akbari, M., Ha, N., & Kok, S. K. (2022). A systematic review of AR/VR in operations and supply chain management: Maturity, current trends and future directions. *Journal of Global Operations and Strategic Sourcing, 15*(5), 534–565. https:// doi.org/10.1108/JGOSS-09-2021-0078

Akbari, M., & Hopkins, J. (2022). Digital technologies as enablers of supply chain sustainability in an emerging economy. *Operations Management Research, 15*, 689–710. https://doi.org/10.1007/s12063-021-00226-8

Alacovska, A., Booth, P., & Fieseler, C. (2020). *The role of the arts in the digital transformation.* Artsformation Report Series, (SSRN). https://papers.ssrn.com/sol3/ papers.cfm?abstract_id=3715612

Australian Bureau of Statistics. (2020). *National, state and territory population.* https:// www.abs.gov.au/statistics/people/population/national-state-and-territory- population/jun-2020

Australian Competition and Consumer Commission. (n.d.). *Digital platform services inquiry 2020–2025.* https://www.accc.gov.au/focus-areas/inquiries-ongoing/digital- platform-services-inquiry-2020-25. Accessed on July 2, 2022.

Culture Counts. (2022). *North Australian festival of arts 2022 evaluation report.* https:// nafa tov.com.au/pages/nafa 2022/. Accessed on January 30, 2023

Drejer, I., Byrge, C., Lyndgaard, D. B., & Lassen, H. M. (2019). Development of new business models: Introducing the cultural elasticity model. *Journal of Business Models, 7*(4), 13–19.

Dutton, W. H., & Reisdorf, B. C. (2019). Cultural divides and digital inequalities: Attitudes shaping internet and social media divides. *Information, Communication & Society, 22*(1), 18–38.

Infrastructure Partnerships Australia. (2022). *Remote communities: Improving access to essential services.* https://infrastructure.org.au/remote-communities-improving- access-to-essential-services/. Accessed on August 1, 2022.

Li, F. (2020). The digital transformation of business models in the creative industries: A holistic framework and emerging trends. *Technovation, 92–93,* 102012. https://doi.org/10.1016/j.technovation.2017.12.004

National Agreement on Closing the Gap. (2020). https://www.closingthegap.gov.au/national-agreement

North Australian Festival of Arts. (2023). https://nafa-tsv.com.au/pages/about-nafa/. Accessed on January 9, 2023.

Osterwalder, A., Pigneur, Y., & Tucci, C. (2005). Clarifying business models: Origins, present, and future of the concept. *Communications of the Association for Information Systems, 16,* 1–25.

PwC. (2022). *Australian entertainment & media outlook 2022–2026.* https://www.pwc.com.au/industry/entertainment-and-media-trends-analysis/outlook.html

Reisdorf, B., & Rhinesmith, C. (2020). Digital inclusion as a core component of social inclusion. *Social Inclusion, 8*(2), 132–137.

Schroeder, A., Ziaee Bigdeli, A., Galera Zarco, C., & Baines, T. (2019). Capturing the benefits of industry 4.0: A business network perspective. *Production Planning & Control, 30*(16), 1305–1321.

Stark, J. (2020). *Digital transformation of industry.* Springer International Publishing.

Thomas, J., Barraket, J., Wilson, C. K., Holcombe-James, I., Kennedy, J., Rennie, E., Ewing, S., & MacDonald, T. (2020). *Measuring Australia's digital divide: The Australian digital inclusion index 2020.* RMIT and Swinburne University of Technology, Melbourne, for Telstra. https://doi.org/10.25916/5f6eb9949c832

Section 5

Synthesis, Tools, and Policy

Chapter 15

Teaching ADEI in Taiwan

Tobie S. Stein

National Sun Yat-sen University, Taiwan

Abstract

In 2021, Dr Shang-Ying Chen, chair of the Department of Theatre Arts at National Sun Yat-sen University, invited me to teach in Taiwan for the 2022 academic year. I taught six 16- to 18-week courses, including creativity, marketing, theater management, and research methods, to 100 undergraduate and graduate college students in English.

As a published sociologist and practitioner of accessibility, diversity, equity, and inclusion (ADEI), I seek to center ADEI in every aspect of my own life, which includes my teaching. My chapter "Teaching ADEI in Taiwan" is an autoethnographic study, utilizing participant observation in documenting the ways in which inclusive pedagogies of ADEI impact teaching and learning in Taiwan. As a Jewish white English-speaking researcher-teacher, I also interrogate my own racial awareness and the impact it has on my efforts to provide my Taiwanese students with an education that is culturally responsive.[1]

Keywords: Taiwan; ADEI; inclusive pedagogy; culturally responsive teaching in higher education; native English-speaking professor; racial awareness

---

[1]I am grateful to Antonio C. Cuyler, who encouraged me to name my Jewish ethnicity as a key component of my social identity. While I fully recognize that I have had great privilege being white in the United States, I also understand that the ethnic group to which I belong has been historically marginalized and that violence against Jews across the millennia is significant even today. I believe that my ethnic identity and history of my family and people have greatly influenced my empathy for every individual who has felt marginalized by society as well as impacted my teachings, research, and fierce advocacy for global human rights.

Accessibility, Diversity, Equity and Inclusion in the Cultural Sector, 229–242
Copyright © 2024 Tobie S. Stein
Published under exclusive licence by Emerald Publishing Limited
doi:10.1108/978-1-83753-034-220241034

Introduction

I have been a Visiting Professor in 10 Taiwan universities during the past 11 years. In 2021, Dr Shang-Ying Chen, Department of Theatre Arts Chair at National Sun Yat-sen University, invited me to teach six courses (three per semester) in English to both undergraduate and graduate students. As both a Sociologist and Practitioner of ADEI, I was ready to infuse inclusive learner-centered pedagogies in each of my classes.

This chapter "Teaching ADEI in Taiwan" is an autoethnographic study of the inclusive pedagogy I used to teach two spring 2022 undergraduate courses to 55 undergraduate Taiwanese students at National Sun Yat-sen University in Taiwan. The study explores the following two research questions: (1) How do inclusive pedagogies of ADEI impact teaching and learning in Taiwan? and (2) To what extent is it necessary for a native English-speaking professor to interrogate their own racial awareness and the impact it has on providing Taiwanese students with a culturally responsive education?

In the literature review, I begin by introducing Taiwan's national commitment to a multicultural society with gender equity. I also share Taiwan's policy of becoming a bilingual Mandarin and English-speaking country by 2030 and how hiring native English-speaking teachers is one effort to meet the goals of this policy. The literature review also addresses inclusive learner-centered pedagogies that native English-speaking professors in Confucius Heritage Cultures (CHC) must use, as well as the need for white American English-speaking scholars to interrogate and dismantle teaching practices that might adversely affect their CHC students.

In the next section of the chapter, I use participant observation to document the interactive teaching and learning experiences in the Introduction to Creativity and Introduction to Theater Management classes I taught, highlighting the inclusive pedagogies used in teaching these classes in Taiwan. Within my descriptive analysis of each class, I interrogate my own white English-speaking identity and the ways in which I attempt to dismantle bias that might harm my Taiwanese students. I conclude the chapter with a discussion of my findings and recommendations for further study.

Literature Review

Taiwan (Republic of China [ROC]) is a democratic sovereign island nation, and Mandarin is considered the official language (Chou et al., 2018, p. 119). Taiwan seeks to become a bilingual Mandarin and English-speaking country by 2030 to "optimize national development, prosperity, and security" (Whittle, 2022). Taiwan's Ministry of Education plans on supporting this national bilingual policy with the hiring of international professors who are native English speakers (Fang et al., 2022).

According to Taiwan's Ministry of Foreign Affairs, Taiwan is "a multicultural society, comprising diverse Han subgroups, as well as Indigenous Malayo-Polynesian people and immigrants from all over the world" ("People," 2020).

Taiwan supports a population of over 23 million people, the majority of whom (95%) have Han Chinese ancestry.[2] There are 16 officially recognized Indigenous Peoples, representing 2.4% of Taiwan's population. New immigrants, primarily from China and Southeast Asia, comprise 2.6% of Taiwan's population ("People," 2020). In addition to its public multicultural statement, Taiwan's government is the first in Asia to support a same-sex marriage law in 2019 (Chiang, 2022). Another bill that would allow transgender people to change their gender identity on their national identity card without submitting proof of surgery is now under consideration by the Constitutional Court (Chiang, 2022).

Though there has been a growing trend toward multiculturalism and gender equity in Taiwan, "[Han] ethnocentrism embedded in Confucian tradition takes the view of cultural deprivation for granted" (Chou et al., 2018, p. 125).[3] In a cultural deprivation or deficit model of teaching, multicultural students are automatically viewed as being disadvantaged by the teacher (Chou et al., 2018). CHC countries, which include Taiwan, also value "hierarchy, social order, and harmonious relationships" (Sun et al., 2019). In a classroom culture that favors CHC principles, the teacher has full authority; students are tested on what they have learned in class (2019). Ikpeze (2015, p. 60) stated that "most Asian born teachers grew up in classrooms where teachers were the sole authority figures." Ho (2020, p. 139) argued that CHC classroom practices center "'xue wen,' meaning knowledge, stressing the importance of questioning and inquiry" and that Confucius traditions place a high value on individual competence within the collective. Ho also advised that "team-based learning [in small groups] is culturally appropriate for CHC learners" (p. 145).

Team-based learning is an important part of an inclusive pedagogy where "learning is welcoming and accessible" (Sanger, 2020, pp. 32, 50). As I enter Taiwan's higher education classroom, with the intention of teaching the arts through the inclusive pedagogical lens of ADEI, what does this mean in a CHC country such as Taiwan? In defining ADEI as an inclusive learner-centered pedagogy in Taiwan's English-speaking classroom, I must first remain aware of the context in which Taiwanese students learn English as a second language.

College students in Taiwan are required to take certain college courses in English, and native English speakers are hired to teach these courses ("Job Description, National Sun Yat-sen University," 2021). However, while Taiwan's college students may have done well in their English exams in high school, some students may not have had the opportunity to practice their listening and speaking skills and thus lack proficiency in these necessary language skills. For example, the students may exhibit a fear of speaking in class (Hsu, 2015, pp. 62–65). In a study of 354 Taiwanese college freshmen, for instance, Hsu (2015)

---

[2]The Han Dynasty (202 BCE-220CE) made Confucianism "an official system of education and scholarship. . ." Classical texts encouraged the individual to cultivate "benevolence toward others, a general sense of doing what is right, and loyalty and diligence in serving one's superiors" ("Confucius and the 'Confusion Tradition'").

[3]"Ascribing superior meaning to their own racial or ethnic group and negative or inferior meanings to people outside their racial or ethnic group" (Stein, 2020, p. 67).

found that while students felt that participation was important to learning, the students exhibited "low overall involvement" in class (p. 61).

Thus, inclusive learner-centered pedagogies that emphasize *accessibility* must allow CHC students to fully participate in the class without the fear of "making mistakes and loosing face" (Hsu, 2015, p. 63). Team-based learning and the ability of the student to cocreate the learning experience with their fellow classmates with encouragement from the professor are examples of inclusive pedagogies that emphasize accessibility (Ho, 2020, p. 127).

How does a native English speaker approach the inclusive pedological concept of *diversity* in the Taiwan college classroom? In my study of underrepresented people of the Global majority in the US majority white performing arts workforce, *Racial and Ethnic Diversity in the Performing Arts Workforce*, I defined diversity as the "practice of valuing and intentionally recognizing, including, and affirming the representation and engagement of a workforce with a multiplicity of cultural identities, experiences, perspectives, and traditions . . ., reflecting the entire community" (Stein, 2020, p. 1).

Teaching diversity as an inclusive pedagogy requires recognizing and affirming the rich diverse cultural identities of the college students by presenting lectures and assignments that are culturally responsive and reflect and embrace the "experiences and perspectives . . .values, communication, learning styles, traditions, language, and language in use" of the students in the classroom (Heidelberg, 2020, p. 177). Culturally responsive pedagogies in Taiwan specifically require the native English-speaking professor to learn and understand the diverse learning styles of the college students and provide equitable opportunities for all students to learn (Chou et al., 2018; Sanger, 2020, p. 3). For example, if the classroom is comprised of students who may have had the opportunity to practice listening and speaking English, as well as students who have not had that opportunity, "an equity-minded [teaching and learning] framework recognizes the structural inequities that exist in a larger society and considers how these inequities disenfranchise certain students" (Fuentes et al., 2021). In other words, in teaching *equity* as an inclusive pedagogy, the native English speaker must remain aware that Taiwan's secondary school system may structurally disadvantage a student's English-speaking and listening abilities in a college classroom (Hsu, 2015). In an equity-minded classroom, the English-speaking professor must recognize structural disadvantages by "intentionally pair[ing] students with more and less prior experience, so that the more experienced students can help guide their less experienced peers" (Sanger, 2020, p. 39).[4]

Native English-speaking professors must make a commitment to pedagogies that emphasize *inclusion*, belonging, and a path to success (Mcleod, 2023; Sanger, 2020, p. 33). When students are socially included in the classroom, they have a voice: The students's lived experiences matter (Mack, 2012). In her study of social

---

[4]It is important to acknowledge Russian psychologist Lev Vygotsky's concept of the zone of proximal development (ZPD), which measures the "difference between what a learner can do without help and what they can achieve with guidance and encouragement from a skilled partner" (Mcleod, 2023).

inclusion and student voice at a multicultural university in Japan, Mack (2012) defined social inclusion as "acceptance and friendship by the social group" (p. 420). In CHC countries such as Japan and Taiwan, it is critical for the native English-speaking professor, who does not share the same cultural background as the students, to provide an inclusive environment where the students collectively "take part in making decisions about classroom procedures, curriculum, and classroom policies" (Mack, 2012, p. 420). In the inclusive classroom, the pedagogy must emphasize a co-construction of knowledge between the professor and the student (Fuentes et al., 2021; Mcleod, 2023).

In prioritizing the co-construction of knowledge between the students and professor, the white English-speaking professor must use their own racial awareness in interrogating the ways in which white American ethnocentric values are adversely imposed on CHC students (Von Esch et al., 2020). Von Esch, Motha, and Kubota asserted that the English language has long been "associated with whiteness and colonial power . . . and there is a need for teachers to explore their whiteness and how it influences the teacher's perception of language learners and pedagogy" (2020, pp. 397, 406). White English-speaking professors must decenter their whiteness in language pedagogy and programming through critical self-awareness and sharing antiracist counter stories (p. 407). When a white English-speaking professor enters the Taiwanese college classroom, their critical self-awareness of potential ethnocentric bias is essential in their efforts to cocreate inclusive ADEI pedagogies with the Taiwanese college students. In the next section, I share the methodology that I used, along with my students, to cocreate inclusive pedagogies to impact teaching and learning in Taiwan, and to interrogate my own racial awareness and the impact it had on providing Taiwanese students with a culturally responsive education.

Methodology

I used participant observation in developing this autoethnographic study of my interactions with 55 students during two undergraduate classes held in the spring 2022 at National Sun Yat-sen University in Taiwan: Introduction to Creativity and Introduction to Theater Management.[5,6] As an autoethnographer, my goal is to both participate in and observe the impact of the inclusive learner-centered pedagogy of ADEI on my Taiwanese students. For example, in the classroom, I ask my students to conduct interviews with Taiwanese artists through a culturally responsive lens of collective identity, confidence, experience, and achievement (Chou et al., 2018; Heidelberg, 2020; Hsu, 2015; Ikpeze, 2015; Sanger, 2020). I placed students with varying degrees of English proficiency in groups who each

---

[5]A research method where the researcher has "direct experiential and observational access to the insiders' world of meaning" (Jorgenson, 1989, p. 15).
[6]An autoethnography focuses on the "scholar's life circumstances as a way to understand larger social or cultural phenomena and uses personal narrative writing as a representational strategy that incorporates affect and emotion into their analyses" (Butz & Besio, 2009).

week collectively gave oral presentations to bolster collective belonging, social inclusion, and individual achievement within the collective (Ho, 2020; Mack, 2012; Mcleod, 2023; Sanger, 2020). I also interrogated my own role as a native English speaker, intentionally attempting to dismantle my own colonizing and biased behaviors in the classroom through critical self-awareness of my spoken and unspoken language and the unintended harm it might have on my students if left unchecked (Von Esch et al., 2020).

Introduction to Creativity

For every class I taught in Taiwan, I placed my entire oral presentation on Microsoft PowerPoint slides so that the class could read each slide in accordance with my oral presentation. I suggested that students audio record the class so that they could review the spoken class lessons on their own or in teams, improve their English reading and listening skills, and develop a deeper confidence in their abilities to verbally participate in class (Hsu, 2015).

In preparing the class for my expectations regarding the use of spoken English in class, I prepared a slide that stated:

> I will ask that you speak in English because this is the only way to learn and practice the language. I will help you and I want every person in this class to share your English knowledge with each other inside the classroom. If someone is struggling with the words, please be a peer teacher and help your classmate.

Looking back on this slide, I realize that some of the students in the class may have felt very uncomfortable with the fact that I formally prioritized spoken English in class. It may have inhibited some students from speaking. Using definitive language like "this is the only way to learn and practice the language" may have been off-putting, not to mention inaccurate. The words I chose did not convey a good use of welcoming and belonging learner-centered language, and I learned through experience to refine my culturally responsive teaching practice.

Early on in my first Creativity class session, I asked each of my 10 students to share their student identity with me: This exercise has been very successful in helping me to build a rapport with my class (Hsu, 2015). Below is the content from the slide that asks the students to share their student identities with each other and me.

- Please share your name, year in college, and where you are from (city, country).
- What are you studying in college?
- What do you hope to learn in this class?
- What is your definition of creativity? Share a moment in your life where you felt creative.

After the students introduced themselves, I created five groups with two students in each group. I also introduced my student assistant to the students and shared that she would send the class the homework assignment each week. I gave the students my email address and invited them to contact me should they have any questions. However, my student assistant became the contact person in flagging concerns and questions from her classmates. The students recognized her as an insider, given that she had a similar cultural background. As a Western white professor teaching English as my first language, I accepted my role as the cultural outsider (please see Robert K. Merton's work "Insiders and Outsiders").

I then presented the goals to the class:

> The Introduction to Creativity course will be taught in English and will utilize lectures, interviews, group and individual presentation exercises, and case studies focusing on supporting the development and practice of creativity in leadership, innovation, and entrepreneurship in everyday life and the workforce.

I then shared the teaching methods I would use to teach the class:

> The main sources of learning will be the assigned text, lectures, group and individual oral and written presentations, role playing, and case study analysis. Based on the readings and lectures each week, student assignments will include PowerPoint presentations and role playing based on problem solving and critical analysis.

For the first homework assignment, I asked the students to write and orally present a personal story using this sentence: I wonder what it would be like to enjoy X and discover Y.

The following week, I was still in New York, waiting for my visa's approval, and so we conducted the class on Google Meet. When I asked the students to orally present their personal stories, each student made the decision, without my interference, to come up to the camera and softly share their story in English. The students' oral individual answers included stories about writing letters using an "old fashioned typewriter," being comfortable being alone with oneself, having the courage to dream, getting in touch with depression, and being aware of not trying new things and being afraid to take risks.

I was so moved that my new students shared these insightful and courageous thoughts with me in English. And I realized that centering the student's learning in the assignment (Lee, 2021), as well as encouraging each student to informally and softly speak to me on camera with positive feedback, engendered a rich sharing of self-reflection and cultural narrative (Hsu, 2015).

In teaching a course on creativity, I wanted to infuse the course with the career trajectories of artists of the Global majority from the United States, including Pulitzer Prize-winning composer Tania León; the first African American female principal dancer of American Ballet Theater, Misty Copeland; and poet Maya Angelou. One related assignment focused on the role that Misty Copeland's mentor had on her career in becoming the first African American female principal dancer of the American Ballet Theatre. After watching a video about Misty Copeland's life journey, I asked the students to create an oral assignment, reflecting upon the role Misty Copeland's mentor had in Copeland overcoming personal and professional obstacles. I also asked the students to reflect upon how their own mentors had influenced their lives. Below, I share the assignment:

> What are the ways in which Misty Copeland achieved her creative goals of becoming a professional dancer? What are Misty's creative traits? What are her obstacles? How does she overcome them? Why must she overcome them? Who helps her overcome these obstacles? Why is it necessary to have a mentor? Who are your mentors in life and school? What have your mentors done to help you achieve your creative goals?

The students' oral presentations in class, without exception, were unanimous in empathizing with the difficulties that Misty Copeland experienced as a result of socially constructed racial barriers in the US performing arts workforce (Stein, 2020). The students recognized the critical role that Copeland's mentor played in helping Copeland break down the structural societal barriers facing her, and the need for Copeland and her mentor to cocreate and sustain an anti-racist counternarrative career story (Von Esch et al., 2020). After discussing the role Copeland's mentor played in her life, each student shared a personal culturally responsive mentorship story, detailing the ways in which family members and teachers have impacted their lives (Chou et al., 2018; Heidelberg, 2020; Ikpeze, 2015).

For the midterm assignment, I asked the students to interview a creative professional from Taiwan. While the students interviewed their creative professional in Mandarin, I asked the students to give an oral report in English. The majority of the students were successful in securing their first choice of artist to interview, which included a Taiwanese fashion designer, a lighting designer, a poet, a professor of art, a painter, and an actress. Approximately 1 week before the students were to present their oral reports, I received an email from one of my students. While he had conducted the interview, he insisted that he could not present the oral report in class. He told me that he would not come to class for 2 weeks, during which time his fellow students would present their oral reports in class. I asked my teaching assistant to intervene, but the student still would not come to class. I asked the office administrator what to do. She gave me the email address of the student's professor-mentor. When I spoke to him, he advised that the student drop the class. I told the professor-mentor that the student had been doing well and that perhaps he might come to my office and share what he learned in the interview. The professor-mentor told me he would share my alternative method of presenting the oral report with my student. The student agreed to meet me in my office. When I spoke to the student, he shared how terrified he was to speak English in front of the class. I said but you have been sharing informal creative stories throughout the class. The structured oral report felt different from the student, as opposed to informally sharing his homework. In the end, the student shared his oral report to me online, as COVID-19 protocols prevented us from meeting in person. After our discussion, I observed that he became a lot more confident in his classroom assignments (Hsu, 2015; Sanger, 2020).

In the final project, the students presented their projects as oral reports in groups of two or three. The assignment follows:

> Each group creates a creative project scenario for your chosen organization. The creative project must have a name, a goal, and a series of five objectives in reaching the goal. Within the project, there must be evidence of encouragement, obstacles (people who stand in your way), creative traits, creative confidence, learning, mistakes made, risk taking, perseverance, innovation, empathetic leadership, and entrepreneurship. On the day of your final project in class, each group will both perform and present (via PowerPoint) your creative project scenario, sharing your creative choices.

I found the final projects impressive! One student group created an arts exhibition in a local night market. Using empathetic leadership skills learned in class, each student in the group spoke about the need to build trusting relationships with local night market business people so that the arts exhibition would be supported by the night market community. Another student group created a scenario between the student association president and the theater department's office administrator. In the presentation, the student president asks the department administrator for more space to park student scooters, additional toilet paper, and the ability to have greater participation in scheduling department rehearsal rooms. The department administrator listens attentively and understands that there are problems but is reluctant to support the student president's request because the students in the department contribute to a "trash crisis." The department administrator asks the student president, "How can you help solve that problem?" Together, they collectively agree that if the students help reduce trash, the administrator will empower the students to share in scheduling the rehearsal room.

Another final project scenario involved two students trying to build an antiwar campaign to end the war in Ukraine. The students recommended that the refugees in both Russia and Ukraine sign a petition to end the war. Through the collective action of refugees from both countries and the use of social media, the refugees would attract international attention, placing pressure on both countries to end the war. The students created the slogan: "Antiwar, Any war."

Each student group learner-centered final project featured an understanding of the creative concepts learned in the class as well as notable English language competency in verbally communicating the creative concepts (Ho, 2020; Hsu, 2015; Lee, 2021; Sanger, 2020).

Introduction to Theater Management

Having 10–12 college students in a class is optimal for learning (Hsu, 2015, p. 63). But organizing a class for 45 students to learn theater management, while at the same time becoming more proficient in English listening and speaking, is indeed a challenge! On the first day of class, I asked each of my 45 students to introduce themselves to me. And after 30 or so minutes of student introductions, there was an outburst in Mandarin from one of the students who was most likely echoing what his fellow students were thinking. Since I was holding the class online, it was hard to decipher exactly what was happening. I can only share that my teaching assistant and at least two additional students jumped into action and stopped the student from sharing his displeasure with my assignment. I then proceeded to let the class know that my online status prevented me from getting to know them and that I wanted very much to know each student (Lee, 2021). This type of outburst never happened again. And throughout the remainder of that class and to this day, the student who showed his displeasure welcomed me into his class every week with a smile and a greeting, "Hello, Professor." I reciprocated with a heartfelt response. He was never absent and grew substantially throughout the class. I am grateful that I did not allow the barriers of online learning or the assignment, which admittedly does not always work with a large number of students, hurt our relationship (Hsu, 2015; Lee, 2021).

On the first day of class, I explained that I would use PowerPoint slides to convey my lessons and that I would conduct the class assignments in leadership teams. I created nine leadership teams of five students. I communicated the goals of the class in this PowerPoint slide:

> This class will be taught in English and student teams must practice their spoken and written English knowledge in class through class discussion, group and individual written and oral class assignments, and presentations. By the end of the semester, students should have a broad understanding of the processes involved in creating a commercial theatrical production and a nonprofit theater company. In addition to learning the best practices of professional theaters and commercial productions, student teams will create their own nonprofit theater/or commercial production, incorporating knowledge of motives, mission, core values, and goals.

The first homework assignment asked the student leadership teams to create their own nonprofit or commercial organization and present it via PowerPoint in class. Student leadership teams created theater organizations that largely focused on Taiwan's local identity as it pertained to culture, artists, and the environment (Ho, 2020; Sanger, 2020).

The second weekly homework assignment worked on creating core values for each of the theater organizations created by the student teams. Again, the students developed highly impactful statements about their own cultural core values.

One team named "The Human Being Arts Festival" had core values that embraced "politics, life inspiration, educating people, bringing art to life, and communicating with people more closely." Another leadership team called the "Wukuaicu Theater" emphasized core values, including "educational programming, cooperation with the local arts government, and achieving audience diversity through producing plays on social conditions." A third leadership team named "Maipu" shared that "promoting Taiwanese culture and drama, bringing art closer to our life, cultural exchange, and co-existence" were important cultural core values (Chou et al., 2018; Heidelberg, 2020; Ikpeze, 2015).

Throughout the Introduction to Theater Management course, I intentionally included case studies supporting culturally plural artists and managers working in the United States (Stein, 2020). In the seventh week of the 18-week course, I added a homework assignment that asked the students to use their own culturally responsive social equity solutions in solving the scenarios concerning culturally plural casting and gender affirming hiring practices (Chou et al., 2018; Heidelberg, 2020; Ikpeze, 2015; Sanger, 2020). I share the assignment below:

> Scenario #1: You are negotiating a contract with a director for your next show. She is quite established and it would be amazing if you could get her to join the production. She wants to cast the show with a racially diverse group of actors and there is one person on your team that doesn't like this idea and won't agree to her demands. How do the other members of the "team" encourage the one dissonant team member to accept the vision of the director? What is the final outcome?

> Scenario #2: You are a nonprofit presenting organization in Kaohsiung and you have booked a well-known Broadway play as part of your subscription series. Soon after you have secured the show, the playwright informs you that he doesn't want his show in your season because you don't have any women playwrights represented on the series. As a theater, how do you handle this? The playwright that wants to cancel has a contract with the theater. You have sold tickets to the public. Does the playwright have the right to cancel, according to the contract you both signed? How will you handle this? What will you say to the public?

Each leadership team wanted to support the diversity and inclusion goals of the artist in each scenario and create opportunities for racial and gender diversity.

For example, in response to the first scenario, one leadership team responded: "All human beings are created equal and no one should be treated unfairly by race, country, color, or class. We are open to recruitment and hiring programs that promote racial diversity." Another leadership team then shared, "We believe that we should sit down with our co-worker and discuss the organization's shared values concerning diversity and inclusion. Communication in this situation is important. We will tell our co-worker: 'If you don't accept our value [diversity in casting], you will miss a rare opportunity. We hope you will stay with us.'"

The leadership teams charged with providing gender equity solutions (scenario #2) were also thoughtful and intentional in their presentations. One leadership team reported: "We will tell the playwright that we will add one special production written by a woman playwright in this season. In the future, we will invite artists of all genders to our theater." Another leadership team shared,

"We will apologize to the playwright. We will donate a part of the season's income to feminist groups. We will create public activities to support gender equity. We will add new regulations that state that 'artists of any gender will have equal opportunity to be part of our family in the future.'" It was apparent that the student teams had used the ADEI principles learned through the US case studies to solve problems in their own cultural organizations. The important point here is that the students were responsible for constructing their own learning directives within a culturally responsive inclusive class (Chou et al., 2018; Fuentes et al., 2021; Heidelberg, 2020; Ho, 2020; Hsu, 2015; Ikpeze, 2015; Lee, 2021; Mack, 2012; Mcleod, 2023; Sanger, 2020).

Conclusion

When I used ADEI as a culturally responsive teaching and learning pedagogy in Taiwan, the students believed that their collective cultural experiences matter in transforming the inclusive curriculum. I found creating small-group student teams essential in helping the students shape and learn subject matter together, building confidence, self-worth, and proficiency in the subject matter and in the English language.

Taiwanese students learned the social practices of ADEI by infusing these practices in their own courageous, insightful, and meaningful personal stories and by creating their own theaters, professional missions, artistic visions, and organizational core values. The students learned to empathize with the challenges faced by artists of the Global majority in the United States, and then, the same students created classroom policies for Taiwanese theaters that supported equity and inclusion for women, people of the Global majority, and LGBTQ+ rights. The impact of utilizing ADEI as a culturally responsive student-centered pedagogy was evident in every assignment. I am forever grateful for the student evaluations and feedback from my colleagues who supported my observations.

It is also essential that native white English-speaking professors become racially aware of how their own racialized experiences may adversely impact their students in CHC countries.

Remaining flexible with expectations and reflecting upon whether those expectations are grounded in notions of whiteness are essential to preventing harm to students in the classroom. In my case, I requested that I have Taiwanese student assistants who were exceptional in showing me the cultural nuances of serving as a professor in Taiwan. These students became my cultural experts, and I am forever grateful to them for leading me in my efforts to remain inclusive and anti-racist. ADEI is an essential tool in creating inclusive teaching and learning pedagogies, and it is my hope to continue writing autoethnographies of my ADEI pedagogical experiences in universities throughout the world. I would also hope that this chapter would inspire cross-cultural professors to consider ADEI-inclusive pedagogies when they teach in countries outside their country of origin.

Acknowledgment

I would like to thank Shang-Ying Chen, PhD, chair, Department of Theatre Arts, National Sun Yat-sen University for granting me the opportunity to teach and practice ADEI in the classroom with 100 undergraduate and graduate students over the course of the 2022 academic year.

References

Butz, D., & Besio, K. (2009, September 15). Autoethnography. *Geography Compass, 3*, 1660–1674. https://compass.onlinelibrary.wiley.com/doi/abs/10.1111/j.1749-8198.2009.00279.x

Chiang, Y. C. (2022, June 11). LGBTQ rights/Transgender people hope for change in ID regulations after landmark court rulings. *Focus Taiwan*. https://focustaiwan.tw/society/202206110011

Chou, P. I., Su, M. H., & Wang, Y. T. (2018). Transforming teacher preparation for culturally responsive teaching in Taiwan. *Teaching and Teacher Education, 75*, 116–127.

Confucius and the 'Confucian Tradition'. http://afe.easia.columbia.edu/cosmos/ort/confucianism.htm

Fang, T., Wang, L. Y., Lin, T. B., & Huang, C. K. (2022). To stay or leave: A multiple-case study of the retention of native English-speaking teachers in Taiwan. *Asia Pacific Education Review, 23*, 325–340. https://link.springer.com/article/10.1007/s12564-022-09756-7

Fuentes, M. A., Zelaya, D. G., & Madsen, J. W. (2021). Rethinking the course syllabus: Considerations for promoting equity, diversity, and inclusion. *Teaching of Psychology, 48*(1), 69–79. https://psycnet.apa.org/record/2020-97521-012

Heidelberg, B. M. (2020). Teaching culturally responsive performing arts management in higher education. In T. S. Stein (Ed.), *Racial and ethnic diversity in the performing arts workforce* (pp. 176–186). Routledge.

Ho, S. (2020). Culture and learning: Confucian heritage learners, social-oriented achievement, and innovative pedagogies. In C. S. Sanger & N. W. Gleason (Eds.), *Diversity and inclusion in global education: Lessons from across Asia* (pp. 117–159). Palgrave Macmillan.

Hsu, W. H. (2015). Transitioning to a communication-oriented pedagogy: Taiwanese university freshman's views on class participation. *System, 49*, 61–72.

Ikpeze, C. H. (2015). *Teaching across cultures*. Sense Publishers.

Job Description, National Sun Yat-sen University. (2021).

Jorgensen, D. L. (1989). *Participant observation: A methodology for human studies*. Sage Publications.

Lee, Y. L. (2021). The meaning of learner centeredness in college online environments revisited. In R. Lee, S. K. S. Cheung, C. Iwasaki, L. F. Kwok, & M. Kageto (Eds.), *Blended learning: Re-thinking and re-defining the learning process* (pp. 26–35). Springer International Publishing.

Mack, L. (2012). Does every student have a voice? Critical action research on equitable classroom participation practices. *Language Teaching Research, 16*(3), 417–434. https://eric.ed.gov/?id=EJ973566

Mcleod, S. (2023, May 14). Vygotsky's zone of proximal development. *Simple Psychology*. https://www.simplypsychology.org/zone-of-proximal-development.html

Merton, R. K. (1972). Insiders and outsiders: A chapter in the sociology of knowledge. *American Journal of Sociology, 78*(1), 9–47.

People. (2020). https://www.taiwan.gov.tw/content_2.php

Sanger, C. S. (2020). Inclusive pedagogy and universal design approaches for diverse learning environments. In C. S. Sanger & N. W. Gleason (Eds.), *Diversity and inclusion in global education: Lessons from across Asia* (pp. 31–71). Palgrave Macmillan.

Stein, T. S. (2020). *Racial and ethnic diversity in the performing arts workforce.* Routledge.

Sun, Q., Kang, H., Chang, B., & Lausch, D. (2019). Teaching international students from Confucian heritage culture countries: Perspectives from three U.S. host campuses. *Asia Pacific Education Review, 20*, 559–572. https://link.springer.com/article/10.1007/s12564-019-09604-1

Von Esch, K. S., Motha, S., & Kubota, R. (2020). Race and language teaching. *Language Teaching, 53*(4), 391–421.

Whittle, P. (2022, June 2). Bilingual policy deserves support. *Taipei Times*. https://www.taipeitimes.com/News/editorials/archives/2022/06/02/2003779194

Chapter 16

Managing Diversity in Federal Cultural Administrations: The Example of Heritage Canada and Library and Archives Canada

Julien Doris

University of Ottawa, Canada

Abstract

Since the 1980s, the Canadian federal public service has implemented employment equity legislation.[1] However, the management of diversity in the workplace and its issues have undergone significant changes over the past 30 years.[2] A recent 2021 directive from the Clerk of the Privy Council Office ordered that each department and agency have an accessibility, diversity, equity, and inclusion (ADEI) management strategy.[3] What about the measures and strategies implemented by the federal administrations in relation to culture? Based on a field survey and institutional documentary sources, the article will deal with ADEI management at Heritage Canada and Library and Archives Canada. It will present some innovations in diversity management and put them in perspective with some recent developments in the mandate entrusted to these two institutions. It will thus highlight that the evolution of the mandate of a public cultural administration in favor of the audiences it serves can impact choices and strategies for both the employees and the organizational environment.

---

[1]Agócs, Carol. 2014. "The making of the Abella report: Reflections on the thirtieth anniversary of the Report of the Royal Commission on Equality in Employment." In *Employment Equity in Canada: The Legacy of the Abella Report*, edited by Carol Agócs. Toronto: University of Toronto Press.
[2]Riccucci, Norma M., Gregg G. Van Ryzin, and Cecilia F. Lavena. 2014. "Representative bureaucracy in policing: Does it increase perceived legitimacy?" *Journal of Public Administration Research and Theory*. Vol. 24 (3): 537–551.
[3]Clerk of the Privy Council Office (2021). Call to Action on Anti-Racism, Equity, and Inclusion in the Federal Public Service.

Accessibility, Diversity, Equity and Inclusion in the Cultural Sector, 243–254
Copyright © 2024 Julien Doris
Published under exclusive licence by Emerald Publishing Limited
doi:10.1108/978-1-83753-034-220241037

Keywords: Accessibility, diversity, equity, and inclusion (ADEI); public management; culture; Heritage Canada; Library and Archives Canada

Introduction

Since the report of the Abella Royal Commission, the concept of employment equity has become a leading legal and political principle in Canada that has underpinned many federal public policies in favor of a public service that is both more diverse and more inclusive. This commission documented the professional marginalization of certain groups and was at the origin of the first employment equity legislation, adopted in 1986 by Mulroney's Progressive Conservative government. This legislation initially only applied to private employers. A more extensive version came in 1995 establishing the responsibility of the federal public employer to adopt employment equity plans. These plans tended to ensure the employment equal opportunity of women, people with disabilities, members of Indigenous communities, and other visible minorities.

Although progress and changes have been made since then, the Employment Equity Act has seen very few revisions and updates since 1995. A working group recently issued a report in which it formulated several recommendations to modernize the approach to diversity management in the federal context. While the law is currently under review, it is no longer simply a question of employment equity but of diversity, accessibility, and inclusion. In other words, the body of standards and practices structuring diversity management in the context of Canadian federal public administrations has gradually expanded. In the same way, the role of diversity managers has undergone a progressive professionalization over the years.

This chapter intends to question this institutionalization of the management of diversity in public administrations by taking the example of two ministries whose mandate is oriented toward the promotion of arts, culture, and heritage: Canadian Heritage and Library and Archives Canada (LAC). In a broader survey, carried out across the federal public service, it emerged that these two departments had historically contributed to thinking about the management of diversity as much with regard to the external (*in their relationships in connection with the public*) as well as internally in the management of the workplace. Each of these two departments implements organizational action plans in favor of integrated diversity management, which I will review later in this chapter. Also, to what extent do these two organizations make the management of accessibility, diversity, equity, and inclusion (ADEI) an essential imperative for improving the workplace and the public policies?

Methodology and Chapter Overview

This chapter is taken from the published results of my doctoral thesis (Doris, 2023). The doctoral thesis is a case study (Roy, 2016) aimed at documenting the field of activity of managing ADEI in the Canadian federal public service. An ethics certificate was issued on May 3, 2020, by the Office of Research Ethics and Integrity of the University of Ottawa. The final data collection report was submitted and approved on June 2, 2022. The data and results of the study were based on the analysis of public and open access archives of the Canadian federal government. These archives included parliamentary debates, working documents and reports of the Abella Royal Commission as well as reports and documentation of key bodies of the federal public service involved in the implementation of the employment equity Act. Finally, the documentary analysis also integrated action plans of federal departments in terms of diversity management. In addition, a series of interviews was conducted with managers from 17 federal organizations, from the core public administration including LAC and Canadian Heritage. The 40 hours of interviews were entirely recorded and then transcribed. Data from the interviews and the documentary analysis were processed using NVivo.

After returning in a first section to certain milestones in the development of the accessibility, diversity, equity and inclusion (ADEI) field in the Canadian federal context, I will present in a second section the action plans and visions prevailing in the two departments. Certain fragments of interviews will also complement the institutional measures and priorities followed in the two institutions. These declarations from managers will also highlight the trajectory followed by these two institutions regarding the rest of the federal public service, also subject to the regulatory corpus making the management of ADEI a new imperative in public management.

Accessibility, Equity, Diversity, and Inclusion as a New Field of Public Management?

Representative Bureaucracy and Employment Equity

Diversity management is far from a new subject in public administration. Several studies have historically examined representation regimes in public administrations. Dolan and Rosenbloom (2003) investigated the distinction made by Mosher (1968) between an active and a passive form of bureaucratic representation. Mosher himself drew this distinction from the work of the philosopher and political scientist Pitkin (1967). "An administration is passively representative if it reproduces the characteristics of the population in terms of race, social class, ethnic origin, religion, gender parity, profession, etc. A bureaucracy is considered actively representative if it defends the interests of a particular category of the population" (Meier & Hawes, 2006, p. 266). In the context of political federalism, work on representative bureaucracy has examined several parameters of the representation of sociodemographic identities, for example, the work of Gagnon et al. who mobilized the concept of representative bureaucracy to question the relationship between ethnocultural representation and linguistic representation in the public service (2006).

In the Canadian context, several studies have focused on employment equity policies, although little work has truly examined the recent changes brought about in the broadening of the legal and political foundations in favor of management of diversity (Riccucci et al., 2014). Agocs et al. (1992) analyzed the institution-alization of the employment equity policy before its revision in 1995. These authors queried the self-referential nature (Jobert & Muller, 1987) of the employment equity policy: "When they implement employment equity, organizations identify and change policies and practices that impede the access and retention of members of marginalized groups and work to create an organizational culture free of harassment and responsive to diversity" (Jain et al., 2000, p. 53). One could link the notion of employment equity to organizational culture (Schein, 1990). In 2016, McGowan and Ng explored the discursive foundations and forms of resistance or support with regard to employment equity policy in the *Canadian Journal of Public Administration*. After listing the legal bases, they used the results of a questionnaire addressed to public servants. They found that men, on average, are more inclined than women to report that they are familiar with the employment equity policy (McGowan & Ng, 2016, p. 315). People with disabilities and members of visible minorities, on the other hand, seemed unfamiliar with this public policy. "Many respondents simply did not know or understand the intent of Employment Equity as a public policy tool aimed at increasing the representation of historically disadvantaged groups" (p. 322). Finally, in the Canadian context, work in public administration on the concept of employment equity has also been understood from a comparative perspective aimed at highlighting the analogies and variations depending on the different levels of governments. Not only Bakan and Kobayashi (2000, 2007) but also Turgeon et al. (2022) compared the (first) provincial employment equity programs, seeing them through an extension or adaptation of the federal policy.

Managing Diversity in the Context of the Canadian Public Service

Although the government intended the Employment Equity Act of 1995 to apply to the Canadian public service and to provide the Canadian Human Rights Commission with powers of control and verification over all public and private employers under federal labor jurisdiction, many federal departments and agencies already implemented employment equity programs, prior to the promulgation of Bill C-64. The Act had the effect of boosting the institutionalization of the field of diversity management in public organizations.

Since then, several texts and management obligations have gradually extended the scope of activity of diversity managers. For example, the recent Accessible Canada Act, adopted in 2019, broadened the scope of action regarding the management of employment equity by addressing disability status. This includes the replacement of the Treasury Board employment equity policy of 1999 by the directive on "employment equity, diversity, and inclusion" of 2020. This new directive is a real paradigm shift. It has in fact reversed the responsibility for diversity management, by requiring that each deputy head designate a senior public servant responsible to "consult, mobilize and collaborate with employees of groups designated under the employment equity act, as well as with managers, departmental bargaining agents and other employees, in all aspects of employment equity, diversity and inclusion, including plans, systems, policies, practices and processes" (Treasury Board, 2020). More recently, the Clerk of the Privy Council's call to action in favor of the fight against racism, equity, and inclusion in the federal public service, as well as the formation of a working group for the modernization of the Employment Equity Act have broadened the scope given to the management of ADEI in the context of Canadian federal public administrations.

Some Principles and Obligations on the ADEI Field Operation in the Federal Context

Some work in the field of public policy has highlighted the incremental dimensions of organizational change. The sociological neo-institutionalist movement has explained the isomorphic dynamics which govern the functioning of public organizations. DiMaggio and Powell (1983, 1991) showed that organizations, to cope with the uncertainty of organizational change, tend to take advantage of the practices of various organizations to ensure their own functioning and respond to external pressures. This extension of ADEI responsibilities which characterizes all Canadian federal organizations is largely due to a normative isomorphism mostly resulting from the progressive liberal agenda of Trudeau's government which has made the management of diversity a mandated priority.

Since 2015 under the liberal leadership of Trudeau, ADEI management has experienced an unprecedented phase of politicization calling for a battery of measures aimed at broadening the scope of organizational action (Birch & Pétry, 2019). The Treasury Board Directive provided multiyear action plans in favor of ADEI. Responsibility for ADEI in the federal departments and agencies comes directly from the deputy heads and no longer from the human resources divisions. Each department has direct access to the Office of the Chief Human Resources Officer (OCHRO) of the Treasury Board of Canada Secretariat (Treasury Board, 2020). In addition to deputy head, managers, as well as employee networks, contribute to the follow-up and monitoring of initiatives implemented both internally and externally. These incremental changes evolving the management of employment equity toward the management of ADEI are the result of a broader involvement in terms of actors and organizational resources. This expansion also results from a gradual professionalization of civil servants who have contributed to developing and disseminating expertise in the field of diversity management.

Managing Diversity at Canadian Heritage and LAC

As central agencies responsible for arts and culture, Canadian Heritage and LAC are two small federal departments. While Canadian Heritage had 1,776 employees in 2021, LAC had 909 employees (Treasury Board of Canada Secretariat, 2021). Taking into consideration the availability of labor in the active population for the four designated groups in the Employment Equity Act, I see the following data (See Table 16.1):

Table 16.1.   Distribution of Public Service of Canada Employees as of March
31, 2021, According to Treasury Board of Canada Secretariat.

Department	Women	Visible Minorities	People with Disabilities	Indigenous People
Overall workforce availability	52.7%	15.3%	9%	4%
Canadian Heritage	67.6%	16.6%	6.6%	4.6%
Library and Archives Canada	63%	8.9%	4.7%	4.2%

Reviewing the Treasury Board of Canada Secretariat statistics, it appears that
the two ministries both encounter a lack of people with disabilities compared to
their overall workforce availability (WFA). On the other hand, and as presented
above, LAC lacks visible minorities unlike Canadian Heritage. The two departments both met their targets for women and Indigenous people. It is important to
look at institutional strategies in ADEI to understand the scope of the measures
taken in these two organizations, to not only achieve the equity targets in
employment matters but, more broadly, to ensure a system of active representation and therefore a general improvement in the climate of diversity (Choi,
2013; Gonzalez & Denisi, 2009; Oberfield, 2016).

Performative Strategies Aimed at Transforming the Workplace

Although organizations tend to converge from the point of view of their standards
and their practices via the tendency to mimicry highlighted by the neo-
institutionalist current, the comparative study of ministerial action plans in
ADEI revealed that despite a relatively similar overall structure, the strategies
pursued aimed to define objectives and initiatives adapted to the context and the
real needs of the organizations. The reactions of the employees can also be similar
from an organization to another one. For example, although the management of
ADEI is at the forefront of organizational priorities, it appeared that some
reluctance could emerge among employees to the initiatives contained in the
action plans. Federal Managers have sometimes spoken out on the subject,
indicating certain employees' discomfort to be placed in a box.

In the context of Canadian Heritage, the action plan for employment ADEI
covers the period from 2021 to 2024. In the message from the deputy minister,
clearly "Heritage Canada is committed to creating a welcoming and healthy work
environment, whether in a virtual or hybrid environment, where diversity is
sought and celebrated, where all employees have the opportunity to share their
ideas, perspectives and experiences without fear of reprisal, and where their well-
being is protected." The action plan is structured around four pillars aimed at
following up on the call to action from the Clerk of the Privy Council on

antiracism and ADEI. In 2018, 80 Canadian Heritage employees participated in a consultation and reported on their experience and the obstacles they encountered. Pillar 1 targets recruitment and specifies that "Heritage Canada must intentionally strive to diversify its workforce horizontally and vertically, so that it reflects Canada." A first objective of Pillar 1 of the action plan aims to increase the awareness of Canadian Heritage managers about achieving a representative workforce. A second objective concerns the integration of ADEI into human resources planning to remove obstacles and increase the representation of certain targeted groups, particularly in recruitment committees. A third objective aims to increase student recruitment, while the fourth objective aims to reduce barriers related to official languages.

The second pillar concerns retention and professional advancement. Improved promotion of qualified internal employees and members of equity-seeking groups as well as the review of integration documents and the association of employees before their arrival to identify their needs before taking office have appeared as specific objectives of the strategy. The third pillar aims to create a healthy environment and a change of culture through actions to raise awareness of cultural diversity, through the fight against harassment and discrimination in the workplace and through the promotion of resources and initiatives to ensure mental health and well-being of employees. The last pillar concerns governance and provides in particular that the various ADEI committees of the ministry can have strategic, administrative, and logistical support to carry out their activities. The governance pillar also aims to establish permanent commitments to ADEI in performance management agreements to hold managers and deputy heads accountable for obtaining results such as increasing the representation of different groups.

In the context of LAC, the action plan obtained from managers for diversity and employment equity extends from 2019 to 2022. This follows a joint union-management working group on ADEI which produced a report in favor of a more diverse and more inclusive public service. In the introduction to its action plan, LAC stated that it "is committed to fostering a healthy, respectful, inclusive, safe and modern work environment in which employees are treated fairly and whose workforce composition reflects the Canadian population" (p. 3). Similar to Canadian Heritage, the strategy contains different pillars that target workforce recruitment, workplace management, and governance. The diversity of the composition of recruitment panels, the use of tools to improve selection and evaluation practices, and the intensification of contacts with community organizations and recruitment partners are identified as priorities in relation with the first pillar. To ensure staff retention, the agency plans to establish an exit evaluation to find out the reasons that employees leave the organization.

Always linked to recruitment and retention, mentorship programs for groups seeking equity, as well as awareness of self-identification, remain strategies followed by LAC. Targeted actions, such as the implementation of activities and events linked to diversity, improve the quality workplace. The department offers training on unconscious bias or on the realities of LGBTQ2+. Finally, the action plan provides access to data for managers. It plans a review of human resources practices to verify that they do not create obstacles for designated groups. The action plan is under the responsibility of the Human Resources and Security General Director, who facilitates a committee on ADEI. This brings together managers and senior executives, including a champion of ADEI and multiculturalism responsible for exercising influence in achieving results. As highlighted, these institutional strategies in favor of ADEI at LAC and at Canadian Heritage aim to influence the transition from a passive type of representation (focused on the representativeness of civil servants) to an active bureaucratic representation regime which intends to modify both standards and management practices. These measures in favor of diversity are, however, not without in-depth work on organizations from the point of view of their mandate and their relationship with the public they serve.

Thinking ADEI Measures in Relation With the Evolution of Mandates and Priorities of Departments

As noted in the field survey conducted among federal managers, this momentum in favor of ADEI results in both politicization dynamics (due to the progressive government agenda) but can also be reflected in the need for organizational rationalization. Concerned about ensuring ever greater transparency and better serving the public, LAC and Canadian Heritage have both undergone recent developments in terms of their mandates and institutional priorities. LAC, for example, has made the openness and accessibility of its collections a key issue in rethinking its connection to the public:

> Everything related to employment equity and diversity is really at the heart of our thinking about everything we do. In fact, we had a meeting with the management team to find out not only what we can do in terms of staff but also the services we provide to Canadians given that our mandate is to acquire, preserve, to make Canadian heritage accessible and therefore, how we can ensure that our collection reflects Canadian diversity but also the way in which we make the collection accessible. Are we succeeding in reaching the diversity of our population? (Manager, Library and Archives Canada)

This attention to the mandate is presented as the way of thinking about ADEI actions which are adapted to the entire organization and goes well beyond the sphere of human resources. The managers interviewed indicated the newness of this paradigm shift. From now on, managers will share the ADEI portfolio across the entire organization and involve partnerships across several departments or agencies of similar size and mandates.

> It is up to each organization to develop its own program according to its own organizational needs. Being small, we are examining the possibility of establishing a partnership with Canadian Heritage.

Why them? Because we have a mandate that overlaps, and it would be interesting for the participants to talk about subjects that directly affect them in their work. Another possibility is to establish a partnership with other small organizations that could help us. So, several tools exist and it's about developing a program that will meet the needs of our organization. This is what we are examining at the moment. (Manager, Library and Archives Canada)

LAC and Canadian Heritage, as part of the same ministerial portfolio, formed an interdepartmental committee to deal with ADEI issues in cultural administration with certain heritage or television organizations such as Radio Canada and which fall under the Employment Equity Act. This interdepartmental committee is above all a space for the exchange of good practices across organizations. On the question of the integration of ADEI into LAC policies whose mandate is to acquire, preserve, and make accessible the collections, the ADEI manager specified that accessibility is a transversal issue applying to all ministerial actions and services:

For people with disabilities, we have an action plan to make everything online accessible and to ensure that visually, the characters are large enough and the colors and many other things. Also, we have forms that the public must complete to access some of our services and again, it is about using the right formats so that they are accessible. Also, we have the exercise of reviewing the terminologies of the forms to ensure that they are gender neutral. So, these are all things that are less the responsibility of human resources, but which are managed elsewhere in the organization, precisely to ensure that diversity is reflected elsewhere, in the delivery of programs and services to Canadians. (Manager, Library and Archives Canada)

Soliciting the public in preservation is also a ministerial priority. An initiative to establish a series of indigenous portraits made it possible to better represent indigenous peoples in the collections and to consult them on the documentary preservation plan while giving them space to create projects disseminated by the ministry.

Regarding Canadian Heritage, the managers interviewed specified that ADEI principles are an integral part of the department's mandate. ADEI programs not only shape the management of the public servants but also the public policy making:

On diversity and equity at Canadian Heritage, everyone considers themselves very "pro" on these issues and after all, we are the department of sports, arts, and culture. (Manager of Canadian Heritage)

As highlighted by the managers interviewed, Canadian Heritage adopts certain strategies by seeking to stand out from other departments or by a certain leadership in the management of diversity. A change in terminology without changing the definitions, for example, circumvented the terms of the Employment Equity Act which very often appear obsolete. The managers interviewed also insisted on the culture of participation which would become important and which would make it possible to better highlight the systemic barriers and obstacles of the organization:

> The fact is that at Canadian Heritage everyone thinks they are "woke" and many are, and others are much less so, I think. The other thing is that the employees are very much heard. Employee committees have direct access to the deputy minister. I don't think this is the case everywhere. We hear a lot about the problems and sometimes we have the impression that there could be more problems. That remains to be seen because in the workplace I have really seen things that are truly unhealthier than what I observe. (Manager, Canadian Heritage)

In summary, the interest in ADEI issues, both for internal management and for the planning of programs and public policies aimed at the Canadian population, is not just the result of legislated obligations or the political agenda. As the field survey revealed, this all-out interest in the field of ADEI is also the result of a gradual professionalization of a new body of professional managers who work within their organization but also at the interdepartmental level to define new organizational standards and practices. This work is now going beyond employment equity to include broader issues.

Conclusion

This chapter aimed to investigate the following questions: (1) How is the field of management of ADEI structured in the light of ministerial action plans? (2) How are the mandates of federal departments' arts and culture portfolio worked on by the ADEI as much as they contribute to shaping innovative approaches and initiatives adapted to the reality and priorities of the departments or central agencies? (3) Finally, how can ADEI constitute an approach that is both positive and participatory, making it possible to involve all employees in the management processes but also the publics and groups seeking ADEI in the development of organizational priorities and policies?

The comparison of action plans as well as the interview process of ADEI managers at LAC and Canadian Heritage, however, made it possible to raise certain mechanisms of resistance toward the strategies pursued in terms of diversity management, which one could explore further. For example, both contexts highlighted self-identification in questionnaires addressed to employees as a process aimed at producing reliable data in terms of organizational diversity but which in small organizations sometimes raises reluctance and distrust of the share of employees who do not always seem to want to identify with a particular category. Most of the managers interviewed recognized that the terminologies used could prove divisive due to their outdated nature. Despite these reluctances and resistance, managers unanimously recognized the importance of following up on the management of ADEI due to its great relevance but also to the social innovations it generates to improve work environments and think about the public service of tomorrow.

References

Agocs, C., Burr, C., & Somerset, F. (1992). *Employment equity. Co-operative strategies for organizational change* (p. 420). Prentice-Hall Canada.

Bakan, A., & Kobayashi, A. (2000). *Employment equity policy in Canada: An interprovincial comparison.* Status of Women Canada.

Bakan, B., & Kobayashi, A. (2007). Affirmative action and employment equity: Policy, ideology, and backlash in Canadian context. *Studies in Political Economy,* *79*(1), 145–166.

Birch, L., & Pétry, F. (Dir). (2019). *Bilan du gouvernement libéral de Justin Trudeau. 353 promesses et un mandat de changement* (p. 278). Presses de l'Université Laval.

Choi, S. (2013). Demographic diversity of managers and employee job satisfaction: Empirical analysis of the federal case. *Review of Public Personnel Administration,* *33*(3), 275–298.

Clerk of the Privy Council Office. (2021). *Call to action on anti-racism, equity, and inclusion in the federal public service.* https://www.canada.ca/en/privy-council/corporate/clerk/call-to-action-anti-racism-equity-inclusion-federal-public-service.html

DiMaggio, P. J., & Powell, W. W. (1983). The iron cage revisited: Institutional isomorphism and collective rationality in organizational fields. *American Sociological Review,* *48*(1), 147–160.

DiMaggio, P. J., & Powell, W. W. (1991). *The new institutionalism in organizational analysis.* University of Chicago Press.

Dolan, J., & Rosenbloom, D. H. (2003). *Representative bureaucracy: Classic readings and continuing controversies.* Routledge.

Doris, J. (2023). *La diversité en tant que champ organisationnel : le cas des gestionnaires de l'équité en matière d'emploi dans les ministères et agences du gouvernement du Canada* (p. 365). Doctoral Dissertation, University of Ottawa. https://ruor.uottawa.ca/handle/10393/44946?locale=en

Gagnon, A.-G., Turgeon, L., & De Champlain, O. (2006). La bureaucratie représentative au sein des états multinationaux. *Revue Française d'Administration Publique,* *118*(2), 291–306.

Gonzalez, J., & Denisi, A. (2009). Cross-level effects of demography and diversity climate on organizational attachment and firm effectiveness. *Journal of Organizational Behavior,* *30*(1), 21–40.

Jain, H. C., Singh, P., & Agocs, C. (2000). Recruitment, selection and promotion of visible-minority and aboriginal police officers in selected Canadian police services. *Canadian Public Administration,* *43*(1), 46–74.

Jobertet, B., & Muller, P. (1987). *L'État en action. Politiques publiques et corporatismes*. PUF.

McGowan, R. A., & Ng, E. S. (2016). Employment equity in Canada: Making sense of employee discourses of misunderstanding, resistance, and support. *Canadian Public Administration Review*, *59*(1), 310–329.

Meier, K. J., & Hawes, D. P. (2006). Le lien entre représentativité passive et active de l'administration. *Revue Française d'Administration Publique*, *118*(2), 265–279.

Mosher, F. C. (1968). *Democracy and the public service*. Oxford University Press.

Oberfield, Z. W. (2016). Why are some agencies perceived as more committed to diversity than others? An analysis of public-sector diversity climates. *Public Management Review*, *18*(5), 763–790.

Pitkin, H. F. (1967). *The concept of representation*. University of California Press.

Riccucci, N. M., Van Ryzin, G. G., & Lavena, C. F. (2014). Representative bureaucracy in policing: Does it increase perceived legitimacy? *Journal of Public Administration Research and Theory*, *24*(3), 537–551.

Roy, S. N. (2016). « L'étude de cas » dans Gauthier. In I. B et Bourgeois (Ed.), *Recherche sociale: de la problématique à la collecte des données* (pp. 195–221). Presses de l'université du Québec.

Schein, E. H. (1990). Organizational culture. *American Psychologist*, *45*(2), 109–119.

Treasury Board of Canada. (2020). *Directive on employment equity, diversity, and inclusion*. https://www.tbs-sct.canada.ca/pol/doc-eng.aspx?id=32635&section=html

Treasury Board of Canada Secretariat. (2020). *Employment equity in the public service of Canada for fiscal year 2018 to 2019*. Canada.ca. https://www.canada.ca/fr/gouvernement/fonctionpublique/mieux-etre-inclusion-diversite-fonction-publique/diversite-equite-matiere-emploi/equite-emploi-rapports-annuel/equite-emploi-fonction-publique-canada-2018-2019

Treasury Board of Canada Secretariat. (2021). *Distribution of public service of Canada employees as of March, 31, 2021*. https://www.canada.ca/en/government/publicservice/wellness-inclusion-diversity-public-service/diversity-inclusion-public-service/employment-equity-annual-reports/employment-equity-public-service-canada-2020-2021.html

Turgeon, L., Doris, J., Gagnon, A. G., & Caruso, J. L. (2022). Varieties of employment equity architecture in Canada: An interprovincial comparison. *Canadian Public Administration*, *65*(1), 188–205.

What Can We Learn From the Case Studies About ADEI Issues?: Conclusion

Marie-Laure Dioh

Université du Québec en Outaouais, Canada

With the aim of analyzing accessibility, diversity, equity, and inclusion (ADEI) practices and initiatives in the cultural sector (performing arts, visual arts, music, and events) from several regions of the world (Australia, Canada, Chile, Colombia, Haiti, South Africa, Taiwan, and the United States), this book presents highly instructive case studies as a basis for understanding the issues involved in implementing ADEI principles.

Readers will first observe the broad range of issues linked to ADEI in the cultural sector: lack of representativeness of certain communities (chapters by Cuyler; Boucher; Doris; Aguado et al.; Galaise), lack of representation of women (chapters by Aumais and Senac; Galaise), lack of recognition of certain groups (chapters by Larose; Stein; Bourgeois; Heidelberg), lack of accessibility to cultural environments by certain individuals (chapters by Cuyler; Doris; Boyle et al.; Heredia-Carroza et al.; Ndzuta; Doris et al.), or even risks of loss of cultural identity and risk of assimilation in the face of majority populations (chapters by Ravi and Leclair; Ndzuta).

A second observation concerns the range of actions and reactions responding to ADEI issues described in the cases which materialize in different ways: through the roles and functions occupied by leaders in decision-making bodies such as in the opera sector (chapter by Cuyler), through the leadership and mentoring they embody in their communities (chapters by Cuyler; Larose; Aumais and Senac), or through defending identity and refusing linguistic and cultural assimilation (chapters by Ravi and Leclair; Aguado et al.). ADEI initiatives are also linked to the promotion of ethnic diversity (chapters by Aguado et al.; Ravi and Leclair; Galaise), to a concern for representing and valorizing certain communities (chapters by Doris; Stein; Boucher) and gender identities (chapters by Aumais and Senac; Galaise), and by a concern for the economic integration of marginalized and disadvantaged populations (chapters by Aguado et al.; Larose; Aumais and Senac; Ndzuta). We noted actions to facilitate access to cultural platforms for certain groups, while enabling artists to perform by eliminating physical, financial, societal, and other barriers to participation (chapter by Boyle et al.; Doris

Accessibility, Diversity, Equity and Inclusion in the Cultural Sector, 255–257
Copyright © 2024 Marie-Laure Dioh
Published under exclusive licence by Emerald Publishing Limited
doi:10.1108/978-1-83753-034-220241040

et al.), thus facilitating diversity and digital access for a greater number of individuals (chapters by Boyle et al.; Ndzuta). One can also see ADEI anchoring the demand for rights based on inclusion, equity, and emancipation for marginalized populations in Haiti (chapter by Larose), or South Africa (chapter by Ndzura), or the defense of social justice for marginalized populations in the city of Atlanta (chapter by Bourgeois). Finally, our readers will remark on how ADEI is embedded in actions to implement management policies and programs in public administration (chapter by Doris) or to establish an organizational culture that favors equity (chapter by Heidelberg). Other such actions include andragogical and pedagogical practices that value the diversity of learners (chapter by Stein) and implementation of effective cultural policies to promote access to museums for people with disabilities, consequently guaranteeing their cultural rights (chapter by Heredia-Carroza et al.).

This book stimulates a third observation that by presenting a range of perspectives through the cases, the reader may compare arguments and principles for coherence or discord. For some authors, such as Cuyler, racial identity should instill in Black leaders a desire for justice, social commitment, and the defense of ADEI values. But this same racial and cultural claim can create a tension in other communities between the desire to preserve their identity and the need to let this heritage develop in response to an ever-changing cultural context. This debate is very well explained in Ravi and Leclair's chapter. We can also see how laudable initiatives can create other problems. In this respect, Boucher's chapter is very edifying, pointing out how museums that aim to make their collections more representative, equitable, and diversified can unintentionally perpetuate the effects of ghettoization and labeling of certain communities or perpetuate ideas of subordination. Doris's chapter also illustrates how legislators and public administrators aspire to achieve inclusion proactively by continually improving laws and programs. However, Heidelberg's chapter juxtaposes organizational buy-in and material support for workplace equity against ideological barriers, such as organizational excellence, which can outweigh and block efforts to instill equity in the organization's culture. However, Heidelberg's chapter described very well how, in another organizational environment where there is organizational buy-in for workplace equity and material support for it, ideological barriers such as organizational excellence can still block efforts, negatively impact the culture, and thus organizational equity efforts.

Finally, the chapters by Larose and Ndzuta demonstrate how on two different continents, similar geopolitical situations render musicians in Haiti and South Africa unable to earn a living from their art. Without the benefit of public policies for ADEI, these artists are forced to implement individual strategies for concrete action to claim their civil rights and improve their lot.

The final takeaway from this book concerns the integrated nature of the initiatives themselves that are featured in the chapters. First, there are the cultural productions observed in Alberta to perpetuate Francophone cultures (chapter by Ravi and Leclair). One can also identify cultural initiatives that enable intergenerational and intercultural mixing and cultural blending within communities (chapter by Ravi and Leclair; Aguado et al.). In addition, some museums strive to become more equitable, diverse, and representative and reinvest in their art collections to embrace ADEI ideals (chapter by Boucher). Some of the other initiatives described in the chapters show how communities left behind are fighting against the social and economic inequalities they suffer, prioritizing values of mutual aid and collaboration over self-interest (chapters by Larose; Aumais and Senac). One can also point out the strategies of struggle for recognition (chapter by Larose) and claims for a place within a cultural milieu (chapter by Aumais and Senac). Other proactive initiatives are linked to establishing new organizational standards and practices, notably in the Canadian public service. These efforts take into account contemporary issues in ADEI, progressing beyond employment equity legislation which is becoming obsolete (chapter by Doris). The book also sheds light on inclusive practices in education, where self-reflexivity leads teachers to question their own racial awareness and its influence on their andragogical and pedagogical relationships (chapter by Stein). Similarly, how a global event such as the Super Bowl can have even more ethical and social repercussions in local communities whose socioeconomic conditions would otherwise isolate them (chapter by Bourgeois). Finally, the case of the Melbourne Symphony Orchestra inspires fortitude because even in spite of the ongoing challenge of defending ADEI values, success was achieved in attaining gender equality in its board of directors, board committees, management team, administrative staff, and musicians.

Readers of this book will observe the relevant contributions the authors collectively make to the academic, organizational, and societal debates surrounding ADEI, by taking as its point of entry real initiatives in a little-studied sector of activity: the cultural sector. This book adds to the body of knowledge around ADEI issues, by analyzing examples from several cultural disciplines in several countries. To date, no other book has assembled research pursuing this avenue of study. It presents original case studies from both the practical and academic spheres, which will prove useful to researchers, cultural workers, artists, managers, practitioners, and political decision-makers alike, as they reflect on and implement management practices that promote ADEI in the cultural sector. One can replicate these practices in other cultural and creative sectors not covered here: audiovisual, video games, cinema, design, architecture, literature, and journalism or the related sectors of fashion and communications. They could also feed into programs enabling cultural and creative companies to develop innovative projects around ADEI and open international networks to interested players. One succinct thought remains at the end of this book – author Galaise's quotation from Arthur Chan – which should guide all researchers and practitioners: "Diversity is a fact. Equity is a choice. Inclusion is an action. Belonging is a result." How can each individual, group, and organization contribute individually and collectively to ADEI implementation? The debate continues...

Printed and bound by CPI Group (UK) Ltd, Croydon, CR0 4YY

19/11/2024

14595311-0002